LABOR
in the Capitalist
World-Economy

POLITICAL ECONOMY OF THE WORLD-SYSTEM ANNUALS

Series Editor: IMMANUEL WALLERSTEIN

Published in cooperation with the Section on the Political Economy of the World-System of the American Sociological Association

About the Series

The intent of this series of annuals is to reflect and inform the intense theoretical and empirical debates about the "political economy of the world-system." These debates assume that the phenomena of the real world cannot be separated into three (or more) categories—political, economic, and social—which can be studied by different methods and in closed spheres. The economy is "institutionally" rooted; the polity is the expression of socioeconomic forces; and "societal" structures are a consequence of politico-economic pressures. The phrase "world-system" also tells us that we believe there is a working social system larger than any state whose operations are themselves a focus of social analysis. How states and parties, firms and classes, status groups and social institutions operate within the framework and constraints of the world-system is precisely what is debated.

These theme-focused annuals will be the outlet for original theoretical and empirical findings of social scientists coming from all the traditional "disciplines." The series will draw upon papers presented at meetings and conferences, as well as papers from those who share in these concerns.

Volumes in this series:

LABOR
in the Capitalist
World-Economy

Edited by **Charles Bergquist**

Volume 7, **Political Economy of the World-System Annuals**
Series Editor: Immanuel Wallerstein

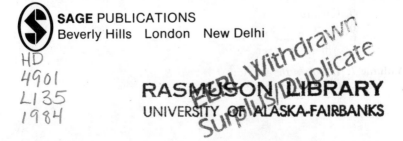

SAGE PUBLICATIONS
Beverly Hills   London   New Delhi

Copyright © 1984 by Sage Publications, Inc.

For information address:

SAGE Publications, Inc.
275 South Beverly Drive
Beverly Hills, California 90212

SAGE Publications India Pvt. Ltd.
C-236 Defence Colony
New Delhi 110 024, India

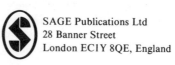

SAGE Publications Ltd
28 Banner Street
London EC1Y 8QE, England

Printed in the United States of America

Library of Congress Cataloging in Publication Data

Main entry under title:

Labor in the capitalist world-economy.
    (Political economy of the world-system annuals ; v. 7)
    Includes bibliographies.
    1. Labor and laboring classes—Addresses, essays, lectures. I. Bergquist, Charles. II. Series.
HD4901.L135   1984   305.5′62   83-27015
ISBN 0-8039-2266-3
ISBN 0-8039-2267-1 (pbk.)

FIRST PRINTING

CONTENTS

PLACING LABOR AT THE CENTER:
INTRODUCTION

Charles Bergquist
Duke University

The world-system approach to modern world history has failed to come to terms fully with the meaning of the struggles of working people. This failure is neither surprising nor especially remarkable. The neglect of labor's struggle in the world historical process is much more blatant in the dominant liberal paradigm against which world-system analysis reacted. And it is a neglect that is also characteristic of the structuralist and neo-Marxist approaches from which world-system theory borrowed extensively and with which it continues to coexist in uneasy intellectual alliance.[1]

The validity of these bald assertions is not widely accepted, even among the authors of the essays collected in this volume. Nor can it be fully demonstrated here. This is true not only because of the individual limitations of the contributors to the volume and of its editor, but because the problem itself has barely begun to be acknowledged and confronted collectively by those who seek to better comprehend the global dynamics of the past so as to work more effectively to mold a future world order that is at once more egalitarian and more free.[2] What can be attempted in this introduction, however, is first, to sketch an explanation of how and why social scientists of virtually all ideological persuasions writing in the decades following World War II could have constructed theories of world development and historical change that placed the workers' struggle so far from the focus of their analysis; second, to show how the dynamic of world developments has worked, over the course of the last decade, to deepen our consciousness of the importance of labor's struggle and to move that struggle progressively toward the center of our theoretical and practical (that is, political) concerns; and finally, to suggest how focusing on labor promises to clarify and help resolve many of the philosophical, methodological, and political issues that have preoccupied proponents and critics of world-systems analysis alike. Bringing labor more fully into the center of world-system analysis is a task that has just begun, but one that holds great promise for the theoretical power of the approach, and for the democratic resolution of the struggle for a more humane world social system.

Out of the last great crisis of world capitalism (1914-1947) emerged a world order that, we see now in retrospect, created the economic, political, and institutional conditions for an unprecedented expansion of capitalism on a world scale (see especially Arrighi, "A Crisis of Hegemony," in Amin et al., 1982). The military and political dimensions of that remarkable era, which lasted for more than two decades, are now widely appreciated. They involved the emergence and maintenance of United States political and economic hegemony over developed and semideveloped capitalist nations and over a progressively decolonized Third World. The role of the world monetary, banking, trade, and "welfare" institutions that accompanied and facilitated capitalist expansion in this period is also well known, as is the importance of the primary vehicle for the massive transnationalization of productive investment of this era, the multinational corporation.

What has not been widely recognized, and is only now becoming clear, is the extent to which this remarkable capitalist success story, and the specific institutional form it took, had its origins in the great victories won by popular forces during the crisis of world capitalism in the prewar period. In the developed, industrialized core of the world-economy, particularly in the preeminent capitalist power, the United States, popular forces, spearheaded by the labor movement, confronted capital at the end of the war with a dual victory. Powerful syndical organizations, particularly in basic industry, threatened the logic of capitalist accumulation in the work place (Arrighi and Silver, this volume). And at the level of the state, popular forces had won effective protection from the capitalist market place through institutionalization of basic social security and welfare measures (Polanyi, 1944).

Outside the United States, the victories of popular forces were no less impressive—and no less threatening to capitalist accumulation. The end of the war found labor movements outside the core closely allied with other classes in effective pursuit of national independence and nationalistic development strategies (Freund, 1983; Furtado, 1970; Ahmad and Weiss, this volume). The first kind of movement, characteristic of the least developed regions of the Third World, threatened not only colonialism but the future of capitalism itself in the periphery. The second kind of movement, typical of the more developed peripheral nations, sought to further transform the old international division of labor through continuing redistribution and industrialization, and threatened to limit the access of international capital to semiperipheral economies. Finally, in the war-torn developed capitalist economies of Western Europe and Japan, the left emerged from the world war against fascism ideologically strengthened, its socialist project intact.

As a result of these victories and the challenge to worldwide capitalist accumulation they represented, capitalists in the core were forced to acquiesce in an unprecedented series of compromises with all these sets of popular forces. Out of these compromises evolved the main institutional vehicle of the postwar world capitalist order: the multinational corporation. It was to protect and foster the activities of this institution for the transnational investment of productive capital that the whole political, military, monetary, and financial superstructure of the postwar capitalist order was created. Yet the transnational corporation was not some marvelous idea that sprang full-blown from the minds of particularly inventive, progressive, or prescient metropolitan capitalists. It was in fact a product of class struggle forced on capitalists by the logic of the compromises they were compelled to make with labor in particular and with popular forces in general in the different parts of the world system as the crisis of the world capitalist order came to an end.

Important among these concessions was a historic compromise with popular forces in the core, particularly in the United States. Capitalists and the state were forced to recognize a significant redistribution of wealth and a weakening of the disciplinary power of the capitalist labor market by leaving in place the social welfare institutions won by popular forces during the world crisis. Even more importantly (since this redistributive mechanism was shortlived once the accumulation process got fully underway), capitalists were forced to validate and sanction in law the organizational gains and growing power of labor in the work place (Montgomery, 1979; Arrighi and Silver, this volume). As a result, the right of workers to organize, to bargain collectively, and to strike for greater returns to their labor was expressly recognized by capitalists and the state. To be sure these historic gains by labor were limited to basic and big industry, and they were won at a great cost to labor. In exchange for these advances, organized labor formally or informally abandoned its commitment to a socialist project and renounced its historic struggle to influence the way work was organized (Montgomery, 1979).

Under United States auspices, this historic compromise between capital and labor in the United States subsequently came to inform industrial relations in the other capitalist core powers (Meier, 1981) and much of the industrializing periphery as well (Spalding, 1977). Everywhere this compromise was effected, organized labor effectively renounced its class project, acquiesced to the capitalist logic of continuing revolution in the forces of production, and lent its bureaucratic weight toward disciplining the labor force and regularizing industrial conflict. It did so, however, in exchange for the promise of a share in resulting productivity gains, the expectation of steadily rising real wages, and the guarantee of the preservation—even strengthening—of its syndical organizations.

Outside the United States this workplace compromise was complemented by others designed to contain popular forces and reconstruct the world market for capitalist accumulation. The economies of Western Europe were rebuilt through a massive transfer of resources from the United States (the Marshall Plan), the economy of Japan through large-scale internal redistribution and reform under the United States occupation. In the colonized periphery, the United States was forced to compromise with the forces for national liberation by seeking to limit their social and economic objectives by supporting their political ones. The rapidly industrializing nations of the semiperiphery, however, presented metropolitan capital with a particularly thorny problem. Thanks to the pressures of reformist political coalitions during the world crisis, development of these economies benefitted from a significant redistribution of wealth, both internationally (as a consequence of default on the foreign debt and the partial suspension of unequal exchange through trade with the core) and domestically (as a result of the transfer of resources from the export sector to urban industrial, middle, and working class groups). The relative development of these semiperipheral economies, the size of their internal markets, and the extent of their resources made them especially attractive to metropolitan capital after 1945. But these states emerged from the crisis governed by popular, distributionist, and developmentalist political coalitions in which organized labor played a prominent role. These coalitions were jealous of their nation's new-found industrial development and relative economic independence, and they were armed with an ideology of development that rejected the old liberal international division of labor.

The multinational corporation evolved as an effort by capital to take advantage of the opportunities for accumulation, and avoid constraints on that process, that were embodied in these various victories of popular forces. In the United States core it could serve as a vehicle for disinvestment, thus enabling capitalists to elude high and expanding labor and taxation costs at home, yet take advantage of increased domestic demand fostered by those wages and the redistributionist policies of the social welfare regime. In the rest of the core and in the semideveloped periphery the multinational corporation enabled metropolitan capitalists to link their investment abroad to the goals of national reconstruction and national industrialization while, at the same time, gaining access to cheaper labor and large internal markets. Finally, in the least developed parts of the periphery, investment by multinational corporations could allegedly promote capitalist development through primary commodity extraction and, increasingly (as labor costs rose in the core and semiperiphery), promote a kind of industrialization there as well (Deyo, this volume).

Each of these overlapping strategies, embodied in the transnationalization of productive investment by the multinational corporation, however, unleashed a new set of contradictions; and each defined a new level of struggle between labor and capital. In time these contradictions and struggles brought about a new crisis of accumulation on a world scale—a crisis first manifest in the periphery, where the compromises worked least well, then in the semiperiphery, where they worked less well, and finally in the core itself.

The dynamics of this whole process are only now becoming clear, but they can be briefly sketched here. In the parts of the periphery where the activities of multinational corporations were limited or where the nature of their investment was primarily in traditional extractive primary export production, the influence of capital investment and the limited development it fostered often proved insufficient to contain fully the ongoing struggle of popular forces to establish a nationalist and socialist order. In fact, where investment in extractive economies in the periphery intensified, the result seems to have deepened the struggle between domestic labor and foreign capital and to have galvanized popular forces in their struggle against metropolitan capitalism. Be that as it may, what is certain is that the ability of multinational investment to promote and maintain a favorable climate for its operations in much of the periphery proved illusory in the postwar world. Efforts by the United States government to protect and expand such investment soon involved the government in a serious of extremely costly and, over the long haul, often ineffectual and self-defeating endeavors—the most important of which was the war in Vietnam.

In the semiperiphery, penetration by manufacturing multinationals initially promoted rapid growth as it denationalized and expanded domestic industrial production. But because these economies were burdened by inefficient agrarian structures (themselves a product of previous incorporation into the world economy as primary producers) and because of the economic drain involved in foreign ownership (interfirm transfers, profit remittances, costs of inappropriate technology), this kind of development rapidly generated severe foreign exchange bottlenecks, serious balance of payments problems, chronic inflation and currency devaluation, and growing unemployment. Under these conditions the postwar compromise between organized labor and capital broke down rapidly, and the reformist popular developmental coalitions in power after the war fell apart. A favorable climate for foreign investors was temporarily preserved by massive loans from foreign sources to ease the economic crisis, and by the institutionalization of United States-backed authoritarian regimes to repress the labor movement and popular forces generally. But these measures only delayed the economic and political crisis in the semiperiphery. By the start of the 1980s the effectiveness of these stop-gap measures had been exhausted: Semiperipheral governments could no longer meet the payments on their staggering foreign debts; their efforts to do so at the expense of the domestic working class unleashed social and political forces that threatened the very existence of the authoritarian regimes themselves.

Finally, as capitalists in the United States core gradually divested from light and heavy manufacturing and transferred production sites to Western Europe and East Asia and beyond, they increased the competitive position of rival national economies in the world market. Disinvestment thus seriously undercut the vitality of the United States economy, and undermined the hegemony of the nation-state that capitalists everywhere had come to depend upon. This whole process strained and then broke apart parts of the superstructure of monetary, banking, and trade agreements on which the postwar expansion had depended. Moreover, as unemployment in the United States rose and real wages stagnated, the compromise with organized labor fell apart; and as the government balanced the deficit from imperial defense through an attack on the social welfare budget, internal demand further stagnated and effective redistribution of surplus declined.

During the 1970s the contradictions inherent in the postwar compromises between capital and popular forces fully revealed themselves. And as the compromises broke down, the whole fabric of accumulation in the postwar world economy began to unravel. As the decade advanced, class conflict within nations escalated; and consequently, tensions between them multiplied. Their confidence shaken, capitalists all over the world proved increasingly unwilling to invest productively at home or abroad. They turned instead to speculation in commodities, in currencies, and in foreign loans. In their desperate effort to reduce their costs they began to attack labor unions directly.

They launched full scale offensives on the social measures that protected consumers, the unemployed, the sick, the old, and the young. Most ominously, with the assistance of an ever more bellicose capitalist state, they began massive investment of their capital in the highly profitable, unproductive, and grossly antisocial manufacture of awesome military arsenals.

This whole history seems so obvious now that it is hard to realize that it is only in the past few years that social scientists could begin to contemplate such a state of affairs. Until the 1970s, the contradictions inherent in the remarkable postwar expansion of capitalism, especially those of the core, went largely unnoticed. For more than two blissful decades the compromises between capitalists and popular forces created conditions that fostered an explosion of growth and accumulation that seemed to eliminate class conflict in the developed world. Contemplating this new era most social scientists writing in the 1950s and 1960s— liberals and many Marxists alike—interpreted this state of affairs not for what it was—a temporary compromise—but as the beginning of a new world order where the prospects for capitalist expansion seemed limitless and where the old idea of socialist transformation, spearheaded by the industrial proletariat, had no place.

It was during this heyday of postwar capitalist expansion that a growing army of liberal social scientists in the core began to celebrate "an end to ideology" and elaborated theories of the "convergence" of postindustrial societies, capitalist and "socialist" alike. It was in the formulation of "modernization theory," however, that their assumptions about the end of class conflict, and the beneficial effects of the spread of "Western" and "modern" values, advanced technology, and capitalist investment from the core were most systematically worked out. Conceived as a rationale for the postwar expansion of United States economic and cultural influence into the rest of the world, modernization theory was projected back in time and became the orthodox liberal explanation of the evolution of the whole of modern world history (Black, 1966).

Much more surprising, given the classical assumptions on which they built their interpretations, were the development theories of Marxist scholars in the core. Some abandoned hope in the revolutionary potential of the industrial working class altogether and focused their theories of social transformation on the alienation of minorities, students, women, and "one-dimensional men" outside the workplace. Others kept their classical Marxism intact in the face of the loss of their natural constituency, the organized working class. They did so by casting their analysis of inevitable socialist transformation in increasingly structuralist, abstract, and economistic terms—terms practically devoid of active human intervention. Even those like Paul Baran (1957) and Andre Gunder Frank (1967), who concentrated their attention on the periphery (where the contradictions of postwar capitalist development were severe and revealed themselves early), rested their case on a mechanical, economistic recipe for socialist transformation. Capitalist extraction of surplus made development in the periphery impossible; world socialism would somehow result from the revolt of the dispossessed in the Third World.

It was therefore appropriate that the major breakthrough in social science analysis of modern world history came not from liberals and Marxists in the core, but from reformist nationalists in the periphery (Furtado, 1970; Sunkel and Paz, 1971). These thinkers undertook to explain and to justify the emergence of the broad popular, developmentalist, and nationalist political coalitions in the semideveloped periphery during the previous world crisis. They sought to promote continued redistribution and national capitalist development through deepening the industrial transformation of the semiperiphery. Because these scholars indirectly challenged liberal development theory, especially its assumption of comparative advantage in world trade; because they argued that, historically, the world capitalist system had distorted and stunted peripheral development (and thus, implicitly, fostered the development of the core); and because they developed a sophisticated, comparative methodology to calibrate the full range of developmental opportunities and constraints in the periphery over time, their thought has proven to be a much more useful—and enduring—contribution to world development theory than that of their liberal and neo-Marxist contemporaries in the core. Yet, true to its corporativist intellectual wellsprings and populist political underpinnings—and its commitment to a national capitalist development strategy—dependency or structural analysis relied on a conception of change that was economistic and technologically deterministic, and wrote class conflict out of its historical analysis. Moreover, its prescription for industrial development in the periphery proved essentially compatible with the major economic trend of the postwar world, the expansion of the manufacturing multinational corporation. Consequently, like liberal and Marxist thought in the core, dependency theory largely ignored the developmental implications of the victories of popular forces in the past. And it proved ill prepared for the emergence of organized labor as the primary impediment to capitalist development in semiperipheral nations as the postwar compromise between capital and labor first foundered and then broke down completely.

In contrast to these rival postwar intellectual traditions, the world-system approach has proven much more receptive to incorporating the workers' struggle into its mode of analysis. No doubt part of the reason lies in the fact that it emerged in the 1970s as the postwar class compromises began to break down. Yet it also sought consciously to build a Marxist conception of class conflict into its model of global historical dynamics (Wallerstein, 1974). As the essays in this volume demonstrate, and as the activities of the labor group at the Braudel Center have long attested, labor as subject within world-system analysis has for some time been a primary focus of attention within the approach.

Yet, in a curious way, world-system analysts—even those who focus on labor itself—have been wont to subordinate labor's struggles, like the class struggle generally, to the "logic" of impersonal forces—to the "demands" of the world market, to the "exigencies" of capital accumulation, to the "periodicity" of the famous long waves. Even the best recent work on this last issue (Gorden et al., 1982), for example, despite its efforts to meet this very criticism, provides only half a loaf. That work is an admirable attempt to link historical analysis of the United States economy over a century and a half with the whole panoply of concrete institutional and human responses by classes in struggle. Those classes battle to mold labor process and control, to influence the climate for investment and for distribution, to innovate tactically and strategically. Nevertheless, despite its best efforts, this work grants workers a role only in disrupting the institutional arrangements that bring an end to the expansionary phase of the long wave of capitalist accumulation. It does not recognize their significant role in creating through struggle the very economic and political conditions that mold the nature and success of the expansionary phase itself.

It is for that reason that this chapter has emphasized the victories of popular forces in the global system during the last world crisis. Those victories set the conditions for the next expansionary phase, and determined in large part its institutional form. Casting the issue in this way—placing labor's struggle and its progressive victories at the center of global analysis—is to empower not capitalists and their world-system but rather the workers and their struggle to overcome it. Doing so helps correct against the teleological and mechanistic tendencies of much world-system analysis because it grounds that analysis in the concrete and human struggle of the class that alone has the power to overthrow the system. Only by recognizing the progressive victories of popular forces as responsible both for capitalist expansion and contraction will it be possible to combat and to minimize the chauvinistic and divisive strategies available to capitalists as they seek to impoverish and divide the working class once the contradictions of expansion begin to reveal themselves, stagnation in the world economy sets in, and the rollback of past working class victories is attempted.[3]

Readers of world-systems analysis and of this volume may or may not accept this evaluation of the promise and failings of the approach. There is one area, however, in which the expressed goal of world-system analysis, and its means to achieve that goal, stand in naked contradiction. Like much of the social science written in all the rival paradigms, world-system analysis—even that which focuses on the working class itself—has proven inaccessible to the very class it seeks to empower. By this I do not mean that it is physically inaccessible, although that is also true. I mean primarily that abstract discussion of the kind engaged in in this introduction and in the bulk of the following chapters is, by itself, congenitally incapable of touching and moving its human subject matter. Only by focusing on labor's story, and learning to tell it creatively[4] will our work be able to link heart and mind, and emotion and intellect, in the human agency, the working class, that drives the system forward and wields the power capable of transforming it.

If world-system analysis is serious about its conception of historical development and change, it must increasingly place working people at the center of analysis. Doing so can both illuminate and make politically relevant the undeniable, and democratic, conceptual breakthrough associated with the paradigm. Doing so will protect world-system analysis from its structural tendency to reify capital and make capitalist initiatives the primary motor of the capitalist world-economy. Doing so can concretize the human dynamic in the genesis and contraction of the long waves in the world economy, locating the controversy over effective demand or declining rate of profit, over the relative weight of entrepreneurial invention versus working-class resistance, in the human sphere of class struggle where it belongs. Doing so can bring the abstract scholastic debate over consciousness of class, ethnicity, and nation into the concrete realm of historical reality. Doing so, most of all, can place people at the heart of the democratic history world-system analysis seeks to promote. It can empower the people who lie unacknowledged in the bourgeois history of great men, ignored in the neo-Marxist history of abstractions, disdained in the neocorporativist history of the structuralists, and demeaned in the "new" social history that ignores politics and regales the working poor with personalistic sops ("they have a history too"). Placing labor at the heart of the study of modern world history can unite the classical Marxist position of political praxis aimed at the working class, with the global dynamics of class struggle in a world social system. In that unity lies the best hope for peace and a more humane world order.

All this is easy to say, and very difficult to do. But the chapters that follow take important steps toward the goal of placing labor at the center of world-system analysis.

In Part 1, "Theoretical Approaches to the Study of Labor in the World-System," Michael Burawoy leads off with a reassessment, built from the perspective of the shop floor, of the relationship between production and politics in evolving capitalist and socialist societies around the world. Steven Bunker advances an ecological approach to the issues of peripheral labor exploitation in particular and development theory in general. Finally, Christopher Chase-Dunn reviews the tenets of world-system theory to argue that, contrary to appearances, the mechanics of the system have changed very little in the contemporary period.

In Part 2, "Labor Systems in an Evolving Capitalist World Order," Richard Fox emphasizes the relatively independent role of the colonial state in India in promoting economic development based on a variety of labor systems, and in charting its reactions to the forms of resistance and protest of direct producers. Carol Smith uses Guatemalan material to argue that the struggles of direct producers historically distort the logic of capitalism and can explain the remarkable vitality of precapitalist and petty-commodity production arrangements in contemporary peripheral societies. And William Martin constructs a historical overview of South African gold mining labor systems to conclude that the recent decline of immigrant labor to the mines may be a temporary phenomenon.

In Part 3, "Working Class Culture, Organization, and Protest," Giovanni Arrighi and Beverly Silver present a case study of the relationship between capitalist development, workers' bargaining power, and the movement of capital within the world system. This chapter focuses on the effects of labor's struggle in the United States in the 1930s and 1940s on postwar capital migration to Europe and European labor protest in the 1960s. Alice Ingerson uses Portuguese materials to unravel and assess the contradictory evaluations of the culture of textile workers in an evolving world-system. June Nash explores the developing consciousness of United States electrical workers who have faced very different challenges over the course of this century. Frederic Deyo finds the key to the relative weakness of the the labor movements of Hong Kong, Taiwan, South Korea, and Singapore in the special structure of industrialization in those small East Asian societies. Finally, Nesar Ahmad and Lawrence Weiss compare the distinctive roles of industrial workers in the great foreign boycott movements in India and China in the first decades of this century.

The essays collected in this volume evolved out of papers presented at the Seventh Political Economy of the World-System Conference, sponsored by the Center for International Studies, Duke University, March 30 to April 1, 1983. On behalf of the contributors, I wish to thank the director of that Center, A. Kenneth Pye, for that support.

NOTES

1. Readers of previous volumes in this series need no introduction to these paradigmatic schools of thought. Others will want to review the treatment of the world-system paradigm presented by Chase-Dunn in this volume, as well as the introductions to the previous volumes in this series.

2. These goals, which unite those who take world-system analysis seriously, are reaffirmed by four of the most notable contributors to this analytical tradition in the Introduction to their recent *Dynamics of Global Crisis* (Amin et al., 1982: 10).

3. Although attention here has focused on recent history, this kind of analysis is applicable to earlier periods as well. Compare, for example, the economistic logic of Lenin's explanation of imperialism (1939) with the social logic of Walter LaFeber's (1963) brilliant case study of the working-class motor behind United States expansion at the end of the nineteenth century. Moreover, although discussion in this introduction and in the chapters in this volume by Burawoy, Ingerson, Nash, Arrighi and Silver, Deyo, and Ahmad and Weiss focuses on the industrial proletariat in the core and semiperiphery, the essays by Martin, Fox, and especially Smith collected here suggest the centrality of the struggle by agrarian classes to capitalist development in the periphery.

4. Doing so, I believe, will involve learning to link narrative and analytical approaches, the humanities and social science. Compare, for example, the effectiveness in reaching and moving the literate layman of Eric Hobsbawm's *The Age of Revolution* (1962) on the one hand, and most work in the world-system paradigm, on the other. The analysis of economic and social change in a global system is not so different; the method, style, and mode of presentation is.

REFERENCES

AMIN, A., et al. (1982) Dynamics of Global Crisis. New York: Monthly Review.
BARAN, P. (1967) The Political Economy of Growth. New York: Monthly Review.
BLACK, C. (1966) The Dynamics of Modernization. New York: Harper & Row.
FRANK, A. G. (1967) Capitalism and Underdevelopment in Latin America. New York: Monthly Review.

FREUND, B. (1983) "Labor and labor history in Africa, a review of the literature." (unpublished)

FURTADO, C. (1970). The Economic Development of Latin America. Cambridge, England: Cambridge University Press.

GORDON, D., et al. (1982) Segmented Work, Divided Workers. Cambridge, England: Cambridge University Press.

HOBSBAWM, E. (1962) The Age of Revolution, 1789-1948. New York: New American Library.

LaFEBER, W. (1963) The New Empire. New York: Cornell University Press.

LENIN, V. I. (1939) Imperialism. New York: International Publishers.

MEIER, C. (1981) "Two postwar eras and the conditions for stability in twentieth-century Western Europe." American Historical Review 86, 2 (April): 327-352.

MONTGOMERY, D. (1979) Workers' Control in America. Cambridge, England: Cambridge University Press.

POLANYI, K. (1944) The Great Transformation. New York: Farrar and Rinehart.

SPALDING, H. (1977) Organized Labor in Latin America. New York: Harper & Row.

SUNKEL, O. and P. PAZ (1971) El subdesarrollo y la teoría del desarrollo. Mexico: Siglo Veintiuno.

WALLERSTEIN, I. (1974) "The rise and future demise of the world capitalist system: concepts for comparative analysis." Comparative Studies in Society and History 16 (September): 387-415.

PART 1

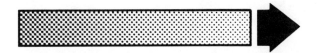

THEORETICAL APPROACHES TO THE STUDY OF LABOR IN THE WORLD-SYSTEM

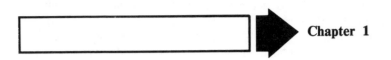

Chapter 1

THE CONTOURS OF PRODUCTION POLITICS

Michael Burawoy
University of California, Berkeley

The connection of labor and politics is at the heart of the Marxist tradition. Classical Marxism held that the working class, forged in production, would project itself into revolutionary struggles against the state. The development of the forces of production would not only lay the material basis for socialism but would also foster the political conditions for the transition from capitalism to socialism. That is, the expansion of the forces of production would prepare the working class for its political role as universal emancipator, establishing the conditions for a working class party to conquer power, transform the state, and usher in the new period of socialism. In the present epoch pessimism has overrun theory as well as practice. Just as working class struggles have only rarely assumed revolutionary fervor and have more generally lost touch with any political mission, so concepts, questions, and analyses have submitted to gloom or voluntarism. Rather than going "beyond the working class" or crying "farewell to the working class," I propose to replace the link between politics and labor at the center of study. If in practice one cannot yet avoid the fragments, at least in theory we can restore their connection. We can avoid the separation of economics from politics, the depoliticization of production and overpoliticization of the state.

AUTHOR'S NOTE: This chapter has benefitted from extensive discussion with Erik Wright and members of the Labor Policy group at the International Institute for Comparative Social Research, Science Center, Berlin.

But there is a second reason for examining the relationship of labor to politics. Not only is that relationship at the heart of the Marxist conception of the struggle for socialism, it is also at the core of the socialist project itself. Although within Marxism there have been utopian impulses that conceive of socialism as the end of "labor" and of "politics," as well as equally powerful anti-utopian themes that refuse even to consider the nature of labor, politics, and their interrelationship under socialism, the socialist revolutions of the twentieth century made nonsense of such pretenses. In a world without socialism it was perhaps permissible to indulge in utopian fantasies and anti-utopian scientism; in a world *with* socialism, and moreover one that is often difficult to recognize as such, we can no longer afford such luxuries. Like any other society, socialism must produce and reproduce its human and material basis, just as it must undertake the regulation of social life. But socialism is distinctive in that it expands the arena of creative labor at the expense of alienated labor, the realm of freedom at the expense of the realm of necessity, and collective regulation at the expense of class domination. Alternative visions suggest different forms and combinations of labor and politics, but both elements must be there.

Necessarily the conception of the future reflects back on the analysis of the present, and vice versa. Thus, a one-sided understanding of capitalism leads to a one-sided understanding of socialism. Studies of the labor process too often project a future of emancipated labor without any consideration of politics under socialism, while studies of the state project a concern with the transformation of societal regulation without rooting it within a transformation of work. The question, therefore, is not whether to adopt an exclusive concern with production or with politics but to understand how the two interrelate. We must already pose these questions within contemporary societies if we are to think of a transition to socialism in other than cataclysmic terms that wipe out the past.

RETURNING POLITICS TO PRODUCTION

The separation of labor and politics has its roots in Marx's critique of Hegel on the one side and classical political economy on the other. Marx imported into his own analysis the separation of state and civil society, politics, and economics as the hallmark of capitalism. In contrast to precapitalist social formations, under capitalism relations between direct producer and appropriator of the product are no longer relations of *political* subordination and *legal* servitude. Once workers are dispossessed of direct access to the means of subsistence, extra-economic coercion is no longer central to the appropriation of the product. The act of production is simultaneously the production of the means of existence of the laborer on the one side and of surplus value—the means of existence of the capitalist qua capitalist—on the other. The coincidence of production and appropriation means that the act of production is simultaneously the reproduction of social relations between labor and capital. For Marx, then, the relations of production reproduce themselves of themselves. Furthermore, that reproduction is viewed as problematic only in the long-run dynamics of capitalism.

To be sure, the reproduction of relations of production requires the domination of capital over labor. But Marx presents that domination as monolithic, undisputed, and inherent to the relations of exploitation. Production and domination are an inseparable couple. Domination is necessitated by the search for profit, by the requirements of exploitation, just as it is made possible by the powerlessness of workers dependent upon capital for their survival. Marx conceived of only one *tendential* form of domination of capital over labor, what we shall refer to as "market despotism." As we shall see, this is actually quite exceptional—its conditions of existence are only rarely realized. The reproduction of alternative modes of domination alongside similar labor processes points to the importance of theorizing the distinction between production and its mode of regulation, between the labor process and the *political apparatuses of production*.

For Marx significant struggles, such as those over the Factory Acts, are political struggles that take place outside production. While their *objective* is to reshape relations of production, their *object* is the state that gives them their distinctive form. No attempt is made to root those struggles in *specific* types of labor process and production apparatuses. Similarly, in his writings on France, preformed classes are wheeled in from the economic arena to participate in political struggles, expressed in the formation of alliances, parties, and so on. That the forms of these struggles were decisively shaped by the organization of work and its regulation is awarded neither theoretical nor political importance (except in the case of the peasantry). So we face a paradox: At the same time that the factory is regarded as the crucible of class consciousness and collective resistance, it is presented as an arena of undisputed domination, of fragmentation, degradation, and mystification. The paradox can be resolved by returning to the nineteenth century and, first, recognizing the variability of domination and, second, focusing on struggles at the point of production as well as in the public sphere—that is, by theorizing a *politics of production*.

Contemporary theories of the labor process close off the openings within Marx's analysis to a politics of production. Harry Braverman's powerful *Labor and Monopoly Capital* has set the framework for the debate of the last decade. Following a certain anthropological reading of Marx, Braverman defines labor as the purposeful transformation of nature; the form of the labor process therefore turns on the relationship between mental and manual labor. Capitalist control becomes the separation of these elements, the separation of conception and execution, the progressive expropriation of skill from the direct producer, which enhances both domination and efficiency. Braverman then offers an historical account of the way capitalism strips away the subjective moments of work for the ascendance of the objective moments of domination. His critics become entangled in this "subject-object dialectic," insisting on the importance of the subjective—in particular, class struggle—as well as the objective (the logic of capital) as a prime mover in history.

Braverman's critics also develop a more differentiated notion of control. Thus, Friedman's *Industry and Labor* offers a historical account of the interaction of control and struggle in England in which "responsible autonomy" complements deskilling as a managerial strategy reproduced and even extended in contemporary capitalism. In a more far-reaching amendment of Braverman's analysis, Richard Edwards's *Contested Terrain* insists on the centrality of struggle in the successive emergence in the United States of three forms of control: simple, technical, and bureaucratic. In the nineteenth century, firms were generally small and markets competitive, so that management exercised arbitrary and personalistic domination over workers. With the twentieth-century growth of large-scale industry, simple control gave way to new forms, in particular to attempts to regulate work through technological arrangements such as the assembly line. This technical mode of control generated its own forms of struggle and, after World War II, gave way to bureaucratic regulation, in which rules are used to define and evaluate work tasks and govern the application of sanctions. Bureaucratic control usually emerged within new industries in the corporate sector without displacing technical and simple control in other industries.

Just as Braverman takes domination as unproblematic, so Friedman and Edwards take resistance as equally unproblematic. Instead of reification and fragmentation spreading through society like a cancerous growth, now it is struggle that is secreted by all corners of life. None of these analyses develops a theory of the formation of interests and of capacities to realize those interests, necessary to go beyond the juxtaposition of subject and object, resistance and domination.

Braverman's scheme cannot be simply reequilibrated to take struggle into account. It cannot be amended or upended; it must be transformed. We must develop a true political economy of production, one that incorporates ideological and political dimensions as well as the material practices that constitute the economic dimension. We must curb the imperial ambitions of the concept of control and unveil its hidden secrets. Thus, Edwards's three historically successive *forms* of control confuse and conceal three *dimensions* of production. Simple control underlines the *relational* dimension of work, technical control underlines the *instruments of production*, and bureaucratic control underlines a concern with *social forms of regulation*. The first two dimensions, when combined with activities of transforming raw materials into useful products, constitute the *labor process*, whereas the third indexes the *political apparatuses of production*. Thus, the historical development of the process of production must be seen in terms of the changing forms of labor process, apparatuses of production, and their interrelationship. With this formulation, we can examine how the labor process on the one side and the production apparatuses on the other generate, first, ideological *effects*—that is, shape interests—and second, political *effects*—that is, determine the realization of those interests through struggles. In turn we can observe how actual or anticipated struggles reshape the labor process and its regulative apparatuses.

The paradox, then, of contemporary Marxist discussions of the labor process is that while they harp on the idea of control, they fail to theorize the political and ideological moments of production. Marxist theories of the state have been complicit in this depoliticization of production. Leninist orthodoxy has always insisted on the unique function of the state as the decisive factor of cohesion in society: To transform the state is a necessary and, under appropriate circumstances, a sufficient condition for the transition to socialism. This perspective rests on erroneous, simplistic, and unexplored assumptions not only about the nature of the state and of the workplace but also about the relationship between the two. It is a perspective that refuses to examine both the relative autonomy and the mutual limitation of the apparatuses of production and the apparatuses of the state. The relationship between the two sets of apparatuses is historically variable, so that the transformation of the state is neither a necessary consequence nor a necessary cause of the transformation of production apparatuses; however, a transition to producer socialism would require that both such transformations take place. The research agenda entailed in this chapter is two-fold. The first objective is to locate the conditions for the transformation of the production apparatuses. Comparative analysis suggests that the labor process, the mode of reproduction of labor power, relations among enterprises, and the state all combine in different ways to limit the form of production apparatuses. The second objective is to examine the political and ideological consequences of different apparatuses of production for both the workplace and the state.

Contemporary theories of the state recognize the interpenetration of economic and political processes. Thus, Jürgen Habermas captures the essence of a wide range of "interventionist" theories of the state in his account of the consequences of the erosion of the market as a mechanism of distribution for politics. On the one hand the state becomes increasingly involved in filling "functional gaps" in the process of capital accumulation so that relations of production are "repoliticized," while on the other hand state politics have become "scientized" with a view to "depoliticizing" the public sphere. In other words, instrumental rationality has overflowed its boundaries into the realm of the state while substantive rationality has entered the realm of production. This notion of interpenetration linked to a functional role of the state (which has informed the work of others such as Offe, O'Connor, Holloway, and Picciotto) precisely fails to acknowledge a genuine politics *indigenous* to production. The labor process is an unexamined given. The analyses begin not with the conditions of production but with the conditions of reproduction.

A second movement toward a concept of production politics can be found in Antonio Gramsci's expansion of the concept of state to include a reformulated civil society. Inasmuch as production apparatuses then become part of the state, this only displaces the problem to one of the relationship among different apparatuses of the state. It is no solution, even if it sensitizes us to the problem. Contemporary theories of the state that follow Gramsci's concern with the organization and repression of class struggle, such as those of Poulantzas and Althusser, insist on a separation of the political and the economic as the hallmark of capitalism. Indeed, the very notion of the relative autonomy of the state, which Poulantzas places on a pedestal in *Political Power and Social Classes*, tends to become a justification for ignoring the economic arena, except at a very abstract level. Relative autonomy is seen to be necessary for the preservation of the cohesion of the entire social formation. The state must act against the economic interests of individual capitalists, fractions of capital, or even collective capital in order to preserve the capitalist order. It must disorganize the subordinate classes at the same time that it organizes the dominant classes into power bloc. How that relative autonomy is produced is never clear in this first work.

Poulantzas's last work, *State, Power, Socialism*, departs radically from his earlier functional notion of the state. The state is now viewed as a "social relation," expressing the balance of class forces. The state is no longer simply the *object* of struggles but becomes the *arena* of struggles both within and between apparatuses. Poulantzas now points beyond assertions about the necessity for the state to produce certain effects toward the conditions and manner of their production—that is, toward the *production of politics*. We must now look at the state (as Therborn also argues in *What Does the Ruling Class Do When It Rules*) as an ensemble of apparatuses with their own distinctive labor processes that, rather than produce commodities (although some, such as nationalized industries, do), produce and reproduce relations (police, law), provide services that socialize the costs of the reproduction of labor power (welfare, education) and of accumulation (postal service), or regulate political struggles within the state (representative apparatuses).

In short, the state is now endowed with productive components—it is no longer simply a superstructure but now has its own base. In the same way, the economy cannot be reduced to technical factors of production, but is a "base" with its own "superstructure." Politics is no longer the monopoly of the state but is found in the economic arena where power is materialized in specific apparatuses. From the *production of politics* we move inexorably to the *politics of production*.

> The economic *is* class struggle, *is* therefore relations of power—and not just economic power. (It is understood that these powers are specific through being attached to exploitation. . . .) In the case of classes, power comes down to objective positions rooted in the division of labor: it designates the capacity of each class to realise its specific interests in a relation of opposition to that capacity in other classes. It is therefore impossible for power to escape economic relations. Rooted in the production of surplus-value and in their relation to the political-ideological powers, these power relations are furthermore concretized in specific institutions—apparatuses: the companies, factories or production units that are the site of the extraction of surplus-value and of the exercise of these powers [Poulantzas, 1978: 36].

Yet the state retains a distinctive position among political apparatuses. It is still the decisive concentration of power in that it guarantees the conditions of and imparts class pertinence to non-state apparatuses. "The state is present in the constitution and reproduction of the relations of production" (Poulantzas, 1978: 18-19). But what does this mean? What indeed is the specificity of factory apparatuses "through being attached to exploitation"? What relations do they reproduce? What struggles do they regulate? Here Poulantzas is particularly unclear because he sets out from an analysis of the state, whereas the answers to these questions can emerge only from a reexamination of the labor process.

The very definition of the labor process becomes critical to the possibility of understanding the relationship between labor and politics. For Marx the basic elements of the labor process are "(1) purposeful activity, that is work itself, (2) the object on which work is performed, and (3) the instruments of that work" (Marx, 1976: 284). We shall add a further dimension—the relations among men and women as they engage in purposeful activity—which Marx explicitly refused to include in his generic definition.

> [The labor process is] the everlasting nature-imposed condition of human existence, and it is therefore independent of every form of that existence, or rather it is common to all forms of society in which human beings live. We did not, therefore, have to present the worker in his relationship with other workers; it was enough to present man and his labour on the one side and its materials on the other [Marx, 1976: 290].

But why should the human relationship to nature be the preeminent and defining characteristic of the labor process? Here Marx is paving the way for a particular meta-history—namely, the transhistorical expansion of the forces of production, the increasing capacity to transform nature. By insisting on the centrality of the social relations of productive activity, I simultaneously suspend Marx's meta-history and lay the foundation for a politics of production. History can no longer be reduced to the interaction of the forces of production and the relations of production but must incorporate the interaction of production politics with state politics.

Production on the one hand is the activity of transforming raw materials into useful products with instruments of production, while on the other hand involves a set of relations into which men and women enter as they transform those raw materials. A mode of production, therefore, consists of two sets of relations: relations *of* production through which surplus is appropriated and redistributed, and the relations *in* production through which nature is appropriated. Although both sets of relations necessarily coexist, the mode of production is defined by the relations of production. These include both *relations of exploitation*, which define the mode of appropriating surplus, and *relations of reproduction*, which define the relations of interdependence among units of production. For it is quite possible for the same relations *in* production to be found under different relations *of* production, for example a capitalist labor process (that is, one produced under capitalist relations of production) within a socialist mode of production.

Unlike Edwards, Friedman, and Braverman, within the sphere of production I distinguish the labor process as defined above from the political apparatuses of production. Political apparatuses are defined by their *effects*, the struggles they regulate. But what shall we mean by politics as such? By politics I understand struggles over or within relations of structured domination, struggles that take as their *objective* the quantitative or qualitative change of those relations. What then is the relationship between politics and apparatuses? I would have liked to claim a one-to-one correspondence between apparatuses and politics—that is, apparatuses guarantee the reproduction of a distinctive set of relations. In particular, apparatuses of the state should guarantee relations *of* production, while apparatuses of the workplace should guarantee relations *in* production. This, however, is patently not the case, as the apparatuses of the workplace are involved in struggles over wages and benefits—that is, relations of exploitation. A better approximation might be that production apparatuses regulate struggles over the labor process and the valorization process—relations in production and relations of exploitation—while state apparatuses regulate struggles over relations of *re*production. Yet this too departs from reality, as the state can be actively involved in the regulation of wages, benefits, working conditions, and even technology, and production apparatuses may regulate struggles designed to transform relations of *re*production, as when wage negotiations are tied to public control of investment.

Considering that there is at best a weak correlation between apparatuses and the relations they regulate—that is, there is not a one-to-one mapping between the two—we must choose between politics defined as struggles regulated by *specific apparatuses*, politics defined as struggles over *certain relations*, and the combination of the two. In the first, politics would have no fixed objective, and in the second it would have no fixed institutional locus. I have therefore opted for the more restrictive third definition, according to which politics refer to struggles within a specific arena aimed at specific sets of relations. Family politics are struggles waged within the family over patriarchal relations. Production politics are struggles waged within the arena of production over relations in and of production and regulated by production apparatuses. State politics, on the other hand, are distinctive in that they cannot be characterized by struggles over any particular set of relations. A given set of relations may or may not be the object of struggle within the arena of the state. This varies historically. What is distinctive about the state is its global character, its function as the factor of cohesion for the entire social formation. The state not only guarantees the reproduction of certain relations but, more distinctly, it is the apparatus that guarantees all other apparatuses. State politics include as their core the politics of politics. The characteristic effects of state apparatuses are to protect and shape family apparatuses, production apparatuses, community apparatuses, and so on.

The restriction of politics to struggle is not uncontroversial. It means, for example, that technology is not in and of itself political. Technology may imply *domination* but not necessarily *politics.* Technology may have political causes and political effects, but it itself is not political until it becomes the object of struggle. The distinction between domination and politics underscores the potentiality for the politicization of relations. It poses the question of the conditions under which, for example, technology, organization of work, investment decisions, and the apparatuses of production themselves become the objects of struggle.

The definition of politics as struggle confined to a particular arena with particular goals has broader political implications to which I shall return in the conclusion of this chapter. The idea of production politics and, perhaps even more clearly, the notion of production apparatuses also shed new insights on the development and transformation of capitalist and state socialist societies. We will show that production apparatuses have effects that cannot be explained by the labor process, alone or in combination with other structures, in particular for class struggles—that is, struggles between classes over the transformation of relations in and of production. As a first step this involves demonstrating that production apparatuses are indeed distinct from and can vary independently of the labor process.

FROM EARLY TO ADVANCED CAPITALISM

Marx's view that the political apparatuses of production would converge on a single form—market despotism—was based on three assumptions. First, it assumed that market competition among capitalists would drive them toward continual intensification and transformation of the labor process. Second, the subordination of labor to capital that is necessary to adapt to market forces would be accomplished through deskilling, so that workers would be transformed from manipulators of instruments into appendages of machines. Third, workers would remain completely dependent on wage labor for their survival. These conditions have rarely held simultaneously, even under early capitalism. It is not surprising, therefore, that their violation has provided the basis for different periodizations of the capitalist labor process. Thus, Braverman conceptualizes such a periodization in terms of deskilling: Monopoly capitalism represents the eclipse of the craft worker. This flies in the face of what we know about early and advanced capitalism: There were many unskilled occupations in the first period, and there were and are many skilled occupations in the second period. It is therefore difficult to periodize capitalism on the basis of the separation of conception and execution. Edwards, on the other hand, upholds a periodization based on market relations among firms. Anarchy of the market in the early period led to simple (often despotic) control, while in the period of advanced capitalism the rise of oligopolies encouraged the development of new forms of control: technical and bureaucratic. Such a periodization of capitalism is not only founded on a certain conceptual confusion but must confront two important anomalies: the persistence of competitive capital (which Edwards acknowledges) and, perhaps more important, its active recreation in the monopoly period.

The periodization I am proposing here is based on Marx's third condition of market despotism: the changing character of the dependence of the reproduction of labor power (the maintenance and renewal of the labor force) on the labor process and its regulation. In the early period the individual was bound through economic and noneconomic ties to the employer; livelihood outside work depended on cooperation at work. In advanced capitalism the state begins to protect labor at work from unfair labor practices and to protect labor outside work with social security. Despotic regimes give way to hegemonic regimes. At the same time, there are variations in factory regimes within early and advanced capitalism—in particular, variations stemming from differences in competition among firms on the one side and deskilling on the other. Nevertheless, as we shall see, the consequences of these factors are decisively shaped by the character of the dependence of the reproduction of labor power on the labor process.

The cotton industry of nineteenth-century Britain, particularly the spinning process (which Marx viewed as the most advanced form of production of his time), underscores the difficulties of adopting competition among firms or levels of skill as criteria for the periodization of capitalism. We can discern the succession of two forms of despotism in nineteenth-century cotton spinning. In the first period, worker control over the instruments of production and fierce competition among capitalists led to a system of inside contracting, which was based on male domination over women and children—patriarchal despotism. In the second period, following crises in the cotton industry that pushed many small firms out of business, competition abated. At the same time deskilling proceeded apace so that the real subsumption of labor replaced its formal subsumption. A new, paternalistic production politics emerged. Under patriarchal production politics, the employer granted the inside contractor the resources and autonomy to dominate his helpers as he wished. Under paternalistic production apparatuses, the employer and his managers themselves intervened into the family, shaping the relationships among men, women, and children. But in both cases survival outside work depended upon cooperation at work. Economic and noneconomic ties of bondage laid the basis of despotism, whether of a patriarchal or a paternalistic character.

With the transition to advanced capitalism these ties were decisively reorganized in two ways. First, the state began to safeguard workers from arbitrary dismissal—negatively through the repeal of Masters and Servants Laws, and positively through trade union recognition and the legalization of strikes. Workers could now appeal against unfair labor practices and collectively resist managerial despotism. On a day-to-day level, managerial autonomy was thereby circumscribed. Second, the state began to recognize, gropingly at first, the idea of a social wage. On the one hand, tacit or explicit minimum wage legislation limited the use of earnings (particularly piece rates) as a means of coercion. On the other hand, social security, particularly in the form of unemployment compensation, reduced the dependence of workers upon the firm. These two forms of state intervention—the one restricting managerial discretion through the regulation of working conditions (labor process) and the form of production apparatuses, while the other increased the independence of the reproduction of labor power from the expenditure of effort—altered the balance of coercion and consent. Capital could no longer depend entirely on the economic whip of the market to exact cooperation but instead had to supplement force with persuasion. Thus, *hegemonic* regimes arose to replace *despotic* regimes. Consent was protected by the armor of coercion and, moreover, the application of coercion itself became the object of consent.

The transition did not take place all at once but was more or less prolonged depending on the development of the relevant state apparatuses. Furthermore, it took place at different times in different countries. But by the end of World War II the basic institutions of state protection for labor were in place. The periodization of production politics presented here should not blind us to variations within early and advanced capitalist societies, particularly variations due to market relations among firms and levels of deskilling in the labor process. We have already illustrated how variations in formal/real subsumption of labor and in competition among firms gave rise to different forms of production politics within early capitalism. Similar variations can be discerned within advanced capitalism. Thus, other things being equal, production politics assume a more despotic form in the competitive sector than in the monopoly sector. However, firms with the same labor process and under similar market forces would not normally exhibit the same production politics under early and advanced capitalism. This is likely to occur only where the advanced capitalist state relinquishes its distinctive regulative functions. California agribusiness, for example, until recently relied on legal or illegal migrant workers from Mexico who had no access to social security and were vulnerable to coercive management practices, facilitated by agriculture's exemption from the National Labor Relations Act. Here we find a monopoly sector industry exhibiting a despotic production politics reminiscent of the nineteenth century. It is an exception that proves the rule. Production politics also vary with skill—craft administration fits into neither despotic nor hegemonic category. Although I have not researched this question, I should expect the craft administration of advanced capitalism to be very different from that of early capitalism.

Production politics vary not only within but also between capitalist societies. Comparative dimensions are never explicitly examined by Braverman, Friedman, or Edwards, although they are implicitly present in their analyses. Thus Braverman's portrait of deskilling as a relatively smooth process, unruffled by resistance from the working class, reflects (albeit in a distorted manner) the relative strengths of capital and labor in the United states. More specifically, it reflects the distinctive forms of production politics that arose with the late development of industrial unionism—so late, in fact, that far from providing an institutional basis for resistance to deskilling they took it as a fait accompli.

Friedman's response to Braverman underscores the importance of class struggle in England for the development of two types of control within the firm—namely, direct control and responsible autonomy. this reflects the fractional production politics that arose from the early development of unionism and craft controls. Simply because England was the first industrial nation, its working class was able to draw on preindustrial legacies to consolidate its resistance to a fledgling class of entrepreneurs. To this day production politics bear the marks of a legacy of unmediated conflict, shaped more by differential bargaining strengths within the working class than by a framework superimposed by the state.

Finally, Edwards's historical account makes a specific comparative claim without a comparative analysis. According to Edwards, the succession of different forms of labor control led to corresponding divisions of the United States' working class, explaining its failure to sustain a radical working-class politics. This claim rests on the unsubstantiated assumption that the European working classes, because less divided, posed a greater challenge to capitalism. My own comparative analysis focuses on the vertical incorporation of the working class through factory regimes insulated from state politics, as more fundamental and causally prior to its horizontal divisions.

Explicit comparative studies underline the significance of state politics for the development of production politics. Precisely because the state was more confined to the protection of the external conditions of production, production politics exhibited greater variation under early capitalism than under advanced capitalism when the state would impose a certain homogeneity by shaping the form of production apparatuses. In contrast to England, where textile workers were cut off from access to subsistence, in the United States ties to family farming led to a more atomized resistance and the development of paternalistic production apparatuses, such as the dormitory system of the women workers at Lowell. However, when immigrant workers, completely dependent upon wage labor, replaced single women in the second half of the nineteenth century, paternalism was replaced by a market despotism based on multiple earner families. Much harsher forms of paternalism, each with its own repressive arm, were common in the Russian mills of the nineteenth and early twentieth centuries. The company state was in part a response to the temporary character of industrial work carried out by peasants whose roots remained on the land and in part shaped by the growing entanglement of the Czarist autocracy in production politics.

Under advanced capitalism, variations *between* countries no longer revolve around differential access to means of production, levels of skill, or different patterns of market competition, but around the form of and extent to which state politics set limits on production politics and vice versa—the form of and extent to which production politics set limits on state politics. We have already observed how the state is instrumental in separating the reproduction of labor power from the labor process and thus tempers managerial despotism. The state may also regulate the conditions of work through stipulating the length of the working day or establishing minimal requirements of health and safety. But my concern here is with the way the state attempts to shape the production apparatuses themselves. Thus, in the United States the state is heavily involved in hedging the form of collective bargaining, grievance machinery, and strike action with legislation. In Britain a "voluntaristic" system obtains in which the state abstains from such regulations—where, for example, collective bargaining is not legally binding and is often continually renegotiated on the shop floor. The abstention of the state, as well as the competition among unions for the allegiance of rank and file workers, lead to fractional bargaining and a more anarchic production politics.

Britain and the United States differ not only in the extent to which the state regulates production politics but also in the extent to which production politics set limits on state politics. Thus in the United States hegemonic regimes rest on the concrete coordination of interests of labor and capital, (based on seniority and collective bargaining) as well as powerful individualizing tendencies based on grievance machinery and internal labor markets, with the consequence of demobilizing collective solidarity on the shop floor. This allows the state greater room to maneuver in formulating labor policies, reflected in the virtual exclusion of labor from the state except as an interest group within the Democratic Party and a very limited presence in the Department of Labor. In Britain, on the other hand, fractional bargaining sets limits on the effectiveness of such government interventions as incomes policy, encouraging productivity deals, and industrial relations legislation. It also provides a base for trade unions and the Labour Party to sustain some presence within the state.

Other advanced capitalist countries exhibit different patterns of mutual intervention of production politics and state politics. In both Germany and Sweden, the state regulates production apparatuses whereas production politics make themselves felt within the state through corporatist bargaining structures involving employers' associations, national unions, and the state. Japan provides a fourth possibility:

Production politics only weakly shape state politics, and state politics provide only the broadest parameters for production politics. Here it is important to stress that it is not simply the institutional presence of the working class in the state (whether in the form of a political party or a corporatist bargaining structure) that limits state politics, but the grounding of that presence in particular forms of production politics.

One can begin to discern the effects of various systems of production and state apparatuses in the responses of working classes to the present slump. But first, we must offer a general characterization of the impact of the slump on production politics. The despotic regimes of early capitalism relied on the capacity of management arbitrarily to fire, fine, and otherwise penalize workers. Under advanced capitalism, ejection has become less arbitrary and more restricted, and less costly (for workers) because of unemployment compensation. The construction of hegemonic regimes was a response not only to working class struggles but also to realization crises. On the one hand, hegemonic regimes organized struggles within limits; on the other, they established new consumption norms, which were not easily eroded and which finally led to a profitability crisis. From the hegemonic regimes there now emerges a new despotism based not on the ejection of individual workers but on the mobility of capital—a mobility facilitated by three developments. First, technological advances have made possible the further fragmentation of the labor process. Second, the revolution in the transportation and communications industries has made possible the geographical separation of the different parts of a single production process. Third, the processes of capitalist development on a world scale have created huge reservoirs of cheap labor power in peripheral or semiperipheral countries, as well as pockets within advanced capitalist countries themselves. The mobility of capital sets in motion competition among enterprises and their labor forces, communities, and governments to attract new capital or maintain old capital. This competition involves concessions that progressively undermine the protections and concessions established by the previous hegemonic regimes.

Labor's response in different countries has been largely shaped by the degree of autonomization of production politics. Thus, in the United States the state created production apparatuses that regulate struggles according to the logic of capital. In this system the concrete coordination of interests of labor and capital, previously based on concessions by capital linked to increasing profits, is replaced by concessions from labor linked to falling profits. Struggles within the labor movement revolve around whether and when to grant concessions. The absence of labor representation in the state, through either party or corporatist bargaining structures, makes alternative strategies aimed at state controlled investment difficult to develop. In England, where labor used its presence in the state to prevent state regulation of production politics, shop-floor militancy has led to localized responses that challenged the logic of capital. Workers have sought to extend collective bargaining to control over investment. Immediate responses to closures have been sit-ins. However, without government support these have generally been unsuccessful. Fractional production politics could establish a bulwark against productivity deals or against more flexible deployment of labor, but they are quite unable to deal with plant closures and capital flight. Moreover, widespread closures and redundancies affect the ability of workers to resist intensification of work, rationalization, and the introduction of labor-saving technology.

In Sweden the state structured production politics in accordance with the logic of capital, but at the same time developed compensatory labor market and welfare policies to deal with redundancies. Profitability crises have affected Swedish firms no less than firms in other countries, so that labor's precarious position can be fought only through the extension of state politics from control over the reproduction of labor power to control over investment. The attempt to collectivize capital through wage-earner funds is one strategy aimed at containing the repercussions of an international economic crisis. Indeed, one aspect of Japan's success in weathering the storm lies in the state's capacity to regulate capital flows on the one hand and the autonomization of production politics in the hands of management on the other.

STATE SOCIALISM

So far we have shown (1) how production politics vary between early and advanced capitalism according to the connection of the reproduction of labor power to the process of the production; (2) how production politics vary within early and advanced capitalism according to levels of deskilling and market forces; and (3) how production politics vary among early capitalist societies and advanced capitalist societies according to the mode of intervention between state and production politics. The plausibility of our arguments that impute the forms and variations of production politics to capitalism and its dynamics is enhanced by the development of different forms of production politics under present-day socialist societies, which I call "state socialism."

Whereas in capitalism, surplus is privately appropriated and redistributed through a market, in state socialism it is centrally appropriated and redistributed through a plan. Capitalist firms compete with one another in the pursuit of profit, whereas state socialist enterprises bargain with central planning agencies for loose plans through concealing capacity and through restriction of output. Whereas demand factors provide a barrier for capitalist enterprises, supply factors generate bottlenecks for state socialist enterprises. Shortages lead to searching, queuing and, most important, forced substitution of inputs and outputs. At the same time, central planners continually change product mixes as a result of rescheduling plan targets so that both horizontal and vertical uncertainties penetrate the enterprise, causing continual reorganization of work. Furthermore, pressures build toward the end of the planning period to intensify output to meet targets. "Rushing" and "storming" are pronounced features of state socialist enterprises. Experienced and skilled workers are essential for continual improvization in work organization to deal with arbitrary variation in inputs and outputs. There are therefore definite limits to deskilling, to the separation of conception and execution. Job control by workers is part and parcel of the state socialist enterprise.

Larger enterprises exercise greater power over supply markets; but they are subject to greater variability in demands from central planners, so uncertainty does not vary systematically according to relationship to the state. Instead of a dualism in production apparatuses developing *between sectors* of the economy, we find it emerging *within enterprises.* A core labor force made up of the more skilled and experienced workers and placed in a strategic position in the labor process continually improvises and reorganizes the work process. Because of the large discretionary component in their jobs, core workers are able to *bargain* for all sorts of inducements (favors, overtime, bonuses, and loose piece rates) in return for their cooperation. Peripheral workers on the other hand carry out the unskilled or semiskilled jobs which are more easily routinized. They face more *despotic* forms of control in which job security may be countered by wage insecurity engendered by tight piece rates, limited bonuses, and overtime. Dual production politics within the enterprise are reinforced by the fixed character of the wage funds, so that what one group gains the other loses, by the absence of effective levelling forces such as a trade union, and by the new hierarchies established by relationship to the party.

Just as under capitalism the transition from early to advanced forms can be characterized by the separation of the reproduction of labor power from the control of the enterprise, so a similar transition can be discerned under state socialism. In the first period of primitive socialist accumulation, the widespread use of piece rates as well as enterprise control over social services such as housing and welfare facilities bound the reproduction of labor power to the expenditure of effort in the workplace, predisposing management toward despotic control. Draconian labor legislation that penalized absenteeism, turnover, and indiscipline at work and established the work book cemented the dependence of the worker upon enterprise management. With the end of primitive accumulation and the inauguration of the period of extended reproduction, labor recovered a certain independence from the enterprise through the relaxation of controls over mobility and the centralization of social services.

Just as the capitalist state modifies the impact of the market on production politics, so the opening of a market economy in consumption goods and services as well as in labor modifies the form of production politics determined by the socialist state. The development of what is known as the "second economy" involves the transformation of the reproduction of labor power in two ways. First, households begin to produce goods that would otherwise be purchased, preeminently housing and food. Such domestic production nevertheless requires substantial income for the purchase of raw materials. It is a drain on wages earned in the state enterprise and thus intensifies vulnerability of workers to despotic regimes. Second, petty commodity production— individual of family production of goods (often, again, food) and services for sale in a rudimentary market—generates income and potentially provides the basis for resistance to managerial despotism.

What distinguishes factory regimes of capitalism from those of state socialism is their relationship to the state. In the one factory apparatuses and state apparatuses are institutionally separated, while in the other they are fused. That is, the capitalist state guarantees and even shapes the form of production apparatuses, but is not present at the point of production. The socialist state, on the other hand, is actually present within production in the form of managerial, party, and trade union functionaries. It is for this reason that I refer to factory regimes under state socialism as "bureaucratic"—bureaucratic despotism and bureaucratic bargaining are both extensions of the state into the factory.

The consequences of the two systems for the development of struggles are as follows. Under capitalism, struggles at the point of production are generally contained within the framework of the firm, whereas under state socialism struggles at the point of production are always potentially struggles against the state. Enterprise struggles under capitalism fragment the working class by virtue of their privatized character, whereas struggles under state socialism potentially bind the working class together by virtue of their common object. Moreover, the operation of the market and the ideology of private property serve to mystify class relations under capitalism, presenting them as natural and inevitable. By contrast, under state socialism the class relations between "conceivers" (planners, teleological redistributors) and "executors" (direct producers) are transparent. They are not mystified but are legitimated by the ideology of socialism in which the central direction of society purports to be based on scientifically derived knowledge of the collective interest. The state is unmistakably an instrument of domination and appropriation. In short, whereas capitalism fragments and incorporates the working class, state socialism engenders the formation of a solidary working class that understands its interests in opposition to those of the "authorities."

How then does one explain variations in the development of class struggle under state socialism? The very tendency toward class formation finds its countertendency in the development of repressive orders that deny workers the opportunity to organize collectively. Typically state socialist regimes do not permit the development of institutions autonomous from the state. But even where civil society has emerged—as occurred to a limited extent in Hungary and Poland (before December 1981)—we find different propensities toward the development of a working-class movement. Why? One can always offer cultural or historical explanations, but the logic of our earlier arguments suggest an alternative approach. Just as the degree of external determination of production politics by state politics and state politics by production politics affected the development of struggles under advanced capitalism, so the degree of decentralization of planning within state socialist societies affects the containment of struggles. The greater the autonomy of enterprises to establish relations among themselves and between managers and workers independently of state supervision, the greater the room for maneuver and the easier it is to divide the labor force through cooptation of core workers and repression of peripheral workers.

A second dimension of variation is the degree of state involvement in welfare and investment planning under capitalism (tending to transform production politics into state politics), and equivalently under state socialism the role of the market in defusing the interconnection of production politics and state politics. In particular the widening of the "second economy" may enhance the resources of the working class at the same time that it promotes individualism at the expense of collective solidarity. Comparative analysis among East European countries would involve examining both dimensions: the degree of decentralization in planning, and the opening of the second economy.

The studies of Braverman, Edwards, Friedman, and others are fundamentally incomplete without a corresponding analysis of existing socialism for at least two reasons. First, there is a latent assumption that the critical attribute of the capitalist labor process—whether it be the separation of conception and execution, or simply domination—will miraculously disappear under socialism. The separation of conception and execution will turn into their unification; domination will be transformed into self-management. There is no attempt to spell out such a productivist vision of socialism and nor to discern whether it would go beyond the bounds of feasibility. Clearly, state socialism fails to meet such criteria; it is therefore not surprising that Braverman, Edwards, and Friedman do not consider the study of such societies to be essential to their projects. Yet, state socialist societies do provide important clues as to what actually might be possible once private or centralized appropriation of surplus gives way to the collective appropriation of surplus.

Second, their analyses attributes the particular developments of the labor process to the capitalist relations of production. Presumably where private appropriation through the market is replaced by central-ized appropriation through the plan one would expect, if the arguments of Braverman and others have any validity, to discover different forms of labor process. Rather than confronting the fact that the capitalist labor process does *not* appear to differ fundamentally from that state socialist labor process, they ignore it, again dismissing state socialism as a species of capitalism and thus siding with the convergence theorists they otherwise abhor. As we have seen, although the labor processes *may* be similar, their forms of regulation under capitalism and state socialism are very different. Because they fail to distinguish between the labor process and the apparatuses of production, Braverman and other writers miss this. We have also observed the importance of the relationship between production apparatuses and state apparatuses as well as the connection between the reproduction of labor power and the enterprise. These same sets of relations also shed light on the development of struggles in peripheral societies, to which we now turn.

PERIPHERAL SOCIETIES

The experience of East European countries testifies to the limits that global politics set on the forms of and the relationship between production politics and state politics. We have also alluded to the responses of different systems of politics in advanced capitalist societies to boom and slump in the global economic order. But international political and economic forces also *directly* shape the form of production politics, of state politics, and of their interrelationship. The process is particularly marked in peripheral societies. Despite the appeal to the analysis of modes of production, there has been little work done on the labor process in underdeveloped countries. My own experience is limited to Southern Africa, particularly Zambia, although the following account has wider applicability to colonies and excolonies whose raw materials are exploited through industrial methods.

We can approach the problem by trying to characterize forms of primitive accumulation under colonialism. Unlike Britain, the expropriation of the means of their agricultural existence from indigenous producers was only partial. While taxation and land expropriations led the colonized people to depend on wage labor, wages were low and insufficient for the support of families in the towns, the urban infrastructure was inadequate, and security for the unemployed, young, and disabled was limited. Urban residence was therefore temporary. The colonial state aimed to reproduce a system of migratory labor, regulating the flow of labor through administrative mechanisms that enforced a dual dependence on the industrial and subsistence economies. This labor system maintained wages at a low level and avoided the expenses and problems of permanent urbanization. The colonial state existed only to exploit the mineral resources of the country and not to undertake broader economic development.

For the duration of their employment, black workers were bound to their industrial employer (in this case mining corporations) through extra-economic means. A company state, with its own repressive apparatuses, was established to organize and regulate life in the compound as well as in the mine. This was truly a state within a state. Whereas the colonial state was responsible for the generation of labor supplies, bringing workers to the mine and making sure they returned to rural areas after the expiration of the contract, the company state was left to regulate the day-to-day life of the employee. Within production, a racial hierarchy established the basis of a despotic production politics in which black subordinates were subject to arbitrary and brutal discipline and punishment—beatings, fines, and verbal abuse—from their white overseers. Colonial despotism rested on the coercive surveillance of the company state, whose racial apparatuses were ultimately guaranteed by the colonial state.

As Africans voluntarily moved to the towns and labor supplies became self-perpetuating, the colonial state lost its raison d'être. It was transformed from an appendage of the metropolitan state to one more responsive to the interests of white settlers and, subsequently, to indigenous African classes. The colonial state became increasingly embroiled in the expanded reproduction of capitalism—that is, with the distribution and extraction of surplus value. The transition to the postcolonial state consolidated the new functions performed by the state, the orchestration of production and the development of a national capitalism. The company state dissolved. Its functions were taken over by the state, on the one side, and by a much weaker administrative bureaucracy on the other. A stable urban population took root in and around the mines, catered for by the postcolonial state. Schools, pension schemes, housing, and social services all expanded to meet the needs of an industrial labor force in the towns.

What effects did these changes in the political order have on the labor process, established on the presupposition of colonial despotism? In some work situations the collapse of the despotic production politics led to the reconstruction of the labor process to conform to the new and weaker production apparatuses. The change often led to greater worker control over production. In other work situations where the technology could not be easily changed and where it also tightly defined the form of the labor process—which in turn depended upon despotic production apparatuses—conflict was inevitable. Workers would organize to resist managerial attempts to reimpose a despotic regime, attempts that often had the implicit or explicit assistance of new state. In short, the persistence of colonial technology—that is, one established under the presumption of colonial production politics—into the postcolonial era became the object of struggle.

We can draw a number of conclusions. First, technology is not neutral. It has political requirements as well as political effects. Second, changes in state politics lead to changes in production politics independent of changes in the labor process. In other words, changes in the form of state occasioned by a multiplicity of local and international factors prepare the way for changes in production politics that may prove to be at odds with the political requirements of the labor process. That is, the labor process on the one side and the international economic and political order on the other set the inner and outer limits of the form and interrelationship between production politics and state politics.

CONCLUSION

In this chapter I have discarded the base/superstructure scheme in which the economic base is the locus of laws, of objective forces, while the political and ideological superstructures are the arena of will, of subjectivity. Instead I have returned politics to production and production to politics. The forces of production, the labor process, and investment decisions are now potential objects of political struggle, of production politics, which in turn set limits on forms of state politics. The hallmark of capitalism is no longer the separation of the economic and the political but the separation of production politics and state politics; the hallmark of socialism is their fusion. At the same time, the specific form of separation/fusion will vary among capitalist and socialist societies.

I have tried to show how production politics are shaped by the reproduction of labor power, the state, the relationship among enterprises, and the labor process itself. Most important, I have made a case for production politics varying independently of the labor process. I have also indicated how these production politics have effects, particularly in the development of struggle both within and outside the enterprise. But there are still other grounds for insisting on a politics of production and for examining their variation and determination.

The expansion of the forces of production—that is, the expansion of the capacity to transform nature—may indeed set limits on the transition to socialism, but the politics of production also set limits. More precisely, the expansion of the forces of production establishes the material basis of socialism, but the consolidation of autonomous units of self-management outside the state establishes the political conditions. Whereas capitalism may guarantee the expansion of the forces of production, it does not guarantee the movement toward worker self-management. Far from it. Both advanced capitalism and state socialism lead away from collectivized councils. In other words, the conditions for transition to producer socialism do not develop automatically but require active intervention at the level of production itself. The capitalist or state socialist factory is not ready-made for producer socialism. The development of workplace self-management not only strengthens resistance to the appropriation of surplus in whatever form but also lays the necessary basis for the political power of the working class in the postrevolutionary period.

As we have seen, the labor process, the reproduction of labor power, relations among enterprises and the state all set limits on the form of production politics, albeit in different ways in different contexts. Any one of the factors may exclude the possibility of collective self-management by workers so that the realization of the necessary conditions for producer socialism may lie in the prior transformation of productive forces, state or family. Nevertheless I am suggesting that to leave the creation of worker self-management until after the inauguration of the socialist state is to abort the project of producer socialism. The socialist factory precedes factory socialism.

REFERENCES

BRAVERMAN, H. (1974) Labor and Monopoly Capital. New York: Monthly Review Press.

BURAWOY, M. (1984) "Karl Marx and the Satanic mills: factory politics under early capitalism in England, United States, and Russia." American Journal of Sociology (September).

——— (1983) "Between the labor process and the state: the changing face of factory regimes under advanced capitalism." American Sociological Review 48: 587-605.

EDWARDS, R. (1979) Contested Terrain. New York: Basic Books.

FRIEDMANN, A. (1977) Industry and Labor. London: Macmillan.

HABERMAS, J. (1975) Legitimation Crisis. Boston: Beacon Press.

MARX, K. (1976) Capital. New York: Viking Penguin.

POULANTZAS, N. (1978) State, Power, Socialism. London: New Left Books.

——— (1973) Political Power and Social Class. London: New Left Books.

THERBORN, S. (1978) What Does the Ruling Class Do When It Rules? London: New Left Books.

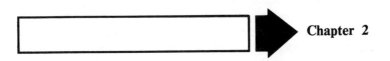

Chapter 2

THE EXPLOITATION OF LABOR IN
THE APPROPRIATION OF NATURE:

TOWARD AN ENERGY THEORY OF VALUE

Stephen G. Bunker
University of Illinois at Urbana-Champaign

The organization of human labor is crucial to the development, or underdevelopment, of regionally bounded social formations. The values created by this labor, however, are ultimately dependent upon other values directly extracted from natural transformations of matter and energy. Extractive and productive economies are typically found in distinct regions. Matter and energy flow from extractive economies, impoverishing the environment in which local populations reproduce themselves, to productive economies, where they enhance the utility of physical infrastructure and organization in ways that accelerate the productivity of labor, the accumulation of capital, and the evolution of complex social organization. Conventional theories of value, of production, and of exchange, and the models of development that draw on those theories have not, however, adequately recognized the absolute physical dependence of production on extraction. Nor have they accounted for the ways that the extraction, transport, and use of natural resources and the social formations that emerge around these processes affect the subsequent developmental potential of the environments from which resources are extracted. Instead, most theories of development have been attempts to extend models derived from systems of industrial production to nonindustrial systems for which they have only limited relevance.

AUTHOR'S NOTE: Parts of the arguments in this chapter were first developed in Bunker (1984a) and have been elaborated further in Bunker (1984b).

Recent theoretical literature on national development has compounded the distortions inherent in this bias to production models. Its primary focus has been a fruitless debate about whether the causes of underdevelopment occur in a global system of exchange dominated by industrial nations, or within specific regional systems of production. Advocates of dependency perspectives criticize theories of modernization for their focus on the internal characteristics of particular economies; Marxist scholars counter world-system models of unequal exchange by insisting on the explanatory primacy of modes of production. Debates over the false issue of whether explanatory primacy should be attributed to global systems of exchange or to regionally specific systems of production are ultimately sterile. A global system of exchange, made up of all importing and exporting regions, determines terms of trade that differentially affect all of these regions, but distinct regional social structures and political arrangements determine how the commodities on which the global system depends are actually extracted or produced.

The organization of labor and its capacity to reproduce itself vary between these regional economies. Understanding the different organization of labor within a world system requires that we examine the internal dynamics of particular regional economies, both as these economies evolve in relation to their own environments and as they are reorganized in response to changing world markets. Neither the internal and external dynamics, however, can be understood unless we take into account regional and global effects of energy flows from extraction to production.

I believe that adequately integrating internal and external perspectives with each other and with explanations of how complex modern organizations operate is finally impossible unless we recast our economic models to take into account (1) the absolute physical dependence of production on extraction; (2) the locational characteristics and regional inequalities that distinguish productive from extractive systems; (3) the very different ecological, demographic, and social structural evolutionary processes in each type of system; and (4) the long-term consequences of net flow of matter and energy from extractive to productive economies. The necessary relations between production and extraction, the fact that they typically occur in different regions, and their different ecological results all fundamentally affect the organization of both regional and global economies and fundamentally determine their long-term potential for social production and reproduction.

Because resource extraction is necessarily anterior to any process of production or transformation, economic models that consider modes of production as bounded and as reproducing themselves are therefore fundamentally wrong, and any economic model that considers that value is created only by human labor is fundamentally wrong. Any theory of international exchange that measures commodity flows between regions only in terms of capital, prices, or the labor incorporated into each, is therefore also wrong.

Instead, our economic models and our theories of development and social change must take account of the physical requirement that the reproduction of any social formation, and of the modes of production that we may discern within it, depends on the reproduction or regeneration of natural energy transformation systems, or, alternately, involves the depletion of a limited stock of energy sources. Once we understand this, we understand as well that a mode of production cannot reproduce itself; rather, it sustains itself only by drawing energy and matter from modes of extraction.

Extraction and production may occur together in social formations bounded by a single regional ecosystem. In such cases, the diversity of human needs may distribute extractive activity across such a wide range of species and minerals that biotic chains can reproduce themselves stably. Once the profit-maximizing logic of extraction for trade across regional ecosystems is introduced, however, price differentials between extractive commodities, and the differential return to extractive labor, stimulate concentrated exploitation of a limited number of resources at rates that disrupt both the regeneration of these resources as well as the biotic chains of coevolved species and associated geological and hydrological regimes. Industrial modes of production depend on this self-depleting form of extractive activity, and therefore inevitably undermine the resource bases on which they depend. Industrial modes of production have evolved the social organizational and the infrastructural capacity to change their own technologies and thereby to find substitutes for essential resources as they are depleted. This process is necessarily finite, however, as each new technology requires other resources from what is, ultimately, a limited stock.

In the immediate or short term, the idea that such modes of production can reproduce themselves or can themselves create value is negated by the physical dependence of production on extraction. In the long run, the logic of maximizing profits or returns to labor accelerates the depletion of different, and eventually of all, natural resources. The acceleration of modes of production accelerates the exhaustion of modes of extraction, and thus hastens the eventual collapse of all production.

Analysis of energy flows between regions and different uses of energy in different regional social formations provides a much fuller explanation of uneven development than any drawn from conventional economic models. If energy and matter necessarily flow from extractive to productive economies, it follows that social and economic processes will be intensified and accelerated in the productive economy and will become more diffuse and eventually decelerate in the extractive economy. The flow of energy and matter to productive societies permits the increased substitution of nonhuman for human energies; allows for increased scale, complexity, and coordination of human activities; stimulates an increasing division of labor and the specialized fields of information that this entails; makes possible increasingly complex systems of transport and communication; and engenders as well the means of technological and administrative innovation by which the industrial mode of production's crises of resource scarcity are solved. The mode of extraction, on the other hand, loses energy, and so becomes socially and economically simpler, less diversified, and completely subject to technologically determined changes in market demand generated by the modes of production. Once we understand this, we can understand as well that while the actual flow of commodities between regions can be explained in terms of markets and labor costs, the consequent uneven development of different regions of the world can be fully understood only if we consider the effects of uneven energy flows on both the physical and social environments of different social formations and on the progressive subordination of simplified, energy-losing societies to increasingly complex, energy-gaining societies.

Our theories of unequal exchange and of uneven development have failed to integrate the internal dynamics of regional social formations with the external dynamic of a world market system because they have not accounted for these necessary relations between extraction and production or for their consequences on the evolution of different societies. These production-based theories can, however, provide essential components for an ecological model of regionally unequal development because their basic assumptions closely match the central belief systems of modes of production that currently dominate the world system. Decisions about production, extraction, and exchange are in fact based on anthropocentric value systems that subordinate nature and nonhuman energy to human strategies for enhancing power and control of other humans and for increasing the effective productivity of human labor. These strategies tend to result in short-term maximization of return to labor and capital with little concern for long-term social reproduction. Conventional theories of development, if properly integrated, can provide us with tools to explain the production and exchange decisions as well as the political and administrative strategies of dominant classes in different kinds of societies. We must go beyond these theories, however, if we wish to understand the consequences of these human decisions for either the short-term development of particular regional social formations or the long-term reproduction of society.

Models of regional and of global systems must be complementary rather than competitive because these systems coevolve. I propose that different regional levels of development result from the interaction between changing world market demand for specific commodities and the local reorganization of modes of production and extraction in response. The cumulative ecological, demographic, and infrastructural effects of the sequence of modes of production and extraction in any region establish limits and potentials for the productive capacities and the living standards of regional populations. The flow of energy from extractive to productive economies reduces the complexity and power of the first and increases complexity and power in the second.

MODES OF EXTRACTION AND THE CREATION OF EXTREME PERIPHERIES

Economic models of industrial production neglect the extractive origins of the materials that industrial processes transform (Georgescu-Roegen, 1975). The internal dynamics of the extractive economies that have provided much of the least-developed regions' exports differ significantly from those of productive economies in their effects on the natural environment, on the distribution of human populations, on the growth of economic infrastructure (understood here as everything humanly constructed or organized that facilitates social and economic activity), and therefore on the subsequent developmental potential of the affected regions. Production models cannot explain the internal dynamics of extractive economies because the exploitation of natural resources uses and destroys values that cannot be calculated in terms of labor or capital. When natural resources are extracted from one regional ecosystem to be transformed and consumed in another, the socioeconomic and ecological linkages to the extracted commodity tend to a loss of value and to economic deceleration in the region of origin, and to accretion of value and economic acceleration in the region of consumption or transformation. Extractive appropriation impoverishes the environment on which local populations depend, both for their own reproduction and for the extraction of commodities for export.

Because this appropriation and its ecological results affect the class structures, the organization of labor, systems of exchange and property, the activities of the state, the demographic distribution of populations, the development of physical infrastructure, and the kinds of information, beliefs, and ideologies that shape social organization and behavior, I introduce the notion, mode of extraction, to suggest the systemic connections between these phenomena. My usage thus parallels the more inclusive definitions of mode of production, which relate multiple aspects of social, legal, political, and commercial activities within single systems of analysis (Anderson, 1974; Hindess and Hirst, 1975). I will argue, however, that both modes of extraction and modes of production can only be understood in terms of their integral interdependence and in terms of their impacts on natural ecosystemic processes. Orthodox Marxist notions of the reproduction of modes of production must be reformulated to account for these ecological interdependencies.

While the specific characteristics and dynamics of particular modes of extraction and of particular extractive commodity markets must be analyzed individually, it is possible to outline some general tendencies in extractive export economies. The following characterization of extractive export economies is elaborated from studies of specific extractive economies (Santos, 1981; Weinstein, 1980; Brockway, 1979; Blair, 1976; Cobbe, 1979) and from more general statements by Levin (1960), Furtado (1970), Daly (1977), Sternberg (1973), and Georgescu-Roegen (1970, 1971, 1975).

The extractive process frequently entails an extremely low ratio of both labor and capital to value, so it may initially produce rapid rises in regional incomes. These may be followed by equally rapid collapses when the depletion of easily accessible resources requires additional inputs of labor and capital without corresponding increases in volume. The rapidly rising cost of extraction usually stimulates a search for substitutes or new sources for the original good. Either alternative profoundly disrupts the economy of the exporting region. The ephemeral nature of extractive economies may lead to a series of demographic and infrastructural dislocations.

Productive enterprises typically are located in close proximity to each other. Transport, communication, and energy transmission costs are thus shared by multiple enterprises. New enterprises can start without assuming the total costs of the infrastructure they require. Populations attracted to these locations provide a labor force that can move easily between enterprises with different rates and directions of growth. While individual enterprises may become obsolete, the infrastructure to which they contribute and the labor they have employed remain for subsequent enterprise.

Extractive enterprises, on the other hand, must be located in close proximity to the natural resources they exploit. These resources are randomly distributed in relation to productive centers, so proximity to other enterprise occurs only by chance, and becomes less likely as the most accessible resources are depleted. Extractive economies, therefore, seldom enjoy the continuities with earlier settlement patterns and infrastructural development provided by shared productive locations. Nor do they usually contribute to the labor and infrastructural requirements of subsequent economies. Instead, whatever changes they bring about in the distribution of population and in the physical environment serve little or no purpose when the specific resources to which they are geared are depleted or are no longer in demand.

Regions whose economic ties to the world system are based almost exclusively on the exchange of extracted commodities, that is, of resources that occur in nature and in whose existence or continued reproduction there is no deliberate human intervention, can be characterized as extreme peripheries because of the low proportions of capital and labor incorporated in the total value of their exports and because of the low level of linkages to other economic activities and social organization in the same region. Even when depletion raises extraction costs, the additional capital and labor are most frequently required for exploration and transport rather than in actual extraction. Even then, these costs constitute a relatively small proportion of eventual price, and an even smaller proportion of what their price would be if depletion rates were taken into account (Schumacher, 1973; Georgescu-Roegen, 1970; Schnaiberg, 1977). Examples of such commodities include not only petroleum and minerals, but also lumber from natural forests; the oils, meats, and hides of wild animals; nuts of undomesticated trees; most fish; and slaves. Cattle raising on pastures formed by burning jungle is also essentially extractive. There is some human intervention in herd management and pasture clearing, but the pasture itself frequently depends on nutrients released from burning vegetation and usually does not last much beyond the rapid depletion of those resources (Hecht, 1981).

While processing and industrialization of most extractive commodities create additional value, extreme peripheries such as the Amazon tend to export them raw or unfinished so that the creation and realization of additional values occur in, and benefit, other economies. Moreover, even the limited contribution of extractive exports to regional economies tends to be unstable: If high demand and expanded scale increase unit costs of extraction by depleting the most accessible resources, entrepreneurs will attempt to domesticate or to synthesize agricultural or industrial substitutes and to transform the extractive economy into a productive one (Brockway, 1979). These new economies, once freed from the need to locate near natural resources, will tend to move to areas where land, labor, and infrastructure are more easily accessible.

The crucial difference between production and extraction is that the dynamics of scale in extractive economies function inversely to the dynamics of scale in the productive economies to which world trade connects them. The forces of production develop progressively in industrial systems because the unit cost of commodity production tends to fall as the scale of production increases. In extractive systems, on the contrary, unit costs tend to rise as the scale of extraction increases. Greater amounts of any extractive commodity can be obtained only by exploiting increasingly distant or difficult sources. Although technological innovation may reduce costs of some extractive processes in the short run, unit costs of extraction will continue to rise in the long run. Therefore when extractive systems respond to increased external demand, they tend to impoverish themselves (1) by depleting non-self-renewing resources, or (2) by exploiting self-renewing resources beyond their capacities for regeneration, thereby (3) forcing the unit cost of commodities to rise so high that the development of synthetic or cultivated alternatives in other regions becomes cost effective. These three results are likely to be aggravated by the disruption of the surrounding ecosystem and the consequent reduction of other useful resources whose existence or reproduction depends on biotic chains that include the extracted resource or are disrupted by the process of extraction. Such disruption limits the human carrying capacity of the extracted environment, and may over time restrict the availability of labor. It also increases the costs of maintaining labor by limiting agricultural potential in areas near the extractive enterprise. Successful plantation or industrial production of formerly extractive commodities completes the cycle of peripheral impoverishment by introducing progressive economies of scale in the new location. The new location's competitive advantages eventually eliminate or seriously reduce the original, and increasingly costly, extractive economy.

Falling unit costs accelerate production-consumption linkages as well as infrastructural concentration and accumulation in expanding articulated production systems. The rising unit costs, further dispersion of labor and investment, and intensified ecological disruption that accompany expanding extractive systems eventually decelerate these economies. The intensified energy flows to and through the socially articulated productive systems permit more rapid accumulation there of physical infrastructure, of specialized technical and social organizational knowledge in an increased division of labor, and of the coordination of research and development of new technologies that enhance these systems' use of nonhuman energy and change the market prices for different extracted resources. This capacity to change world markets through technological innovation frees the production systems from short-run dependence on particular extractive commodities as they become depleted, and enhances both the productive systems' dominance over and periodic disruptions of the decelerating modes of extraction.

Production-dominated technological innovations may involve both plant transfers and synthetic substitutions. Brockway (1979) has shown how the development of the botanical and related sciences in the industrial core responded to and promoted the domestication and genetic adaptation of cultigens extracted in the extreme peripheries to other peripheral regions where center nations controlled both the land and the labor necessary to transform these cultigens into plantation crops. Successful transformation to a plantation system brought these plants—rubber, sisal, and chinchona—into a mode of production in which increased scale progressively reduced unit costs to levels at which extractive systems could no longer compete. (These plantation systems frequently aggravated the impoverishment of other extreme peripheries by requisitioning slave or indentured labor.) The incorporation of these extreme peripheries into the world economy, then, resulted not only in a transfer of value, but also in a direct transfer of resources—both natural and human—to less peripheral regions. These plantation systems themselves were finally impoverished by industrial production of synthetic substitutes. Modern searches for oil substitutes—whether nuclear, solar, or agricultural—respond similarly to rising capital and labor costs as the most accessible oil sources are depleted.

Extractive economies tend to develop fewer lateral linkages than productive economies. The well-documented "enclave" nature of extractive economies (see Levin, 1960) results from several factors. First, the low proportion of capital and labor to market value concentrates profits in the exchange, rather than in the extractive, sector (Katzman, 1976). Second, extractive economies do not respond to the locational advantages that tend to foster the mutual proximity of productive enterprises. Extractive economies necessarily locate at the sources of raw materials, and these sources may be far removed from existing demographic and economic centers. Distance from existing demographic and economic centers increases the costs of labor recruitment, subsistence, and shelter and of infrastructural development. In extreme cases, labor is expeditionary, usually involving the temporary migration of males. The additional costs of migration are increased by a near total dependence on imported foodstuffs and other materials, which further reduces the possibility of local economic linkages. This situation in turn enhances control over the labor force, as the provision of subsistence needs is controlled by those who purchase labor. Distance from established communities further heightens the employers' control, as there are few alternative social organizations to provide support for laborers' resistance to exploitation.

The combination of (1) factors that lead to the eventual impoverishment or collapse of extractive economies in specific regions or subregions, with (2) factors that limit the extent that extractive economies based on remote resources can share with other enterprise the locational advantages of population centers and infrastructure, creates cycles in which costly infrastructure and human settlements are periodically abandoned or suffer a severe reduction in economic utility. Economic and social development based on extractive economies thus tends to be discontinuous in time and space. Production systems tend to build a social and physical environment shared by multiple enterprises. These enterprises suffer the effects of technological and demand changes at different time and rates, so a production system as a whole tends to be more stable and continuous than an extractive one. The locational advantages of shared labor pools and infrastructures that production systems usually enjoy are much more likely to allow adaptation to changing technologies and markets. The fact that most of the infrastructure developed for extractive export economies is specific to the requirements of resource removal and transport exacerbates their loss of utility as the extracted resource is exhausted or substituted.

The concentration of capital in removal and transport infrastructure frequently creates especially severe technological dependencies on the industrial countries. Railroads, steamships, docks, drilling rigs, pipelines, and earth-moving machinery require techniques and capitals that extractive economies are highly unlikely to develop. The concentration of investment in export facilities instead of in a production-enhancing infrastructure further accentuates the concentrated control over exchange—and profit—that emerges from the absence of alternative economic and demographic linkages. (See especially Santos, 1981; Weinstein, 1980; Solberg, 1976; Blair, 1976; Cobbe, 1979; Levin, 1960.)

The particular problem of regions where extractive export economies are predominant is that socioeconomic organization that at one time responds to international demand for specific extractive commodities is likely to lose its utility when the extractive source is depleted or when demand shifts away from it. Predominantly extractive economies disrupt human settlement patterns and the natural environment in ways that are adaptive only in the relatively short run, and maladaptive in the long run. In the absence of self-sustaining and flexible productive systems, there is little or no economic basis for local opposition or resistance to entrepreneurs or to dependent national states that seek to organize the population and environment as to exploit the potential for quick profit. Thus, extractive economies tend toward eventual stagnation, broken by new extractive cycles if new demands for other material resources available in the region emerge.

These factors may vary with the characteristics of the natural environment, with the type and extent of the national resources extracted, and with the policies of the national state. In the Amazon, the tendency for extractive economies at one time to leave the region susceptible to the establishment of subsequent extractive economies (whenever world markets create pressures or opportunities for easy and rapid profits) has led not simply to underdevelopment relative to more rapid increases in productivity in other regions, but to absolute impoverishment and progressive underdevelopment (Bunker, 1984a, 1984b). Where there is little local population to disrupt, however, extractive economies may generate considerable benefits. Valuable minerals or fossil fuels exploited in desert areas with sparse populations may generate revenues that the state can tax or redirect to develop other, more productive economies (see, for example, Palmer and Parsons, 1977, on the very different results of extractive economies in South Africa and Katanga). Even in these cases, however, the benefits are likely to flow to other areas of the nation where the raw materials are transformed and revenues are directed to more productive enterprise.

Theories of imperialism (Luxemburg, 1951; Lenin, 1939; Baran, 1957), of world systems and dependency (see especially Galtung, 1971), of mode-of-production-based unequal exchange, and of modernization have all acknowledged primary material export as a defining characteristic of most forms of underdevelopment, but they have not systematically explored the internal dynamics of extractive systems as a distinct socioeconomic type. Nor have they understood that the complex social organizational, demographic, and infrastructural forms that emerge as technological change and accumulation accelerate the flow of energy through the production-consumption linkages of articulated productive systems ultimately depend on processes that progressively decelerate the economy, disrupt the ecosystem, and simplify social organization in extractive regions.

None of these theories of development has accounted sufficiently for the ways in which the extraction and export of natural resources affect the subsequent developmental potential of the environments from which they are extracted. The extraction of particular commodities from nature has measurable effects on the energy transformation processes in surrounding biotic systems and on the density and distribution of human populations. I expect that extractive economies tend to "build" the surrounding environment and to distribute human populations in ways that limit, rather than enhance, subsequent forces of production. If this is so, understanding the development and underdevelopment of these environments requires models that systematically take the historical sequence of these effects into account.

Theories of value that focus exclusively on labor and capital do not simply err conceptually. Rather, they reflect and legitimate a world view in which nature is subordinated to mankind and where natural resources are considered as flow or income rather than as part of a limited global stock or capital (Schumacher, 1973; Georgescu-Roegen, 1970). Theoretically and practically, nature, values in nature, and the economies that depend on values in nature have been systematically undervalued, while human labor, consumption, and reproduction in articulated societies have been correspondingly overvalued. Revaluing natural energy transformation on a global level would necessarily slow the rate of energy flow from periphery to core, and therefore also slow rates of industrial production and consumption. I believe this is essential for the long-term reproduction of human society in both extractive and productive modes. Specifying the particular characteristics of and values in extractive economies is an essential first step in any attempt to reverse these economies' disruptive effects, but these characteristics and values must be integrated with more general theories of development and of social evolution, both regional and global (see Bunker, 1984b).

TOWARD AN ENERGY CALCULUS OF VALUE

Extractive export economies constitute an extreme case of what de Janvry (1981) has called dependent disarticulation. Socially articulated economies produce goods for internal consumption. The resulting acceleration of social and economic activity through linkages between wages, consumption capacity, and markets enhances return to capital and expands production of goods. This partially resolves the contractions between wage costs and profits, making wage increases systemically rational. The disarticulated economy, in contrast, depends on external markets and therefore lacks any internal consumption-driven accelerator to rationalize high wages. De Janvry invokes the logic and contradictions of accumulation within each economy to explain the necessary relations and interdependencies between these economies. Crises of overproduction and falling rates of profit in the articulated core economies, and the limited consumption capacity of internal markets in disarticulated peripheral economies, create the necessity for each economy to establish external relations with the other; the necessity of each is the other's possibility. The necessary relations between extractive and productive systems are more profound, however, than de Janvry implies.

Matter and energy, the essential components of production, cannot be created; they can only be transformed, and every transformation increases entropy—that is, frees energy into humanly unuseable forms (Georgescu-Roegen, 1970). Productive economies are all, finally, only the molecular, structural, and spatial reorganization of matter and energy extracted from nature. In the precise sense, humans can only produce ideas and symbols. The rest of what we call production is only our intervention in and redirection of natural processes of energy and material transformation. Production (or, more properly, transformation) cannot occur without some form of continued extraction from the natural environment. Extraction and production, although integrally related, usually occur in distinct geographical locations; this tendency is drastically enhanced as industrial production and the division of labor increase social complexity, population density, and urbanization. Typically, some economies specialize in particular extractive exports and depend on the reimportation of transformed commodities for their own consumption. Energy and matter are thus withdrawn from the natural environment of the extractive economies, flow toward, and are concentrated in the social and physical environments of the productive economies, where they fuel the linked and mutually accelerating processes of production and consumption.

Matter stores energy, and can be converted to energy. Adams (1982: 17) argues that all life forms consume and dissipate energy, and that "the process of dissipation constitutes [their] structure. . . . Society is composed of the energy it consumes, hence, it can be treated as a dissipative structure." This formulation provides us a more adequate measure than de Janvry's exchange values for the flows that bind articulated to disarticulated, and extractive to productive, systems. Conventional economic measures can only capture the exchanges or flows between classes and systems in the monetary terms of wages, prices, and profits, or in the ultimately nonquantifiable notions of abstract labor value. Wages can be shown to create consumption capacity and thence the market demand that makes production and return to capital possible. By focusing on the flows and conversions of matter and energy, however, we can extend these measures directly to the accretion of humanly useful forms of knowledge and social organization, modifications of the physical environment, and the environmental costs of matter-energy transformations, as well as to the production and exchange of commodities. We can also show that the relation between extractive and productive economies is not reducible to the accumulation strategies of regionally distinct dominant classes but is a physical requirement of industrial production. Accelerated energy flow to the center permits the social complexity that generates both political and economic power in these systems, permits the rapid technological changes that transform world market demands, and thus creates the conditions both of the core's economic and political dominance and of different, regionally dominant classes' accumulation strategies. Finally, we can show that the exhaustion of a series of modes of extraction must eventually end the modes of production that depend on them.

Adams, however, has not yet realized the sociological implications of his essentially physical formulation. The energy that any organism consumes is dissipated at highly variable rates. Although all conversions of matter and energy heighten entropy, this rate is also highly variable. Human intervention in the conversion of energy and matter accelerates entropy, but it may also direct or embody energy and matter in forms that are both more durable and more humanly useful. Genetic manipulation of plants, the storage of food products, or the treatment of wood are all possible examples. At a more abstract level, human memory and learning—and thus social organization—also involve the partial conservation of experiences that required the consumption of energy but that may make future uses of energy and matter more humanly useful. As well, the capital plant and physical infrastructure of articulated production systems require and embody energy that has been consumed but is being dissipated in ways and at rates that preserve its human utility. The socially and technologically complex organization of the articulated economy is finally only possible if vast amounts of energy are thus "embodied" or conserved in useful ways. Thus, if society is composed of the energy it consumes, articulated societies consume extractive economies and their natural environments and in the process become more complex and more powerful. As long as there are sufficient energy resources to consume, they also remain more flexible (unless the by-products of the energy and matter flow-through impossibly pollute their own environments).

The extractive region, which loses energy and matter, becomes increasingly simplified, both ecologically and socially, and less adaptive or flexible, both through its simplification and its loss of resources and through the disruption of the natural energy transformation processes related to or dependent on the extracted resource. Unable to embody energy in either durable physical infrastructure or in complex and adaptive social organization and technology, it becomes increasingly vulnerable to penetration by and subordination to the productive economies that can concentrate control over nonhuman energies and effectively coordinate much larger and more complex organizations of human energy.

The articulation and acceleration of the productive economy then, does not only depend on nor is it adequately described by a wage-consumption-profit-production treadmill calculated in exchange values. It also requires the concentration and coordination of human and nonhuman energy flows and their embodiment in both complex social organization and durable infrastructure. This it achieves at the cost of the extractive economy and extracted environment.

Conventional economic models do not adequately explain the necessary relations between extraction and production. Nor, because of their derivation from production systems, can they adequately explain the internal dynamics of extractive economies. They limit their concepts of value to measures of labor and capital and so exclude multiple other values essential to human and social reproduction.

The imperfect fit between monetary measures such as wages and prices and theoretical notions of labor value severely distorts the examination of unequal exchange between classes and between regionally bounded social formations (Emmanuel, 1972; Amin, 1977; de Janvry, 1981: 15). The labor theory of value requires concepts of abstract labor that are theoretically coherent only within a fully capitalist economy (see de Janvry, 1981: 79). Such economies do not exist, and the closest approximations to them are intimately bound to noncapitalist formations, both through exchange and through their necessary dependence on resource extraction. A labor theory of value excludes from consideration the usefulness to continued social reproduction of energy transformations in the natural environment. Nor can it take into account the value of the ideas, beliefs, and information that underlie human social organization. These, and all other human experiences, are formed out of previous dissipation of energy. They are all essential to humanly effective uses of natural energy, and may make these uses more efficient in terms of their human energy costs. I believe that the unequal relations between articulated and disarticulated, and between extractive and productive systems, can ultimately be explained by the informational and organizational forms that energy-intensive economies foster in articulated productive systems and that simply cannot evolve in energy-losing extractive systems. The first generates more and more social power and the technology to extend this power over wider geographical areas. The second progressively loses social power.

The survival and reproduction of society itself must be the ultimate criterion of value, so our concept of value must include anything that affects this process and its outcomes. Labor value, or its imperfect monetary measures, cannot do this. Measures of energy and matter and of their conversion, however, touch everything that is humanly useful. Rather than separating human activity from other ecosystemic process-es, these measures allow us to see the interdependencies between human energy use and energy transformation processes which proceed natural-ly (i.e., without human intervention).

If value is defined only in terms of labor, we have no way to assess the costs that contemporary uses of the environment may impose on subsequent generations and social formations. Energy measures can provide us a calculus of costs and values—past, present, and future— for the multiple effects of human intervention in natural energy transformations. These effects include the disruption of the biotic chains that capture and store energy, the incorporation of energy into immediately consumable goods and services, and the partial conserva-tion of energy and matter in more durable physical infrastructure and social organization.

To use these measures, however, we must reject the anthropocentric and temporally biased notions that value occurs only as a cognitive attribution to certain things or processes. We must also reject the idea that resources do not exist until they are humanly discovered. Humans may eat fish without knowing or understanding what the fish eat, but this ignorance does not diminish the value of the fish's sources of nutrients to the survival and reproduction of human society. Human activity at one period may destroy or reduce natural energy transforma-tion processes whose usefulness can only be realized with future knowledge or technology; present ignorance does not reduce the cost, or loss of value, to future human generations.

Temporarily and culturally bound attributions of value are both socially and epistemologically significant, however, because they affect the allocation and distribution of human labor and the forms of energy extracted from the environment. New technologies and new consumption patterns create new value attributions for the resources they require. The attribution of value to labor enormously influences human decisions about both social organization and uses of natural resources. The differential valuation of labor in different modes of production influences the flow of goods between different economies. Most important, labor is essential to the use value of most naturally occurring resources. All of these, however, constitute only part of the energy transformation processes that sustain human life and society. All of them finally depend on values that occur in nature as the result of energy flows largely independent of human intervention.

Pure extractive economies are the extreme case of human appropriation of these values, but many apparently productive processes include elements of extraction. Different agricultural and pastoral economies, for example, present a gradient of the proportions of human labor and natural values incorporated into the final product, ranging from the minimal modifications of the natural environment in ecologically complex swidden systems to the energy-intensive manipulations and simplifications of bounded ecosystems in large-scale monocropping systems. Forestry exhibits similar gradations. Human societies depend on complex and variable combinations of natural and labor values. Energy as a measure can be applied to the creation of both kinds of value, and allows us to relate them through a common currency. It also allows us to see the usefulness, and thus the value, of human learning and social organization. We can examine the ways that human societies reorganize matter to build their own environments, as social inventions that extend the value of portions of the energy that society consumes and dissipates. Finally, it forces us to recognize that there is no possible unidimensional calculus of value because the long-term maintenance of human life depends on energy transformation processes of which we are not yet aware. We cannot yet measure all of the complex energy exchanges in the biotic chains that make up the ecosystems in which we participate. Nor can the value of human organization be directly measured. We can use both human and nonhuman energy more effectively because we have remembered past uses of energy and have stored and transmitted this knowledge through social organization, but we could only measure the value of this knowledge and organization by comparing its presence to its absence in the same society. Even without a unidimensional calculus of value, however, we can analyze the very different potentials for social organizational, infrastructural, and economic development in the societies that concentrate energy from outside and the societies that lose energy to them. We can then also explain how the dominance of productive systems accelerates extraction and ecological destruction.

Focusing our analysis on economies that are predominantly extractive highlights the particular internal dynamics of extraction processes and forces major revisions to theories of value. This is necessary to correct both the temporal and industrial biases of most theories of social and economic development. The ultimate goal of such an exercise, however, must be to reveal both the internal dynamics and the necessary external relations between different regional social formations. Only then can we understand either uneven development or the prospects for long-term, sustained human and social reproduction.

IMPLICATIONS OF AN ENERGY THEORY OF VALUE FOR THEORIES OF UNEQUAL EXCHANGE

Focusing on the ecological successions in extractive regional economies underscores a series of problems in the debate between the externally focused world-systems and the internally focused modes-of-production perspectives on unequal exchange as a cause of underdevelopment. In this section, I examine some of the distortions that follow from the labor theories of value implicit in these perspectives and propose an alternative approach. This approach would integrate ecological and social measures of both return to labor and the possibilities for the long-term reproduction, not just of labor, but of the societies in which labor emerges and is used.

The world-systems perspective tends to ignore the crucial ecological differences between different regional economies in its insistence on a single, global, unit of analysis. Wallerstein's and Franks's insistence that "the world-economy is capitalist through and through" (Wallerstein, 1981), no matter how carefully qualified, goes beyond its valid, intended point about the systemic relations that bind most of the world's economies in a single market. These metaphoric extensions especially distort their understanding of different labor regimes. Frank (1967: 7-8) absurdly reifies the abstract relations that comprise dependency when he extends his metropolis-satellite metaphor to the relationship between *hacendado* and *peón*. Wallerstein (1974: 400) homogenizes all regional class structures when he declares that slavery, coerced sharecropping, and wage labor are equivalent within a world capitalist mode of production because all three are organized to produce exchange values for profit. This extreme reductionism follows from his extrapolation of a single, global capitalist market to imply a single, global production system with a single division of labor (1974: 390-397).

This extrapolation is demonstrably invalid (Brenner, 1977). It is also unnecessary to Wallerstein's argument. I argue instead that the rapid accumulation of capital in the core, which is accelerated by unbalanced energy flows from the periphery, increases the rate of technological and consumption innovation and of consumption capacity. The acceleration of production-consumption-accumulation linkages allows the core to determine most global demand. Rapid innovation at the core subjects the periphery to a constantly changing market over which it has little control. If dominant classes in the peripheral areas reorganize modes of production and extraction in response to this externally dominated, frequently shifting market demand, the populations, social organizations, and ecosystems of these areas are subject to repeated disruption. If the local modes of extraction or production are not so reorganized, the demand shifts subject regional economies to falling terms of trade. Wallerstein's metaphorical extrapolations impede attention to these and other regional processes.

Wallerstein and Frank see politically enforced unequal exchange as the root cause of an international division of labor that profoundly discriminates against the peripheral regions by syphoning off their capital and keeping their labor less productive. Their Marxist adversaries have inverted this formula by maintaining that the differential productivity of labor in different modes of production is the root cause of unequal exchange. The ensuing debate has obscured the need to consider regional production as particular and international exchange as systemic. It has also perpetuated the error of using labor as a standard of value and as the basis of comparison for the exchange of all goods, even when these goods are extracted with relatively little labor from nature or when the social relations of production do not involve wages.

Wage differentials provide the primary mechanism that these Marxist analysts employ to extend the internal concepts of modes of production to the external question of unequal exchange. Emmanuel's (1972), Mandel's (1975), and Amin's (1976, 1977) somewhat different formulations all presuppose a definition of labor and wages appropriate to a capitalist mode of production—that is, one in which labor as a commodity is used and recompensed for production for profit in a market. Thus, they implicitly affirm the pervasive capitalist character of the production relations that concern them, even though they insist on the specificity of the various, noncapitalist, less productive modes of production in the underdeveloped regions. Their focus on the labor incorporated in a product assumes—incorrectly—that this labor is always the primary determinant of value.

The fundamental values in lumber, in minerals, oil, fish, and the like are predominantly in the goods themselves rather than in the labor incorporated in them. Additional value may be created when these materials are transformed by labor. The important point, however, is that this additional value is generally realized in the industrial center, rather than at the periphery. Thus, there are multiple inequalities in international exchange. One, certainly, results from the differential wages of labor. Another, however, is the transfer of the natural value in the raw, unlabored resources from periphery to center. Another is in the location of the full realization of value in the center, rather than in the peripheral sources of the material commodities. Finally, if the resources do not renew themselves naturally, the inequality of the exchange is intensified by the loss of resources to the periphery itself.

The use of labor as a standard of value for unequal exchange ignores the multiple inequalities inherent in the subordination of extractive economies to production economies, when value in nature is appropriated in one region and labor value is incorporated in another. Bettelheim (1972: 300-307), for instance, restricts the concept of exploitation to the appropriation of surplus labor value in specific modes of production, and thus excludes from consideration the international inequalities involved in the exploitation and export of natural resources. De Janvry (1981: 20) extends Bettelheim's restriction in his criticism of dependency and world systems perspectives: "By focusing on the external factors, the underdevelopment school tends to replace the relations of exploitation between social classes with those between geographical areas."

Once we acknowledge, however, that not only the value in labor but also the value in nature can be appropriated, it becomes clear that we cannot counterpose the exploitation between social classes and between geographical areas. Instead, we must consider the effects of the exploitation of labor and the exploitation of entire ecosystems as separate but complementary phenomena that both affect the development of particular regions. We can therefore reject as well Amin's (1977) arguments that unequal exchange occurred only after center wages started to rise above subsistence levels as the result of imperialist strategies that opened world markets and world sources of raw materials for capitalist exploitation. The appropriation of values in nature, from the periphery, in fact initiated unequal exchange between regions and between ecosystems long before the rise of wages and the expansion of consumer demand in the core. Examination of the ecological effects of the ivory trade (Palmer and Parsons, 1977) and of the demographic effects of the slave trade (Wallerstein, 1976) on large parts of Africa demonstrate the impact of exploitation between geographic areas as well as between classes on the evolution of unequal exchange.

If we leave aside the semantic discussion of whether or not the entire world is capitalist, we can abstract from Frank's and Wallerstein's analyses models of unequal exchange that posit an international market that responds to all of its producing and consuming components but within which certain national economies disproportionately influence supply, demand, and prices in ways that permit them to accumulate capital, and thus to expand their own reproduction, far more rapidly than can other national economies (see Wallerstein, 1974: 406; Brenner, 1977). The combination of accelerated capital accumulation and technological innovation in turn enhances the influence of industrial economies on world market demand. Technological innovations and their industrial use in the center create demand for specific extractive commodities such as rubber, bauxite, or cassiterite. New demands emerge with subsequent innovations. Accelerated capital accumulation is associated with rapid technological change, so the center disproportionately influences the global structure of demand. This progressively disrupts the ecological and social bases for social reproduction, and for the expansion of labor's productivity, in the extractive periphery, while enhancing social consumption and the productivity of labor in the productive core.

World-systems perspectives on global exchange should permit consideration of these multiple inequalities, but erroneous insistence on a single world mode of production and on an international division of labor within it does not allow an adequate account of the ecological disruptions and economic deceleration that result from the transfer of natural values (i.e., commodities whose values are primarily extracted from nature rather than produced by labor and capital) from the periphery to the core. Wallerstein's extension of a single world market to imply a single capitalist division of labor is ultimately as biased toward production models and the assumption that labor provides value as are the modes-of-production analyses. His arguments for a single global mode of production are based on commodities in different labor regimes organized to produce exchange values. He thus ignores the special characteristics of the extractive economies predominant in many peripheral areas. Nor, despite his concern with modes of production as elements of an international division of labor, does Wallerstein indicate how historical sequences within particular modes of production or extraction or sets of "articulated" modes of production affect both the ways modes of production reproduce themselves and the ways they are inserted into the world economy over continuous, or sequential, periods of time calculated at the regional, rather than at the global, level.

We can only understand the underdevelopment of extractive economics if we take into account the multiple costs or the loss of value that these entail for natural environments and for the social formations that draw their subsistence from them. A labor theory of value, and models of unequal exchange of labor between regions, are inadequate to such a calculus. The use and reproduction of labor in extractive economies are central to their evolution, however. It is precisely because the market values and the eventual-use values of extracted goods exist in nature, and are considered to be the property of extractive entrepreneurs, that the small portion contributed by extractive labor to their value and to their utility can be, and is, exploited without regard to labor's reproduction. During brief extractive booms, labor not directly involved in the extractive process is usually "in the way" (Gaventa, 1980). The rapid geographical shifts of extractive location, the investment of surplus capital in transport and exchange infrastructure, and the logic of exploiting available resources quickly as the demand rises all militate against the establishment of linkages to local productive communities, even though their absence does raise labor maintenance costs. Labor is expendable in the short-run, profit-maximizing logic of extractive export economies. The continued disruption of populations, however, accelerates the eventual collapse of each particular extractive cycle by contributing to rising labor costs, and constitutes a major component of the labor shortages or maldistributions that cause progressive impoverishment across sequential extractive cycles.

PERIODIZATION AND ECOLOGICAL SUCCESSION

An adequate theory of development requires that we delineate the "chains of historical causation" (Gutkind and Wallerstein, 1976: 7) in ways that permit simultaneous reference to both global and regional units of analysis as historically continuous systems. Analysis at the global level has achieved several effective "periodizations" of the world system, but these have all derived from sequential changes in the structure and composition of capital and in the relations of dominant classes to the state in the industrial core (Lenin, 1939; Frank, 1979; Baran, 1957; Amin, 1974; Preobazhensky, 1965; Mandel, 1975). While these periodizations make reference to the impact of these changes on the periphery, they do so by using different peripheral regions to exemplify the dynamics of the different periods (see e.g., Wallerstein, 1976). They thus sacrifice historical continuity at the local level.

A full account of the intersection between regional and global systems requires separate analysis of each system in terms that recognize the dynamics of each system as an integral unit while simultaneously permitting analysis of their effects on each other. I propose that this can be achieved by (1) organizing regional economic history into periods which correspond to the predominance of particular commodities in a region's export trade; (2) examining the extent to which the combination of political forces and the changes in world system demand structured the relative composition of exports from that region; (3) describing how labor was exploited in the extraction and production of these different commodities, either through reorganization of prior modes of production and extraction or through organization of new modes; and (4) analyzing how the demographic, organizational, infrastructural, and ecological effects of each of these modes of production and extraction established the potential for and the limits on later modes of production and extraction. This articulation of concepts across levels and across time requires precise attention to internal responses to opportunities and pressures generated in external systems. Both the world system and local modes of production and extraction constitute discrete units of analysis whose mutual effects can be seen in the ways that local actors—including those deriving power from organizations that operate beyond the local area—reorganize local modes of production and extraction in order to take advantage of exchange opportunities in the world system. These activities and relationships have demonstrable effects on the physical environment, on social organization, and on demographic distributions that establish the limits, and the opportunities, for subsequent uses of these environments.

Treating each local mode of production and extraction as regionally discrete and historically continuous allows consideration of the internal dynamics by which societies may reproduce themselves independently of their participation in a world system, of the variation between societies, and of their participation in, response to, or occasional withdrawal over time from the world system. This avoids reifying dependency, unequal exchange, or capitalism as causal agents; rather, it permits development and underdevelopment of particular nations or regions to be understood as the ways that particular local classes reorganize modes of production and extraction in response to exchange opportunities and political actions in the world system. It thus allows us to integrate our analysis of class inequalities with analysis of inequalities between world regions. Finally, it allows us to relate the transitions between modes of production and extraction to the ecological successions that structure the physical environments on which these modes depend.

REFERENCES

ADAMS, R. N. (1982) Paradoxical Harvest: Energy and Explanation in British History, 1870-1914. New York: Cambridge University Press.

AMIN, S. (1977) Imperialism and Unequal Development. New York: Monthly Review Press.

———— (1976) Unequal Development. New York: Monthly Review Press.

———— (1974) Accumulation on a World Scale. New York: Monthly Review Press.

ANDERSON, P. (1974) Lineages of the Absolutist State. New York: Monthly Review Press.

BARAN, P. (1957) The Political Economy of Growth. New York: Monthly Review Press.

BLAIR, J. (1976) The Control of Oil. New York: Random House.

BRENNER, R. (1977) "The origins of capitalist development: a critique of neo-Smithian Marxism." New Left Review 104: 27-59.

BROCKWAY, L. H. (1979) Science and Colonial Expansion: The Role of the British Royal Botanic Gardens. New York: Academic Press.

BUNKER, S. G. (1984a) "Modes of Extraction, Unequal Exchange, and the Progressive Underdevelopment of an Extreme Periphery: The Brazilian Amazon, 1600-1980." American Journal of Sociology.

———— (1984b) Underdeveloping the Amazon: Extraction, Unequal Exchange, and the Failure of the Modern State, Urbana: University of Illinois Press.

COBBE, J. H. (1979) Governments and Mining Companies in Developing Countries. Boulder, CO: Westview Press.

DALY, H. E. (1977) Steady-State Economics. San Francisco: W. H. Freeman and Co.

DE JANVRY, A. (1981) The Agrarian Question and Reformism in Latin America. Baltimore: Johns Hopkins Press.

EMMANUEL, A. (1972) Unequal Exchange: A Study in the Imperialism of Trade. New York: Monthly Review Press.

FRANK, A. G. (1979) Dependent Accumulation and Underdevelopment. New York: Monthly Review Press.

———— (1967) Capitalism and Underdevelopment in Latin America: Historical Studies of Chile and Brazil. New York: Monthly Review Press.

FURTADO, C. (1970) Economic Development of Latin America: A Survey from Colonial Times to the Cuban Revolution. London: Cambridge University Press.

GALTUNG, J. (1971) "A structural theory of imperialism." Journal of Peace Research 8, 2: 81-117.

GAVENTA, J. (1980) Power and Powerlessness: Quiescence and Rebellion in an Appalachian Valley. Urbana: University of Illinois Press.

GEORGESCU-ROEGEN, N. (1975) "Energy and economic myths." The Southern Economic Journal 41, 3: 347-381.

————— (1971) The Entropy Law and the Economic Process. Cambridge, MA: Harvard University Press.

————— (1970) "The entropy law and the economic problem." The Ecologist 2, 7 (July): 13-17.

GUTKIND, P.C.W. and I. WALLERSTEIN (1976) "Editors' introduction," pp. 7-29 in P.C.W. Gutkind and I. Wallerstein (eds.) The Political Economy of Contemporary Africa. Beverly Hills: Sage.

HECHT, S. (1979) "Spontaneous legumes of developed pastures of the Amazon and their forage potential," pp. 65-80 in P. A. Sánchez and L. A. Tergas (eds.) Pasture Production in Acid Soils of the Tropics. Cali: CIAT.

HINDESS, B. and P. Q. HIRST (1975) Pre-Capitalist Modes of Production. London: Routledge & Kegan Paul.

KATZMAN, M. (1976) "Paradoxes of Amazonian development in a 'resource starved' world." The Journal of Developing Areas 10: 445-460.

LENIN, V. I. (1939) Imperialism, the Highest Stage of Capitalism. New York: International Publishers.

LEVIN, J. (1960) Export Economics. Cambridge, MA: Harvard University Press.

LUXEMBURG, R. (1951) The Accumulation of Capital. London: Routledge & Kegan Paul.

MANDEL, E. (1975) Late Capitalism. London: New Left Review Editions.

PALMER, R. and N. PARSONS [eds.] (1977) The Roots of Rural Poverty in Central and South Africa. Berkeley: University of California Press.

PREOBAZHENSKY, E. (1965) The New Economics. Oxford, England: Clarendon.

SANTOS, R. (1981) Historia Ecónomica da Amazonia (1800-1920). São Paulo: TAO.

SCHNAIBERG, A. (1980) The Environment: From Surplus to Scarcity. New York: Oxford University Press.

SCHUMACHER, E. F. (1973) Small Is Beautiful: Economics as if People Mattered. New York: Harper & Row.

SOLBERG, C. (1976) Oil Power: The Rise and Imminent Fall of an American Empire. New York: New American Library.

STERNBERG, H. O'Reilly. (1973) "Development and conservation." Erdkunde 23: 253-265.

WALLERSTEIN, I. (1981) "On how accumulation works." Contemporary Sociology 10, 1: 41-43.

————— (1976) "The three stages of African involvement in the world economy." pp. 30-57 in P.C.W. Gutkind and I. Wallerstein (eds.) The Political Economy of Contemporary Africa. Beverly Hills: Sage.

—————(1974) "The rise and future demise of the world capitalist system." Comparative Studies in History and Society 16, 4: 387-415.

WEINSTEIN, B. (1980) "Prosperity without development: the Paraense elite and the Amazon rubber boom (1850-1920)." Ph.D. dissertation, Yale University.

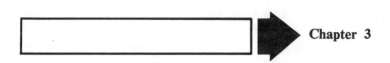

Chapter 3

THE WORLD-SYSTEM SINCE 1950:
WHAT HAS REALLY CHANGED?

Christopher K. Chase-Dunn
Johns Hopkins University

This chapter will examine the contention that, from the point of view of structural features and systemic logic, the capitalist world-economy has not significantly changed since World War II. It can be argued that rapid changes of scale and apparently new institutional forms are interpretable as continuations of processes long in operation. This position requires that we have a fairly clear idea of the deep structural logic of capitalism, and an accurate specification of the processes that maintain the structure of the modern world-system and drive forward its cycles and trends.

First I will present an overview of the current literature that claims that one or another recent development constitutes a new stage or a significant change for the world-economy. Transnational corporations, cabals of a global bourgeoisie, state sovereignty at bay, the peripheralization of the core, the new international division of labor, the emergence of a socialist world-system, and other current phenomena will be subjected to severe scrutiny. Then, the problems of claiming that no significant change has occurred will also be discussed and I shall speculate briefly on the potential for future world-system transformation.

SYSTEM LOGIC, CYCLES, AND TRENDS

In order to study change we must have a clear idea of the basic structure and processes of the capitalist world-economy. At the risk of boring readers already familiar with this discussion I shall outline fundamental concepts and theoretical propositions of the world-system perspective. Such an exercise both serves a pedagogical function and often reveals gaps or theoretical contradictions that have yet to be clearly resolved.

Structural Constants

World-systems are not global, or at least none were until the late nineteenth century when the capitalist world-economy succeeded in incorporating all other socioeconomic systems. Immanuel Wallerstein (1979) distinguishes between two basic kinds of world-system: *world-economies*, which are multicultural, multistate economic networks in which basic goods are exchanged over a wide territory; and *world-empires*, multicultural territorial divisions of labor (economic networks) that are incorporated into a single state apparatus. World-systems of the latter kind are the Chinese Empire, the Roman Empire, the Ottoman Empire, the Aztec Empire, and so on. There have been many precapitalist world-economies as well, but most of them tended to become world-empires, or to disintegrate.

The capitalist world-economy is a world-system in which the capitalist mode of production has become dominant. Thus this historical system contains a deep structural logic of capitalist capital accumulation that drives it to expand and contains systemic contradictions that will provoke its transformation to a different logic once expansion and deepening of capitalist social relations have approached their limits.

The constant structural features of the capitalist world-system are the following.

The interstate system, which is a system of unequally powerful nation-states that compete for resources by supporting profitable commodity production and directly engaging in geopolitical military competition.

A core-periphery division of labor in which the countries that occupy a core position specialize in *core production*—relatively capital intensive production utilizing skilled, high-wage labor. Peripheral areas contain mostly *peripheral production*—labor intensive, low-wage, un-skilled labor, which has historically been subjected to extra-economic coercion.

Production relations in the capitalist world-economy are more complex than Marx (1967) assumed in his basic model of capitalist accumulation. The direct producers differ in their access to political organizations, most importantly, states. Thus there is a reproduced differentiation between core labor and peripheral labor. Labor is commodified, but it is not a perfect commodity. Direct producers (workers) vary in terms of the degree to which their interests are protected or coerced by political organizations. Core workers often enjoy the protection of state-legalized labor unions and welfare laws, although many remain in the condition of "free" laborers subject to the vicissitudes of the labor market. At the other extreme are those peripheral workers who are directly subjected to extra-economic coercion—historically, serfs, slaves, or contract laborers. Thus the continuum from protected to coerced labor is a constant differentiation within the work force of the capitalist world-economy, although, as we shall see below, the trend toward proletarianization moves a greater proportion of the work force toward full-time dependency on capitalist commodity production.

Commodity production for the world market (which includes both national and international markets) is the central form of competition and source of surplus value in the capitalist mode of production. This form of competition is fundamentally interwoven with the competitive political processes of state-formation, nation-building, and geopolitics in the context of the interstate system. The world market is not a perfect price-setting market, although it has long been and remains a very competitive arena. Monopolies are politically guaranteed *within sub-units*, and superprofits deriving from these monopolies are subjected to a long-run competition as the political conditions for maintenance of monopolies are themselves subjected to the forces of competition.

System Cycles

Long business cycles. This is a cycle in which the relative rate of capital accumulation and overall economic activity increases and then decreases toward stagnation in a forty-to-sixty-year period. The causes of this long wave or Kondratieff cycle are explained within a Marxian framework by Mandel (1980).

Core competition. This refers to a cycle of unicentricity versus multicentricity in the distribution of power and competitive advantage in production among core states. Unicentric periods are those in which power and competitive advantage are relatively concentrated in a single hegemonic core state. Multicentric periods are those in which there is a more equal distribution of power and competitive advantage among core states. There have been three hegemonic core states since the sixteenth century: the United Provinces of the Netherlands, the United Kingdom of Great Britain, and the United States of America. The national-level conditions and system-level processes that cause this cycle arc explicated in Chase-Dunn (1982a).[1]

This cycle is also related to periods of peace versus periods of warfare among core powers. During the unicentric period in which a core power is hegemonic, wars among core powers are fewer and world trade is less encumbered by national protectionism. During multicentric periods mercantilist interference with world trade emerges as economic interests try to use political power to protect their markets and investments. There have been four *world wars* in which the entire core of the capitalist world-economy became involved.[2]

Samir Amin (1980) has suggested that world wars represent normal forms of competition within capitalism as a system. The political structure within which peaceful capitalist accumulation proceeds becomes unable to provide stable support after a period of uneven economic growth, and world wars establish a new power framework for continued capitalist accumulation (Chase-Dunn, 1981).

The structure of core-periphery trade and control. A periodic change in the pattern of control and exchange between the core and the periphery has characterized the world-system since 1450. Periods of relatively free market multilateral exchange are followed by periods in which trade is politically controlled and tends to be contained within colonial empires (Bergesen and Schoenberg, 1980). The causal relationships between this cycle and the cycle of core competition (above) are hypothesized in Chase-Dunn (1978).[3]

System Trends

A number of systemic trends increase in waves that (often) correspond in time with the cycles described above.

Expansion to new populations and territories. The capitalist world-system has expanded to take in formerly external arenas in a series of waves since the sixteenth century. The limits of this type of expansion were reached at the end of the nineteenth century when the whole globe became integrated into the world division of labor and the colonial empires.

The intensification and deepening of commodity relations. Land, labor, and wealth have been increasingly commodified in both the core and the periphery.[4] More spheres of life have taken the commodity form in the core than in the periphery, but all areas have experienced a secular increase in every epoch of the modern world-system.

State formation. The power of states over their populations has increased in every period in both the core and the periphery (Boli-Bennett, 1980). States have increasingly expropriated the authority of other actors and organizations, although this trend has been uneven; and there have been periods when state control temporarily decreased or was decentralized.

Increased size of economic enterprises. The average size in terms of assets and employees controlled by economic enterprises has increased in every epoch. Agricultural enterprises and industrial enterprises have gone through periods when this trend has slowed or even reversed temporarily, and the causes of this concentration of capital vary according to the phases of the business cycle (Bergesen, 1981).

The internationalization of capital. Capital has been international since the long sixteenth century, when both commodity exchange by merchants and direct investments by productive capital (plantations, mining) were made both among core states (Barbour, 1963) and in peripheral areas (Frank, 1979). Since then it has become increasingly international in the sense that investment across national boundaries and transnational control of production have increased. The most recent expansion of transnational corporations is thus a continuation of a trend long in operation.

Increasing capital intensity of production. The several industrial revolutions in both agriculture and manufacturing have increased the productivity of labor in both the core and the periphery. Capitalist relations of production have deepened across the system, subjecting the labor process to greater amounts of direct control, although decentralization in the form of small commodity production, subcontracting, or bureaucratization of labor control (Edwards, 1979) reproduces a "competitive sector" of independent producers and forms of autonomy within even the most centralized sectors. The long-run trend among transnational firms has been toward more direct control over production and the expansion of the scale of coordination of production.

Proletarianization. The process of class formation has increased the dependence of the world labor force on participation in labor markets. Subsistence redoubts, urban informal sectors, domestic economies, and newly created "villages" have been allowed to exist for the sustenance of semiproletarianized elements of the work force,[5] but the long-run trend has been to move more and more direct producers into full-time dependence on commodity production. This has been true of both the core and the periphery with a greater lag in the periphery. Similarly the extent of extra-economic coercion used to compel labor in the periphery has been reduced over time, as the alternatives for sustenance have been reduced. Capitalist slavery, serfdom, and contract labor have been largely eliminated, although the relative degree to which political coercion is applied in class relations remains greater in the periphery than in the core. This includes anti-labor union laws, "bureaucratic authoritarian" regimes, and other forms of repression.

The above list of structural constants, cycles, and trends exhibited by the capitalist world-economy constitutes what can be described as a "descriptive model" that seeks to show the causal relations and the relations in time among different empirically observable features. The more difficult theoretical task of formulating a model of the prime movers behind such a system remains to be worked out.[6]

Has The System Changed?

The question to which this chapter is addressed is "Has the world-system really changed since the last World War?" To answer this completely we would need a clear formulation of the deep structural logic of the capitalist world-economy, and an indication of the extent to which new developments have altered its logic. As we do not yet have such a theory we shall have to make some rough estimations in the light of the constants, cycles, and trends outlined above. Of interest in such an exercise is the problem of when quantitative change (the upward movement of trends) becomes qualitative change.

STAGES OF CAPITALISM

Several authors, following the lines of Marxian thought, have reformulated the notion of "stages" of capitalism to fit the capitalist world-economy as a whole.[7] Szymanski (1981: 95) argues that

> imperialism has gone through four qualitatively distinct stages: first, noncapitalist mercantile imperialism from around 1500 to around 1800; second, competitive capitalist imperialism from around 1840 to around 1880; third, early monopoly capitalist imperialism from around 1890 to around 1960; and fourth, late monopoly capitalist imperialism since the 1960's.

Elsewhere I have argued against the periodization into stages presented by Szymanski (Chase-Dunn, 1980/1981). The focus of this chapter urges us to consider only his most recent transformation, from early to late monopoly capitalist imperialism.

In another version of the stages contention Borrego (1982) argues that capitalist accumulation based on the core-periphery hierarchy is becoming transformed into "metanational capitalist accumulation" based on a global, nonterritorially organized bourgeoisie operating through global firms. Szymanski's latest stage is based on what he sees as the importance of decolonization and the industrialization of the periphery, while Borrego's metanationalist stage focuses on the importance of globally operating firms. Both of these contentions will be dealt with in the subsections devoted to these topics below.

My discussion of the various claims about substantial change will be organized into the following topics:

(1)   the internationalization of capital;
(2)   the new international division of labor;
(3)   world class and state formation;
(4)   a socialist world-system: the socialist states.

THE INTERNATIONALIZATION OF CAPITAL

Some social scientists, on discovering the reality of the world-economy, have assumed that its importance as a systemic logic that has major effects on the development of subsystems is of recent origin (Michalet, 1976) or that it has just recently become transnational (Hymer, 1979). These claims may be broken down into their constituent arguments, which involve the logic of investment decisions, monopolization, effects on states, and effects on prices and value. Arguments about the effects of the growth and reorganization of transnational firms on the peripheral countries will be discussed below in the section on the new international division of labor.

It is undeniable that transnational firms have grown in size and importance in the post-World War period. Their expansion has been studied as business history and econometrically as to its extent and effects on the structure of the world-economy. The fact of this growth is presented by some analysts as evidence that the logic of the system must have changed. This assumption needs to be examined.

The great chartered companies were the first transnational corporations, engaging in both merchant capitalism (buying cheap and selling dear) and productive capitalism (the direct organization of commodity production). They were joint stock companies that were allocated monopoly rights and protection by the individual core states that chartered them. These "monopolies," however, were partial because competition among the chartered companies of the core states was rife.

Some authors have alleged that the contemporary transnational corporations are controlled by international groups of capitalists not aligned with any particular core state (Dixon, 1982). In terms of the ownership of stock, it has been shown that the modern transnational firms are, in fact, owned and controlled by capitalists in one or another of the core states (Mandel, 1975). Nevertheless there is some coparticipation in ownership across national boundaries. This feature, however, is not new. Violet Barbour (1963) reports that disgruntled seventeenth-century Amsterdam merchants not able to obtain shares in the Dutch East India Company were instrumental in the formation of the English East India Company.

That capital was transnational in the seventeenth century does not contradict the contention that it is more transnational now. The question is, What difference does that make for the logic of investment decisions? And, granting that the great chartered companies, along with plantations and mines, were operated according to the logic of productive capital rather than merely merchant capital, it is undoubtedly the case that the direct organization of production by capital has become much more firmly entrenched since the seventeenth century. We also know that transport and communications costs have declined in geometric fashion, making the spatial extent of investment strategies expand greatly. Thus the world-economy is more integrated by global investment decisions and international sourcing than ever before. But does this constitute a change in logic or merely a change in scale?

I would argue that the model presented in the first section accounts well for most of the recent changes, especially as it designates trends toward internationalization, capital-intensity, and the increasing size of firms. It could be argued that these quantitative trends have led to qualitative changes in the nature of the game, and some contentions of this kind will be considered below.

One undeniable consequence of the increasing integration of the world-economy by transnational corporations and the shift away from merchant capitalism is to increase the systemness of the system. merchant capitalism trades commodities between regions that have not become fully integrated as systems of production. Marx (1967) describes how merchant capital eventually creates "abstract labor" by subjecting qualitatively different kinds of production to an equivalent standard in terms of the efficient allocation of scarce resources. Unintegrated systems have price structures that vary according to their social structural uniquenesses, and differences in natural endowments.

Merchant capital moves goods from systems where they are cheap to systems where they are dear in what Amin (1980) calls the "exchange of unequals." But the long-run consequence of such exchanges is to alter the allocation of labor time in both systems such that they move toward the formation of a single equilibrated system in terms of the "efficient" allocation of labor and other scarce resources.

No market system is ever in perfect equilibrium in the above sense, and indeed a certain inequality of labor values is part of the institutional nature of the capitalist world-economy—the unequal exchange between the core and the periphery (Emmanuel, 1972). The long-run consequence of the action of market exchange is to produce a single interactional set of prices that reflects the competitive rationality of a market system. The remaining structural barriers to the equalization of wages and other prices are generated by the system itself.

The trends toward the internationalization of capital, the further integration of the world-economy, and the growing importance of production decisions on a global scale reduce the importance of the remnants of precapitalist systems. The capitalist mode of production became dominant in the European world-economy of the long sixteenth century, but it still contained precapitalist modes of production that continued to have some influence on the historical development of the system. As it expanded it incorporated other socioeconomic systems, and these too have left institutional remnants that have influenced the particular configurations of development in each area (Wolf, 1982). Aspects of these precapitalist logics undoubtedly remain, but their importance has certainly decreased with the growing integration of the system.

Some analysts have argued that the growing importance of the transnational corporations has altered the logic of capitalism toward a less competitive, more monopolized and monolithic system. A large and growing component of international trade is made up of *intra*firm transfers. The portion composed of market transactions among independent producers has decreased. The affect of this, it is alleged, is to decrease the overall amount of competition in the system.

This argument is analogous to the discussion of the transition from competitive to monopoly capitalism. It is alleged that there was once a stage of capitalism in which the state did not interfere in production decisions or markets, but merely provided the institutional support for the operation of the free market in land, labor, and capital. Firms were small, start-up costs were low, and thus the competitive market system forced firms to produce as cheaply as possible and to sell their products at the lowest possible prices.

This vision is alleged to describe Britain in the late eighteenth and early nineteenth centuries. In fact it describes certain sectors of the British economy that became idealized in economic myth. It is true that capitalism is a dynamic system that has always had a "competitive sector" of high-risk, small-scale entrepreneurs, and that at certain periods in certain countries something approximating the free market model has come into being.

Once we focus on the world-economy rather than national economies several things become clear. First, most states most of the time have attempted to influence production and market forces in favor of some group of capitalists. The laissez-faire state is merely a special case, in which one set of capitalists has succeeded in reducing the political favoritism formerly offered to another set. Second, although monopolies are granted by states and enforced within municipalities and by other political organizations, cartels, guilds, unions, and so on, *there are no long-run monopolies in the capitalist world-economy*. The political organizations that grant monopolies are themselves in competition with one another and, as no one can really escape interaction in the larger arena for long, protectionist measures and monopoly rights are themselves subjected to a logic of competition.

These observations are no less true today than they were in previous centuries, except that the size of the largest firms has increased relative to the size of states. It is this last development that has caused some authors to argue that competitive capitalism has changed into monopoly capitalism.

Monopoly pricing allows firms to pass on costs to those consumers over whom they have some direct or indirect political influence. If the world-system had a single overarching state apparatus, true and complete monopolies could be maintained. But in a world-economy with a competitive interstate system, monopolies are partial and temporary.

At the global level there are no industries that could be described as uncompetitive, despite the growth of transnational firms. The recent glut of steel, cars, oil, and other world commodities reminds us of the continuing "anarchy of production decisions" that has always been a feature of capitalism (Strange and Tooze, 1981).

Several analysts have suggested that the increased importance of transnational corporations has diminished the power of nation-states. Raymond Vernon stated this thesis most strongly in his *Sovereignty at Bay* (1963). A modified version has been discussed by Marlene Dixon (1982) in her essay on "dual power." It is clearly the case that transnational corporations have increased their power vis-à-vis small peripheral states. And, simply as a function of their size, the largest firms may have increased their influence over core states as well. It should be remembered, however, that states have also increased their powers. The question is whether or not the changing relationship between the size of firms and the size of states has altered the logic of the game.

It has been pointed out that, contrary to the contentions of some authors, most of the world's largest firms continue to be primarily controlled by capitalists from one or another of the core states. Thus there are no truly multinational firms from the point of view of ownership. Among the fifty largest transnational firms only Unilever and Royal Dutch Shell could be considered "binational" in terms of ownership (Bergesen and Sahoo, forthcoming). The extent to which these firms may constitute an integrated world bourgeoisie is discussed below in the section on world class formation. Here I wish to address the relationship between firms and states.

It is obvious that transnational firms do not control their own armies, nor do they have powers of taxation. The usual distinction between "private" firms versus public organizations becomes very problematic when we consider the case of state capitalism. But, even considering the growth of state control in production there remains an important differentiation between economic and political sources of power in the capitalist world-economy.

Firms continue to rely on states for the provision of "order." Frederic Lane (1979) has analyzed the interaction in terms of the notion of "protection rent," and the best state (from the capitalist point of view) is the one that provides the social conditions for profit making at cost. The cost is, of course, raised when class struggle places demands on states to ameliorate some of the negative consequences of market rationality; and states unfortunate enough to be influenced by the interests of workers find that capital will emigrate to areas where taxes and wages are less.

Transnational corporations have contradictory interests vis-à-vis states. On the one hand they need world order, not merely order within national boundaries, and for this they need a fairly stable set of alliances among the strongest core states. On the other hand, they make great profits from their ability to play off states against one another. States compete to offer the best deals to attract the capital investments of the transnationals. And transnationals desire to maintain the maneuverability that the multistate system guarantees.

But we should not overemphasize the power of the transnational firms. Their dependence on individual states is still very great. They cannot suppress strikes, political challenges, or nationalizations without being able to mobilize the police forces and armies controlled by states, and so they must maintain influence and control over states. This cannot be done solely by threat of flight. It must also be done by cajolery, tax paying, and "good citizenship" shown by public affairs campaigns and "social" activities. This is most true of their relations with core states, of course. But even in peripheral states they must coopt some support, even if this only means bribing a few generals.

The "sovereignty at bay" thesis was most believable when it was first put forth in the 1960s. At that time the world economy was still growing. Stagnation had not yet caused a shift toward protectionism and the use of political power to maintain access to markets and profit-making opportunities. When the pie is shrinking the world-system turns toward a much more state-centric system, which provides the basis for neomercantilist interpretations (Krasner, 1978). In reality the dual power thesis is correct. The complicated game of competition in the capitalist world-economy is a combination of profitable commodity production with efficient use of geopolitical power. But this is not a new development. Rather, we have experienced in recent years a shift that has occurred many times before—from capitalist profit making in an expanding market to equally capitalist geopolitical competition involving mercantilism, austerity, and the threat of world war.

THE NEW INTERNATIONAL DIVISION OF LABOR

Several versions of the new international division of labor thesis have been offered. The strongest version of the thesis claims that the core-periphery territorial division of labor has been eliminated, with metanational capitalist accumulation taking place globally irrespective of territorial location. Another version contends that peripheral capitalism (based on "primary" accumulation using coerced labor to produce cheap, labor-intensive raw material inputs) has been eliminated with the industrialization of peripheral countries. Yet another version emphasizes the political autonomy of peripheral states following decolonization and the demise of the colonial empires. We shall examine these arguments in turn.

First let us describe the core-periphery hierarchy as it has been conceptualized in the world-system perspective. The underlying analytic basis of this territorial hierarchy is the distinction between core production and peripheral production. Core production is relatively capital-intensive and employs skilled, high-wage labor; peripheral production is labor-intensive and employs cheap, often politically coerced labor. In core areas there is a predominance of core production, and the obverse condition exists in peripheral areas. This means that there may be backwaters of peripheral production, or simply less capital-intensive, less-skilled labor within core states. Semiperipheral states are defined as areas containing a relatively equal mix of core, peripheral, and intermediate types of production.

One of the main structural features that reproduce this territorial hierarchy is the exercise of political-military power by core states. It is not simply a matter of original differences among areas in terms of wage levels and "historical" standards of living, as Emmanuel (1972) implies. The wage differential between core and peripheral workers is a dynamic and reproduced feature of the system. Core states (the most powerful political organizations in the system) are induced to provide some protection for the wages of their citizens, as well as supplemental benefits composing the social wage. The core-periphery wage differential is greater than that which would be due to differences in productivity alone, and this differential is maintained by restrictions on international labor migration from the periphery to the core. The great differences in capital-intensity between the core and the periphery also account for a good portion of the wage differential.

This territorial division of labor is not static. It has expanded along with the expansion of the whole system, and there has been some upward and downward mobility within the structure (Friedmann,

1982).[8] The whole system moves toward greater capital intensity, so production processes that were core activities in the past may become peripheral activities at a later time.

The international division of labor has been reorganized several times before in the history of the capitalist world-economy (Walton, forthcoming). The original plunder by core states of external arenas (extremely primitive accumulation) was replaced by the production of raw materials using coerced labor. Core investments in plantations and mines were followed by investments in utilities, communications, and transportation infrastructure. As domestic markets in the periphery developed, local and core capital took up profitable opportunities in manufacturing, and, in the most recent phase, industrial production for export has emerged in the periphery.

The core-periphery hierarchy has been reinforced by an unequal distribution of political-military power among core states and peripheral areas. Historically this was organized as a system of colonial empires in which core states exercised direct political domination over peripheral areas. Chirot (1977) and Szymanski (1981) have argued that the complete decolonization of the periphery has reduced the power differential between core and peripheral states. Contrary to most discussions of neocolonialism, Chirot claims that formal sovereignty has eliminated the periphery, and that Asia, Africa, and Latin America can now be categorized as semiperipheral.

Overstating the argument this way causes difficulties. Was Latin America then semiperipheral immediately upon attaining independence from Spain in the early nineteenth century? Nonetheless, the underlying contention that the power differential may have diminished should not be so easily dismissed. The phenomena of OPEC, the Conference of Non-Aligned Nations, and strong presence in the United Nations of peripheral supporters of a New International Economic Order may indicate some truth to the hypothesis of a reduction in the magnitude of the core-periphery power differential.

Clearly some former peripheral countries have become semiperipheral, and the United States has lost some of its former hegemony. But core states as a whole may have gained additional power at the same time that peripheral states have attained formal sovereignty. Only carefully thought-out empirical research on changes in the distribution of military power capabilities, state access to resources, and level of economic development over time can resolve this question. Until this is done we can only surmise about the ways in which a reduction in the overall distribution of power between the core and periphery might affect the logic and operation of world capitalism. This will be done in a concluding section.

Another contention about the new international division of labor focuses on the growth of industrial production in the New Industrializing Countries (Caporaso, 1981). Sometimes this is interpreted as the end of a core-periphery system. Deindustrialization in the core, industrialization in the periphery, and a shift toward control by global transnational corporations are portrayed as the beginning of a new era of metanational capitalism.

The notion of upwardly mobile semiperipheral countries has been convincingly utilized to understand the developmental paths of Brazil, Mexico (Gereffi and Evans, 1981), and India (Vanneman, 1979). The notion of "dependent development" put forth by Cardoso (1973) and applied by Evans (1979) has proven extremely fruitful for understanding the bargaining and collusions among transnational firms, semiperipheral state managers, and national capitalists in Brazil.

Cardoso's (1973) analysis of the shift from classical dependence (production of raw materials for export to the core) to dependent development (Brazilian production of manufactured goods for the domestic market by transnational corporations) claimed that a change had occurred in the effects of dependence on overall economic development. Cardoso argued that the transnational firms would now have an interest in the expansion of the domestic market and so would act economically and politically to foster the growth of the national economy, albeit in a way that would exacerbate inequalities among classes. Cross-national research on the effects of dependence on foreign investments in manufacturing does not support Cardoso's claim. Volker Bornschier (1981) finds that dependence on transnationals in manufacturing has a large long-run negative effect on overall GNP growth in a cross-national comparison. This shows that one of the mechanisms that reproduced the classical core-periphery hierarchy (exploitation through foreign investment) continues to operate in the "new" international division of labor.

Froebel, Heinrichs, and Kreye (1980) have emphasized the importance of manufacturing in the periphery for export to the core. They document the growth of so-called free production zones, areas juridically outside the tariff and labor regulations of peripheral countries that allow transnational firms to have "export platforms" for the utilization of cheap peripheral labor. The industrial exports of the Asian "Gang of Four" (South Korea, Taiwan, Singapore, and Hong Kong) are important cases of the shift toward peripheral industrial production for the world market.[9] Froebel, Heinrichs, and Kreye (1980) contend that this kind of peripheral industrialization steals jobs from core nations by shifting industrial production overseas. Ross and Trachte (1983) have argued that the recent growth of sweatshops employing undocumented immigrant workers in New York City is an instance of the "peripheralization of the core."[10]

The problem is whether or not these developments are the first stages of a shift toward metanational capitalism or are simply the continuation of uneven capitalist development in a period of economic stagnation, with upward and downward mobility occurring in a structural hierarchy that is still intact. The decline of the economic hegemony of the United States has occurred mainly vis-à-vis other core powers, Western Europe, and Japan. This is a continuation of the cycle of core competition, with uneven development occurring within countries (the decline of the industrial Northeast and the rise of the Sunbelt) as well as internationally.

No one could seriously claim that the core-periphery hierarchy has already been eliminated. Immense differences still exist in the level of living and the capital intensity of production. The transnational corporations have their headquarters in the great world cities of the core countries. Industrial production in the periphery has certainly grown but it remains a very small proportion of world industry (Petras et al., 1981: chap. 6). Even if recent trends of the kind described above continued it would be a very long time before the arrival of a metanational world without core and peripheral areas.

Just as the industrialization of the periphery has yet failed to significantly alter the international division of labor, so the deindustrialization of core states, primarily the United States, has not had much overall impact. To claim that core countries have become peripheralized because certain areas within the core have experienced economic decline is certainly an exaggeration. Similarly, discussions of the arrival of "postindustrial" society in the core are certainly premature. The proportion of the work force in services and nonmanual labor has grown in core countries. But, at least for the United States—a declining hegemonic core power—this is the repetition of a pattern that can be seen in the trajectories of hegemonic predecessors—the United Provinces of the Netherlands and the United Kingdom of Great Britain. Both of these hegemonies began their ascent by developing a competitive advantage in consumer goods, followed by the export of capital goods, and finally lived out the twilight of their golden ages as centers of world finance and services. The United States is, in part, following this same sequence (Chase-Dunn, 1982a).

While it is true that industrialization has occurred in some areas of the periphery it should be remembered that industrialization is the application of greater amounts of fixed capital, machinery, and nonhuman energy to production. It is an increase in capital intensity. This increase has continued in the core at the same time as it has occurred in the periphery, and thus the relative distribution of capital intensity may not have changed. Indeed, at least some of the peripheral industrialization has been labor intensive. The free production zones exist primarily to exploit cheap labor.

Very little careful empirical work has been done on changes in the distribution of development characteristics in the world-system. Table 3.1, taken from a review of trends toward convergence or divergence among nation-states (Meyer et al., 1975), is one of the few such comparisons over time. The cutting points are not ideal for our purposes, but we can get a rough idea about the changes in the distribution of economic activities and institutional features associated with "modernization."

This table shows that the poorest countries did not increase their share of Gross World Product between 1950 and 1970, while they did increase very slightly their proportion of world electrical energy consumed. Between 1950 and 1960 they increased their share of the world's nonagricultural work force from 7.3 percent to 9.5 percent. These figures confirm the impression that the economic structure of the peripheral countries has indeed changed, but that they have not increased their share of world output as a result.

The largest increases for the least-developed countries are in the areas of educational enrollments and urbanization. These institutional features (which are often associated with "modernization" of national societies) have grown rapidly. These changes, however, are only superficially similar to the educational expansion and urbanization processes that occurred in core countries.

Education does not expand as a function of the growth of domestic demand for skilled labor in industry and services. Between 1950 and 1970 educational enrollments expanded everywhere in the periphery and semiperiphery of the world-economy (Meyer et al., 1979) regardless of the level or rate of economic development.

TABLE 3.1 Concentration of Resources Among Nations in the
World System[a]

| | Percentages | | |
	1950	1960	1970
Economic Production			
The proportion of Gross World			
Product going to			
the countries highest on GNP per	73.8	69.0	69.2
capita with 20% of world population			
the middle countries on GNP per	23.4	27.8	28.6
capita with 60% of world population			
the countries lowest on GNP per	2.8	3.2	2.2
capita with 20% of world population			
the United States	41.9	35.8	30.4
13 Socialist nations	12.4	18.1	23.2
		129 cases	
		(IBRD, 1971, 1973)	
The proportion of world electrical			
energy consumed by			
the countries highest on KWH per	66.5	64.9	58.9
capita with 20% of world population			
the middle countries on KWH per	32.9	34.4	39.3
capita with 60% of world population			
the countries lowest on KWH per	.6	.7	.8
capita with 20% of world population			
the United States	42.0	38.5	30.4
9 Socialist nations	15.0	19.1	21.8
	75 cases (UN Statistical		
	Yearbook, 1950)		
Economic Structure			
Proportion of the world nonagricultural labor force living			
in			
the countries highest on percentage	44.3	40.0	
of nonagricultural work force with 20%			
of world population			
the middle countries on percentage	48.4	50.5	
of nonagricultural work force with 60% of world popu-			
lation			
the countries lowest on percentage	7.3	9.5	
of nonagricultural work force with 20% of world popu-			
lation			
the United States	15.2	13.6	
14 Socialist nations	22.4	28.5	
		138 cases	
		(ILO, 1971)	

(continued)

Table 3.1 Continued

	Percentages		
	1950	*1960*	*1970*
Educational Enrollments			
Proportion of world primary students enrolled in			
countries highest on percentage of primary students enrolled with 20% world population	27.0	23.1	23.4
middle countries on percentage of primary students enrolled with 60% world population	63.9	65.5	62.4
countries lowest on percentage of primary students enrolled with 20% world population	9.1	11.4	14.2
the United States	15.9	14.7	12.1
13 Socialist nations	37.3	42.7	40.0
		91 cases	
		(UNESCO, 1950)	
Proportion of world secondary students enrolled in			
countries highest on percentage of secondary students enrolled with 20% world population	53.6	44.0	41.4
middle countries on percentage of secondary students enrolled with 60% world population	42.6	50.4	51.3
countries lowest on percentage of secondary students enrolled with 20% world population	3.8	5.6	8.3
the United States	20.3	18.0	21.1
9 Socialist states	13.4	11.5	14.3
		91 cases	
		UNESCO, 1950)	
Proportion of world tertiary students enrolled in			
countries highest on percentage of tertiary students enrolled with 20% world population	58.0	54.3	53.7
middle countries on percentage of tertiary students enrolled with 60% world population	38.9	42.8	42.8
countries lowest on percentage of tertiary students enrolled with 20% world population	2.1	2.9	3.5
the United States	38.8	34.8	34.9
8 Socialist nations	26.6	28.8	24.5
		83 cases	
		(UNESCO, 1950)	

(continued)

Table 3.1 Continued

	Percentages		
	1950	1960	1970
Urbanization			
Proportion of world city-dwellers living in			
countries highest on percentage of urbanization with 20% world population	50.0	46.3	
middle countries on percentage of urbanization with 60% world population	44.7	47.8	
countries lowest on percentage of urbanization with 20% world population	5.3	5.9	
the United States	16.7	15.7	
14 Socialist nations	23.9	25.5	

a. Data are reported only for countries with data at all time points. The totals are calculated similarly. Because some countries are excluded from the total, the absolute numbers cannot be taken seriously; comparisons over time, however, are appropriate.

Similarly, the urbanization explosion in the periphery and semiperiphery has been dubbed "overurbanization" by some observers because it has occurred in the absence of a similar growth rate of industrial employment. The great cities of the periphery most often import capital-intensive technology from the core, which does not create a large demand for workers in industry. Squatter settlements and a teeming "informal sector" of peddlers, domestic servants and small commodity producers swell the urban population. This informal sector provides cheap inputs to large scale enterprises and government by (1) subsidizing the costs of reproducing labor power, and (2) by producing products for sale that are cheap because of the exploitation of unpaid family labor or subminimum wage labor (Portes, 1981). The urban informal sector, then, is a functional equivalent of rural labor reserves, village economies, and the "domestic mode of production" that cheapen the wage bill in classical dependent economies by reproducing part-time proletarians.

In addition, the city systems that have grown up in Latin America are much more centralized around a single large city than those in core countries. This urban primacy emerged, not during the colonial era, but during the 1920s, 1930s, and 1940s (Chase-Dunn, 1982c). Thus, the type of urbanization experienced by peripheral countries has been very different from that in the core. Kentor (1981) has shown that one cause of urbanization in the periphery is dependence on foreign investments by transnational corporations. This dependence has also been shown to cause rises in the levels of tertiary employment that are much greater than the growth in secondary (industrial) employment (Kentor, 1981; Evans and Timberlake, 1980).

WORLD CLASS AND WORLD STATE FORMATION

Although it has been difficult to maintain in the recent period of international squabbles, warmongering, and neomercantilism, some have made the argument that the world bourgeoisie is becoming more integrated as a class (Sklar, 1980; Borrego, 1982). International organizations such as the Trilateral Commission are alleged to form the core of an emergent monolithic world bourgeoisie based on the global transnational corporations. This is a new formulation of the old debate that started at the end of the last century among members of the Second International about superimperialism versus continued imperialist rivalry. Many of the issues discussed above in the section on the internationalization of capital are relevant, but here we shall focus on changes in the interstate system.

There has been a world bourgeoisie since the beginning of the modern world-system, but it has been a very differentiated, competitive, and conflictive class. Peripheral capitalists employing peripheral co-erced labor have produced for export to the core. Core capitalists, divided by nation-state, sector, and access to state power, have made alliances and fought wars among themselves. Often these alliances have crossed the boundaries of core states. It is undeniable that the frequency and importance of intra-core capitalist alliances has increased as the scale of transnational firms has grown.

The question is, does this lower the competitiveness of the system (addressed above) and does it alter the operation of the interstate system. Recent attempts to forge a core-wide common policy against OPEC (organized by the Rockefeller-led fraction of the United States internationally oriented bourgeoisie) were not notably successful. The Trilateral Commission has attempted to coordinate the economic policies of European, North American, and Japanese states in an era of economic contraction, again without much success. That these kinds of international organizations exist is not unique to the contemporary period, and neither is their ineffectiveness novel.

Some may discern a trend toward international political integration in the emergence of the United Nations. Indeed, international organizations have proliferated as the world-economy has become more integrated. The Concert of Europe fell apart to be reorganized as the League of Nations, which was rent by world war, to be followed by the United Nations. Although there undoubtedly has been some progress toward institutionalization of international conflict resolution and collective security in this sequence, no one would contend that the United Nations is capable of preventing war at the present time. The question we must ask is whether or not the importance of military competition among core states has been reduced.

The effect of the spread of nuclear weapons must be discussed here. Do these weapons make obsolete continued competition among fractions of world capital by means of war? Clearly a world war involving nuclear weapons would disrupt the operations of the capitalist system, hardly the most tragic of its effects. Such a war would lead to social devolution, if not the end of our species. This outcome is possible because the contenders who are risking nuclear holocaust are not in control of events.

State managers, world bankers, and transnational firms create war machines as a mechanism to provide investment opportunities, to be sure, but the weapons also have a potential "use value" as threats to maintain or extend political hegemony. These threats involve the risk of a holocaust even though none of the major actors desire this outcome. Thus the existence of nuclear weapons does not change the logic of international political-military competition until they are actually used. Then they change all logics.

The existence of such a threat to the survival of the human species could potentially provide the motivation for the mobilization of a movement to created a real basis for collective security, a world federation capable of preventing warfare among nation-states. The current manifestations of this potential are, however, a long way from that goal.

THE SOCIALIST WORLD-SYSTEM:
SOCIALIST STATES AND THE DOMINO THEORY

Another version of the claim that the current world-system has undergone, or is now experiencing, transformation focuses on the emergence of the socialist states. I have elsewhere presented an interpretation of these states as territories in which intentionally socialist movements have come to state power, but have not yet successfully introduced a self-reproducing socialist mode of production (Chase-Dunn, 1982b). Capitalism provokes movements that try to protect people from market forces and to reorganize the logic of social reproduction and development toward more democratic and collective rationality.

Polanyi (1944) discussed the dialectical interaction between the market principle and the needs of society for protections against certain of the consequences of market rationality, but his analysis focused on national societies. At the level of the world-system and its antisystemic movements we see that the attempts to create noncommodified relations of cooperation become encapsulated politically within organizations: cooperatives, unions, socialist parties, and socialist states. The market principle has, so far, been able to expand its scale to reincorporate these collectivities into the logic of competition within the larger world-system. Thus the contemporary socialist states are important experiments in the construction of socialist institutions that have been perverted to some extent by the necessities of survival and development in the context of the world market and the interstate system.

The large proportion of the world population now living in avowedly socialist states, and recent victories of socialist national liberation movements in Africa, Latin America, and the Caribbean, have been interpreted by Szymanski (1982) as a kind of domino theory of the transition to world socialism. Szymanski contends that the Soviet Union and Eastern Europe constitute a separate socialist world-system and that the logic of world capitalism has been seriously weakened by the growing number of socialist states.

My own interpretation disputes this contention. I see the socialist states (including China) as having been significantly reincorporated into the capitalist world-economy. Whether or not this is true, one of the most disconcerting features of current socialist states is their most unsocialist behavior toward one another. I interpret this as a continuation of the nationalism and interstate competition that has gone on in the capitalist world-system since its beginning. Frank (1980: chapt. 4) draws the same conclusion from recent trends in which the socialist states have increased their exports for sale on the world market, imports from the avowedly capitalist countries, and made deals with transnational firms for investments within their borders.

The national economic planning that is most highly developed in the socialist states may be simply the most complete expression of the trend toward state capitalism that is occurring in most core and peripheral countries. And while distribution is more equal within socialist states, this does not change the competitive logic with which they interact with other states. Thus one possible world is composed of states that are internally socialist but that compete with one another in international markets and geopolitics.

The increasing number of socialist states does not seem to have weakened the logic of world capitalism. Rather the political constraints on the free mobility of capital that these states have organized pushes the logic of capitalist organization to expand its scale. States become firms, and transnational corporations deal with all players in a competitive world that remains subject to the anarchy of investment decisions.

DISCUSSION AND CONCLUSIONS

To argue that the system logic has not altered fundamentally does not imply that this is impossible or even unlikely. Nor is it to argue that the massive expansions, emergent institutions, and shifts of capital from place to place have not had drastic effects on the lives of people. I would like to revisit some of the questions raised in the earlier sections to speculate about the possible consequences of changes that may not have occurred yet but might occur in the future.

What if it were true that recent trends were the beginning of the end of a core-periphery system. Marx's analysis of capitalism does not posit the existence of "peripheral capitalism" in which commodity production employs politically coerced labor. For Marx, the extra-economic coercion occurring in the periphery is merely part of primitive accumulation, the use of force to create the institutional basis of a capitalist mode of production that, once created, will sustain itself. World-system theory has claimed that *peripheral* capitalism is a normal and necessary part of the capitalist mode of production, and that the reproduction of expanded accumulation in the core requires the existence of primary accumulation in the periphery.

This idea is not based on the claim that peripheral production creates the bulk of surplus value in the system, but rather on the insight that the relative harmony of classes in the core—the somewhat peaceful accommodation between capital and labor that exists as social democracy, corporatism, or "business unionism"—is based on the ability of core capital to emphasize nationalist bases of solidarity. Nationalism in the core is sustained by competition among core states and by the ability of core capital to pay off core workers with higher wages, better working conditions, more welfare provisions, and greater access to political power through democratic processes. This is possible, at least in part, because of core exploitation of the periphery, which provides a measure of additional surplus through unequal exchange (cheap bananas for core workers), profits derived from investments in the periphery, and the status-based affects of comparison with "less-developed" countries.

In a pregnant sentence Immanuel Wallerstein predicts that "when labor is everywhere free we shall have socialism" (1974: 127). The implications of this are that if the core-periphery division of labor disappears, capitalism will no longer be able to overcome its own contradictions, and the political structures maintained by the core-periphery hierarchy will crumble. Socialist revolution, predicted by Marx for the most-developed (core) nations, will finally visit them.

If the above analysis were true, the imminent approach of metanational capitalism could be seen as good news for the world socialist movement; and indeed this is the point of view expressed by Borrego (1982). But the formal proletarianization of the world work force (the end of coerced labor and the decreasing availability of alternatives to dependence on the world market) does not necessarily mean the end of "segmented labor markets." Political and ethnic stratification has proven effective in maintaining wage differentials among formally "free" proletarians. And the core-periphery hierarchy might become based on an inequality between *protected* labor and "free" labor. Nevertheless, something like a contraction in the magnitude of the core-periphery hierarchy might be occurring, and this could well exacerbate the contradictions of capitalism, which have been avoided in the past by what David Harvey (1982) has called the "spatial fix."

The expansion of the capitalist world-system has been driven by the search for new markets, cheap inputs, and profitable investment opportunities. Lenin (1956) pointed out that by the end of the nineteenth century the core states could no longer find new worlds to conquer and were forced to divide and redivide the already conquered world. This extensive expansion has been supplemented by intensive expansion, the conversion of more and more aspects of life to the commodity form, and thus expansion of profit-making opportunities in the provision of fast food breakfasts and the like. The potential for further commodification is great, especially in the periphery, where a substantial terrain of production and consumption for use remains.

Nevertheless, continued increases in the commodification of aspects of life should eventually reach limits that will contribute to the decline in the rate of profit in the system as a whole. Along with further extension of commodification, we have antisystemic movements that create political obstacles to the maneuverability of capital and place claims on profits. Capital flight has pitted workers against one another for five hundred years, but the increasing density of political claims on capital decreases the incentive to move. Decolonization and the socialist states should be understood in this way, despite the argument made above about their failure, so far, to transform the logic of the system. Again, however, I must reiterate my skepticism about a domino theory of the transition to world socialism. Only the organization of democratic and collectively rational production, distribution, and development *at the world-system level* can produce a social system in which the logic of socialism is dominant.

Even though I argue that major change has not yet occurred, I am also arguing that it most definitely will occur eventually if present trends continue and if our species survives its adolescence. Whether the demise of world capitalism takes two hundred more years or twenty, we must spend our energies now to move in the direction of a more humane world. The priority of survival is overwhelming, and so we must prevent nuclear holocaust; but we must also move in the direction of a more just political and economic system, and this involves risks. For those of us in the United States, socialist revolution is not on the agenda in our declining hegemonic core power. We may, however, aspire to catch up with Europe regarding the introduction of socialist issues into political culture. National planning will be the main issue following the demise of the current "free enterprise" regime. Liberal corporatism provides a terrain for raising questions about the beneficiaries of the plan and the democratic control of the planners. These are issues that are also relevant for the extant socialist states, and so our American experiment, which may yet benefit from its peculiarities, can yet participate in the search for institutional forms that move the world-system toward socialism.

NOTES

1. The cycle of core competition corresponds to changes in the population size hierarchy of the world city system (Chase-Dunn, forthcoming).

2. The four world wars are as follows: world war I—the struggle between the Habsburgs and the house of Valois described by Wallerstein (1974); world war II—the attempt by Louis XIV to establish dominance over the European core in the War of Spanish Succession; world war III—the Napoleonic Wars; and world war IV—the two twentieth-century attempts by Germany to dominate the core. By this reckoning the next, and probably last world war will be the fifth.

3. Bergesen and Schoenberg (1980) have shown that waves of expansion of colonial empires are correlated in time with wars among states.

4. A product of human labor is a commodity when it is produced for exchange on a market. Thus products consumed by their producers are not commodities. Land and labor become commodities when their uses are determined by market forces.

5. These "precapitalist" forms of production that are articulated with capitalist commodity production have often been analyzed in terms of the way in which they subsidize the lifetime cost of reproducing the work force. It is certainly true that such forms have been allowed to exist, or have even been created by the policies of colonial powers seeking to sustain a low-wage labor force. On the other hand, the struggles of peripheral workers to maintain some independence of capitalist commodity production have also been an important cause of the continued existence of these forms. Excellent studies of the process of reproduction and breakdown of these noncapitalist forms of production are those by Meillassoux (1981), Murray (1980), Rodney (1981), Kahn (1980), and Warman (1980).

6. This distinction is described more fully in Chase-Dunn (1980). Chapters 2 and 3 of Hopkins and Wallerstein (1982) contain an outline of a descriptive model similar to the one presented here. An attempt to move toward a theory of deep structure is outlined in Chase-Dunn (1983a).

7. Gordon (1980) has developed an admirable conceptual structure for a theory of stages, breaking hypothetical qualitatively different stages into general phases based on a Marxian theory of capitalist accumulation. Unfortunately he does not designate the particular stages to which his scheme applies.

8. I have made a preliminary estimation of the amount of upward and downward mobility in the core-periphery hierarchy between 1885 and 1980. Looking only at movements across boundaries between zones (core, semiperiphery, and periphery) it appears that there has been no downward mobility (across zonal boundaries) but that a significant number of countries have moved from the periphery to the semiperiphery, and some have moved from the semiperiphery to the core (Chase-Dunn, 1983b).

9. Although the larger semiperipheral countries have also promoted industrial exports, and these have grown rapidly, they constitute only a small proportion of industrial output in these countries. Gereffi and Evans (1981: 51) show that exports as a percentage of total sales by transnational manufacturing firms has indeed risen in both Mexico and Brazil, but in 1972 it was still only 5.1 percent in Mexico and 3.5 percent in Brazil.

10. Saskia Sassen-Koob (1982) has also explored the effects of international immigration on the structure of New York's economy. A very similar shift occurred in London in the 1880s as Irish immigrants to the East End provided the workers for a swollen informal sector. This development, which occurred during the decline of England's hegemony in industrial production, is studied in fascinating detail by Gareth Stedman Jones (n.d.).

REFERENCES

AMIN, S. (1980) Class and Nation: Historically and in the Current Crisis. New York: Monthly Review Press.

BARBOUR, V. (1963) Capitalism in Amsterdam in the Seventeenth Century. Ann Arbor: University of Michigan Press.

BERGESEN, A. (1981) "Long economic cycles and the size of industrial enterprise," pp. 179-91 in R. Rubinsin (ed.) Dynamics of World Development. Beverly Hills: Sage.
—— and R. SCHOENBERG (1980) "Long waves of colonial expansion and contraction, 1415-1969," pp. 231-278 in A. Bergesen (ed.) Studies of the Modern World-System. New York: Academic Press.
BERGESEN, A. and C. SAHOO (forthcoming) "The changing international distribution of the world's fifty largest corporations, 1956-1980." Review.
BOLI-BENNETT, J. (1980) "Global integration and the universal increase in state dominance, 1910-1970," pp. 77-108 in A. Bergesen (ed.) Studies of the Modern World-System. New York: Academic Press.
BORNSCHIER, V. (1981) "Dependent industrialization in the world-economy." Journal of Conflict Resolution 25, 3: 371-400.
BORREGO, J. (1982) "Metanational capitalist accumulation and the reintegration of socialist states," pp. 111-147 in C. Chase-Dunn (ed.) Socialist States in the World-System. Beverly Hills: Sage.
CAPORASO, J. (1981) "Industrialization in the periphery: the evolving global division of labor," pp. 140-171 in W. L. Hollist and J. Rosenau (eds.) World System Structure: Continuity and Change. Beverly Hills: Sage.
CARDOSO, F. H. (1973) "Associated-dependent development: theoretical and practical implications," in A. Stepan (ed.) Authoritarian Brazil. New Haven, CT: Yale University Press.
CHASE-DUNN, C. (forthcoming) "The system of world cities: 800-1975," in M. Timberlake (ed.) Urbanization in the World-Economy. New York: Academic Press.
—— (1983a) "The kernel of the capitalist world-economy: three approaches," in W. R. Thompson (ed.) Contending Approaches to World-System Analysis. Beverly Hills: Sage.
——(1983b) "Inequality, structural mobility, and dependency reversal in the capitalist world economy," pp. 73-96 in C. F. Doran et al. (eds.) North/South Relations: Studies of Dependency Reversal. New York: Praeger.
—— (1982a) "International economic policy in a declining core state," pp. 77-96 in W. P. Avery and D. P. Rapkin (eds.) America in a Changing World Political Economy. New York: Longman.
—— (1982b) Socialist States in the World-System. Beverly Hills: Sage.
—— (1982c) "The coming of urban primacy in Latin America." Presented to the Working Group on Latin American Urbanization, Tepotzlan, Morelos, Mexico, August 22.
—— (1981) "Interstate system and capitalist world-economy: one logic or two?" International Studies Quarterly 23, 4: 601-623.
—— (1980/1981) "Stages of dependency or cycles of world-system development?" Humboldt Journal of Social Relations 8, 1: 1-24.
—— (1980) "Models and interpretation in world-system research: comments on Bach," pp. 311-314 in T. K. Hopkins and I. Wallerstein (eds.) Processes of the World-System. Beverly Hills: Sage.
—— (1978) "Core-periphery relations: the effects of core competition," pp. 159-176 in B. H. Kaplan (ed.) Social Change in the Capitalist World-Economy. Beverly Hills: Sage.
CHIROT, D. (1977) Social Change in the Twentieth Century. New York: Harcourt Brace Jovanovich.
DIXON, M. (1982) "Dual power: the rise of the transnational corporation and the nation-state." Contemporary Marxism 5: 129-146 (Summer).

EMMANUEL, A. (1972) Unequal Exchange. New York: Monthly Review Press.

EVANS, P. (1979) Dependent Development: The Alliance of Multinational, State, and Local Capital in Brazil. Princeton, NJ: Princeton University Press.

—— and M. TIMBERLAKE (1980) "Dependence, inequality and growth in less developed countries." American Sociological Review 45: 531-552

FRANK, A. G. (1980) "Long live transideological enterprise!" pp. 178-262 in Crisis: In the World Economy. New York: Holmes and Meier.

—— (1979) Mexican Agriculture, 1521-1630: Transformation of the Mode of Production. Cambridge: Cambridge University Press.

FROEBEL, F. J. HEINRICHS, and O. KREYE (1980) The New International Division of Labor. Cambridge: Cambridge University Press.

GORDON, D. M. (1980) "Stages of accumulation and long economic cycles," pp. 9-45 in T. K. Hopkins and I. Wallerstein (ed.) Processes of the World-System. Beverly Hills: Sage.

GEREFFI, G. and P. EVANS (1981) "Transnational corporations, dependent development, and state policy in the semi-periphery: a comparison of Brazil and Mexico," Latin American Research Review 16, 3: 31-64.

HARVEY, D. (1982) The Limits to Capital. Chicago: University of Chicago Press.

HOPKINS, T. K. and I. Wallerstein [eds.] (1982) World-Systems Analysis: Theory and Methodology. Beverly Hills: Sage.

HYMER, S. (1979). The Multinational Corporation: A Radical Approach. Cambridge, MA: Cambridge University Press.

JONES, G. S. (n.d.) Outcaste London: A Study in the Relationship Between Classes in Victorian Society. New York: Viking.

KAHN, J. S. (1980) Minangkabau Social Formations: Indonesian Peasants and the World-Economy. Cambridge: Cambridge University Press.

KENTOR, J. (1981) "Structural determinants of peripheral urbanization: the effects of international dependence." American Sociological Review 46: 201-211.

KRASNER, S. D. (1978) Defending the National Interest: Raw Materials Investments and U.S. Foreign Policy. Princeton, NJ: Princeton University Press.

LANE, F. (1979). Profits from Power. Albany: SUNY Press.

LENIN, V. I. (1965) Imperialism: The Highest Stage of Capitalism. Peking: Foreign Languages Press. (originally published in 1916)

MANDEL, E. (1975). *Late Capitalism.* London: New Left Books.

MARX, K. (1967) Capital, Volume 1. New York: International Publishers. (originally published in 1867)

MEILLASSOUX, C. (1981). Maidens, Meal, and Money: Capitalism and the Domestic Economy. Cambridge: Cambridge University Press.

MEYER, J. W., J. BOLI - BENNETT, and C. CHASE-DUNN (1975) "Convergence and divergence in development." Annual Review of Sociology 1: 223-246.

MICHALET, C. A. (1976). Le Capitalisme Mondial. Paris: Presses Universitaires de France.

MURRAY, M. (1980). The Development of Capitalism in Colonial Indochina: 1870-1940. Berkeley: University of California Press.

PORTES, A. (1981). Unequal exchange and the urban informal sector," in A. Portes and J. Walton, Labor, Class and the International System. New York: Academic Press.

PETRAS, J. with A. E. HAVENS, M. H. MORLEY, and P. DeWitt (1981). Class, State and Power in the Third World. Montclair, NJ: Allanheld, Osmun.

POLANYI, K. (1944). The Great Transformation. Boston: Beacon Press.

RODNEY, W. (1981) A History of the Guyanese Working People, 1881-1905. Baltimore: John Hopkins University Press.

ROSS, R. and K. TRACHTE (1983) "Global cities and global classes: the peripheralization of labor in New York City." Review 6, 3: 393-431.

SASSEN-KOOB, S. (1982) "Changing composition and labor market location of hispanic immigrants in New York City, 1960-1980." New York Institute for the Humanities. (unpublished)

SKLAR, H. [ed.] (1980) Trilateralism: The Trilateral Commission and Elite Planning for World Management. Boston: South End Press.

STRANGE, S. and R. TOOZE [eds.] (1981) The International Politics of Surplus Capacity: Competition for Market Shares in the World Recession. London: Allen and Unwin.

SZYMANSKI, A. (1982). "The socialist world-system," pp. 57-84 in C. Chase-Dunn (ed.) Socialist States in the World-System. Beverly Hills: Sage.

——— (1981) The Logic of Imperialism. New York: Praeger.

VANNEMAN, R. (1979) "Strategies for the Southasian semi-periphery: cashews and crankshafts." Presented at the annual meetings of the Association for Asian Studies, Los Angeles.

VERNON, R. (1971) Sovereignty at Bay. New York: Basic Books.

WALLERSTEIN, I. (1979) The Capitalist World-Economy. New York: Cambridge University Press.

——— (1974) The Modern World-System, Volume 1. New York: Academic Press.

WALTON, John (forthcoming) "The third "new" international division of labor," in J. Walton (ed.) Capital and Labor in the Urbanized World. Beverly Hills: Sage.

WARMAN, A. (1980) We Come to Object: The Peasants of Morelos and the National State. Baltimore: John Hopkins University Press.

WOLF, E. R. (1982) Europe and the People Without History. Berkeley: University of California Press.

PART 2

**LABOR SYSTEMS IN
AN EVOLVING CAPITALIST WORLD ORDER**

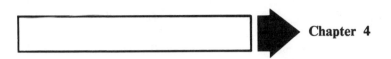

Chapter 4

BRITISH COLONIALISM
AND PUNJABI LABOR

Richard G. Fox
Duke University

British colonialism in India constantly negotiated a difficult balance between two contradictory objectives. Depending on which one of these objectives was of greater weight during a particular period or in a particular place, different systems of Indian agricultural production and labor grew up over the course of British colonialism. Because these production and labor systems reflected contradictory aspects of colonialism and world-systems penetration, they too were in a state of contradiction—which often took the form of rural resistance against the overarching powers of the colonial state to make or break them. The pivotal colonial institution that expressed this contradiction—that is, which was victimized by it and therefore tried to resolve it—was the Government of India.

This chapter relates the changing system of production and labor in one region of India, the Punjab, to these contradictory objectives within British colonialism. I try to show how conflicting labor systems came to regulate agricultural production in the Punjab and how a class of petty commodity producers, itself a creation of the world system, came to resist a subsequent penetration of the world economy that threatened its economic position. I also argue that the policies of the colonial state were the major factor in bringing these labor systems and classes into existence and then destroying them. In conclusion, the chapter joins in the criticism of the "functionalist theory of imperialism" associated with world-system and dependency theory. But I also critique the argument that an effective resistance to capitalist penetration arises from the maintenance of noncapitalist forms of production and their nonarticulation with capitalism. Instead, I argue that effective resistance to capitalist penetration is a result of contradictory objectives pursued by the colonial state, which subsidize conflicting production and labor systems. My argument, following Banaji (1977) and Alavi (1980)—who, in turn, follow Marx—is that capitalism works to transform into its own image production and labor everywhere; that is, there is no necessary "development of underdevelopment" or unequal specialization in the world economy. Dependency relations are historically transitory and structurally transitional. They exist in the interim between the initial penetration of capitalism and its full subsumption of labor and production. These periods of transition occur because (1) capitalism usually must accommodate to the indigenous pattern of labor and production it finds in a colony and (2) this accommodation may create colonial labor systems that are not yet fully capitalist, which (3) may continue because of contradictions in colonial exploitation, until (4) a time when these contradictions are resolved and the labor systems destroyed.

COLONIAL INDIA: DEVELOPMENT AND CONTRADICTIONS

The two contradictory colonial objectives involved the commercial and fiscal relations between Britain and India and between the home government and the colonial Government of India.

One objective was that India should supply raw materials to Britain and purchase British manufactured goods. This traditional form of mercantilism, or colonial appropriation "on the cheap," required no investment in the growth of India's industry; in fact, colonial policy often worked to destroy indigenous artisanry (see Alavi, 1980). It also took the precapitalist forms of agricultural production and labor as it found them—based on "feudal" landlords or peasant smallholders— and appropriated their surplus production without radically transforming their productivity through capital investment or through substantial revision of the labor process. For this colonialism, it was sufficient and necessary to commercialize or monetize agriculture—that is, to force agrarian production and rural labor into the market. This "mercantilization of precapitalist relations," as Amin (1976: 204-205) sees it, is a form of primitive accumulation that "compels people to go in search of money, and so either to become commodity producers or to sell their labor power." The commercialization of agriculture everywhere facilitated the collection of government revenues in coin, and it also provided cultivators with money incomes with which to purchase British imports. The need for money rooted export crops in the agrarian production of ecologically favored regions.

Indigenous merchants and moneylenders became the willing accomplices of this commercialization: unofficial agents for the British, formidable parasites on the rural cultivator. They forced peasants (and even landlords) into a debt peonage that eventually fully converted agriculture into petty commodity production for the market. Through high interests charges, forced sales at below-market prices, and other such devices the moneylenders reaped the profits from agricultural commercialization, and each advance in British domination further bloated this class until it achieved a size and power unprecedented before colonialism.

This typical "development of underdevelopment" prevailed during the early years of the East India Company's domination, up until the onset of crown rule in the middle of the nineteenth century. Its ascendancy during this period resulted either from the inability of the colonial administration to penetrate the localized political economy, as Washbrook (1976), Stokes (1978), and Frykenberg (1965) argue; or it grew out of the general mercantile character of the world economy and the success of a mercantile class in controlling that economy, as Kahn (n.d.) suggests.

This colonial objective made the colonial government depend on the same tributary sources of revenue as had the Moghuls and previous rulers of India (for the concept of a tributary mode of production, see Wolf, 1982, or Amin, 1976). The main form of tribute income consisted of a portion of agricultural productivity, which the government extracted through an assessment on cultivators' holdings. Given the precapitalist agricultural system, which was not reformed by British capital investment, productivity increases were limited. Pax Britannica brought some increases in productivity in the early years of company rule, just as a strong indigenous dynasty would have, but even the most powerful state eventually became stymied by the constraints on productivity imposed by the precapitalist technology and labor relations. The constant pursuit of new territories by the East India Company's Indian administration during the late eighteenth and early nineteenth centuries probably developed out of fiscal necessity, even though it often departed from the express policy of the home company directors. New lands promised new revenues more cheaply and more readily to a colonial power than a state-imposed and state-funded revolution in agricultural production in the conquered territories would have.

This colonial objective of quick and cheap exploitation has its limits, however. On the one hand, the British soon reached the practical limits of their colonial expansion in India. On the other, in pursuit of increased land revenue, the British pressed the rural social system under their control to the breaking point. After the conquest of the Punjab, that is, by the middle of the nineteenth century, the colonial government's fiscal resources had already proved limited and relatively unexpandable by further conquest. Somewhat earlier, the colonial power, hoping thereby to extract more revenue, had deposed large prebendaries and landlords in favor of collecting revenues directly from cultivators in the recently acquired North-Western provinces and Oudh. At this point and in these actions, the British reached the limits of their initial colonial exploitation of India and, attempting to accede them, precipitated the Mutiny of 1857-1859. Disgruntled "native" soldiers joined with dispossessed landed magnates in rebellion against John Company—the soldiers protesting against a company become miserly and no longer "Bahadur" ("courageous")—there were no new territories that it payed to conquer and therefore no bonuses for active duty, the princes protesting against a colonial rule that was both shrewd and rapacious. Both thus protested the necessary and ultimate character of British colonialism on the cheap.

After the mutiny, the government of India, now under crown rule, realized the folly of pressing excessive revenue demands on the precapitalist agriculture and rural society of India. But alternative sources for expanding government income were not readily available. The home government prevented the Government of India from an obvious remedy—placing tariffs on British manufactures—because that would have harmed British industry and Britain's balance of trade. Tomlinson suggests that the increasing devolution of limited political and taxation power to Indian provincial legislatures, district councils, and municipal boards, which began in the late nineteenth century, came about to legitimate new government exactions (Tomlinson, 1979). But the interests of the home government in building British industry and exports meant that no policy could effectively address Indian interests, and throughout the last half of the nineteenth century, the Government of India suffered a continuous fiscal crisis.

Because it was ascendent in the early period, this policy of cheap colonialism distorted India in several features other than the agrarian economy, but just as important. Cheap government required but also sanctioned (because penurious colonial administration, whatever its necessity, was seen as a virtue) the creation of a class of indigenous low-level bureaucrats and clerks, the *babus*. Then followed the colleges to train them, the physicians to heal them, and the lawyers to protect people from their decisions, which they sometimes reached as agents of government and other times to advantage themselves. Cheap colonialism also meant the British relied on a predominantly indigenous Indian Army to maintain their rule. Even after the mutiny, when they feared their dependence on Indian soldiers most deeply, economics dictated that the troops of colonialism should come from the villages of the colonized. I shall show later how British dependence on Indian troops greatly influenced colonial state policies in the Punjab, especially late in the nineteenth and early in the twentieth centuries when the army came increasingly to suppress the dissent generated by the growing nationalism of the babus, lawyers, physicians, and other "educated classes" whom cheap colonialism had produced.

The poverty forced upon the Government of India by this development of underdevelopment contradicted the other objective of British colonialism: that a financially secure Indian administration bear all the costs of the British colonial enterprise and that these costs be paid by conversion of rupees into sterling. A related goal was that India should continue to have a trade surplus with nations other than Britain, so that India's surplus would eliminate Britain's negative balance of payments. This objective required a flow of resources from India to Britain, and it was accomplished through the notorious form of economic drain called the "home charges." From its revenue collections, the Government of India has to remit large sums to the home government in payment of the costs of the British administration of India, costs incurred both in India and Britain; the support of an army in India, including the British units temporarily stationed there; the pensions paid to retired civil servants and military officers; and a multitude of other so-called home charges that drained India's wealth and converted rupees into shillings. Although this objective also aimed at colonialism on the cheap—in the sense that British revenue should never have to pay for Indian administration—it required a fiscally secure government and a strong Indian currency. It was thus exactly opposite to the penurious government and weak rupee that the first objective enjoined. It if were not counterbalanced by the development of underdevelopment, the second objective should have led the Government of India to attempt a capitalist transformation and development of its colonial realm. It should have led the government, for example, to try to raise the productivity of Indian agriculture so that revenue collections might grow. It should also have led the government to subsidize indigenous industrial production so that export earnings might grow, and to protect the nascent industries for the enhanced revenues protective tariffs would have brought.

The "laws of motion" of British Indian colonialism grew out of these two contradictory objectives. The contradictory objectives of the development of underdevelopment and of development coexisted throughout the course of British colonialism in India, but each had a different period of ascendancy. Initial British colonialism, as I have indicated, mainly satisfied the objective of underdevelopment and free trade. However, changes in the world system in the middle of the nineteenth century and then again after World War I eventually forced the colonial government to champion the second objective, development and protectionism.

The silver mines of western America had a major impact on British colonial policy in India during the last third of the nineteenth century. The large amounts of silver bullion produced by these mines lowered the value of India's silver coinage in relation to the gold-based currency of Britain. The home charges became an increasingly difficult burden for the Government of India, and it eventually won permission for a temporary tariff on manufactured cotton goods as a source of revenue (see Dewey, 1978). This movement away from laissez-faire to protectionism took on a much more substantial character after World War I, again because this period was one of great fiscal strain on the government but also because Japan and other countries had ousted Britain from its monopolization of exports to India. Government revenue requirements outweighed British economic chauvanism, and India was launched on an active development of native industry, in part with British subsidy and protection. By its independence in 1947, India was hardly a typical colonial economy: Local manufacture and import substitution were strong; multinational capital was relatively weak; and a lower-middle class of rich farmers and urban small businessmen, bureaucrats, and professionals dominated the country (see Tomlinson, 1979; Raj, 1973).

Increased capital investment in India, mainly under government auspices, marked the ascendancy of the development objective. Railroad construction was one of the earliest manifestations of this state capitalism. Rather than fundamentally reordering Indian labor and production, however, railroads mainly hastened the commercialization of the countryside and the removal of export crops from the middle of the nineteenth century on. Much more transformative of Indian production and labor were the major irrigation projects undertaken by the colonial state in the late nineteenth century, as I shall show below for the Punjab.

Depending on their date of conquest, fertility, and indigenous social system, different regions of India experienced British colonialism in distinctive ways. In some, such as eastern U.P. and Bihar, the initial objective of cheap colonialism was hardly balanced by a later movement to capital investment and development. In the Punjab, however, the colonial government's investment in transforming agricultural production was great, as were the consequences of this investment on the labor and production system previously fashioned by colonialism on the cheap.

EXPORT CROPS, PETTY COMMODITY PRODUCTION, AND PUNJAB'S UNDERDEVELOPMENT

In their initial colonial tenure—that is, from annexation in 1849 until the 1890s—the British successfully harnessed the Punjab's agricultural production and labor to the world system without radical transformation or major capital investment. Late in the nineteenth century, the Punjab, especially the fertile "central" districts, served British interests by producing wheat for export to other parts of India and to Britain. By 1881, three distinctive labor and production regions had been fashioned by this colonialism on the cheap. Cultivation in southeastern Punjab characteristically involved nonirrigated land (*barani*) worked either by peasant proprietors or landlords and sharecroppers. The major crops were "inferior" grains like barley, which had little market value, or gram, which was to become a cash crop at the zenith of wheat export. In the central Punjab, peasant proprietors predominated, growing a mixture of wheat and gram on well-irrigated lands. Western and especially southwestern Punjab was heavily committed to wheat production on well-irrigated lands given out by large landlords to sharecroppers (see Table 4.1, which gives agricultural data for 1901, the first year they are available).

The labor processes typifying the three regions in the late nineteenth century arose from a combination of ecological constraints, indigenous precolonial land tenures, and British modifications. The primary ecological factor was rainfall; a sufficiency thereof permitted nonirrigated cultivation on small properties worked intensively by peasant proprietors. The submontane districts running along the northern and northeastern borders had higher proportions of peasant proprietors than the almost desertic southwestern and southeastern areas. The land

TABLE 4.1 Punjab Regions in 1901-1902*

Characteristic	Southeastern Region	Central Region	Southwestern Region
Population density (per thousand acres)	.2848	.3646	.1856
Population density, (cultivated land (per thousand acres)	.5667	.7996	.7964
Percentage of land cultivated	.7052	.6610	.2461
Well irrigation, percentage	.0875	.2113	.2377
Canal irrigation, percentage	.1537	.1208	.1588
Dry cultivation, percentage	.6413	.6447	.4100
Wheat acreage, percentage	.1103	.2724	.2885
Gram acreage	.0511	.0908	.0260
Jowar-bajra acreage	.1345	.1564	.1030
Owner-worked land, percentage of total cultivated	.5309	.5062	.4747
Tenants-at-will lands, percentage of total cultivated	.2983	.3398	.4315

SOURCE: Computed from Government of India, Punjab District Gazetteers.
NOTES: *Southeastern region*: Districts of Delhi, Gurgaon, Karnal, Hissar, Rohtak, Ambala, and Native States of Jind and Kalsia. *Central region*: Districts of Ludhiana, Jullundur, Hoshiarpur, Amritsar, Gurdaspur, Ferozepore, and Native States of Patiala, Nabha, Kapurthala, Faridkote, and Malerkotla. *Southwestern region*: Districts of Sialkot, Lahore, Gujranwala, Rawalpindi, Attock, Jhelum, Gujrat, Shahpur, Multan, Montgomery, Muzzarfargarh, Mianwali, Dera Ghazi Khan, Peshawar, Hazara.
* Excludes the Jhang district.

tenure arrangements introduced by successive rulers of the Punjab were probably more determinative than was ecology, however. British policy, for example, aimed at leveling the agrarian class structure by eliminating large landlords and equalizing the rights of tenants and proprietors. Its purpose was to maximize government revenues by removing all intermediaries between the peasant producer and the state. This policy continued and extended the land tenure arrangements and the removal of intermediaries begun by the former ruler of the Punjab, Ranjit Singh. It is a clear instance of how the early colonialism of the British acted to improve but not to revolutionize the precapitalist forms of production and labor. The British implemented their leveling policy most successfully in areas of the Punjab where Ranjit's administration had held sway longest. That is, in the central Punjab, the most fertile region of the province, the British successfully maintained and/or instituted peasant proprietorship; this region became the primary source of export wheat and land revenue under the "development of underdevelopment" of the early colonial period.

Because wheat can serve as a subsistence crop, peasants can choose whether to sell or to eat it. There had be some mechanism to force the peasant's wheat production into the market place consistently. This market determination of agricultural production was to require no massive British capital investment; it did not call forth radical transformation of agrarian ownership and labor relations. It was accomplished by a combination of British revenue policy and the self-interested actions of indigenous moneylenders and merchants. The British required peasants to pay their land revenue in money, while the merchant/moneylenders advanced the required cash to peasants on the collateral of their lands or crops or in exchange for preemptive rights of purchase. The result was a form of debt peonage in which merchant capital began to reorganize peasant productivity so that it was necessarily and fully determined by market forces (see Banaji, 1977). By late in the nineteenth century, the independent peasantry of the central Punjab had turned into debt-ridden petty commodity producers, Punjab agriculture had been commercialized, and an indigenous class of merchants and moneylenders had become large and well-to-do.

Rural debt in central Punjab had other, probably unforseen, advantages for British colonialism on the cheap. It facilitated the wholesale recruitment of Punjabis to the British Indian army; it led them to accept, indeed to seek actively, proletarianization as migrant labor in Southeast Asia and North America. The remittances from those in military service and laboring abroad helped maintain the system of peasant smallholdings and family labor—that is, petty commodity production—against the inroads of merchant capital.

The colonial state helped shore up the petty commodity production system by constructing new canals or refurbishing indigenous ones in the 1850s and 1860s, especially in the central districts. The British later labeled these canals "protective" because their primary function was to even out seasonal differences in rainfall and thus give peasant small-holders greater security. They did not represent the massive capital input into the transformation of rural production that later irrigation works represented; their cost was borne out of the land revenue collections of the government (Paustian, 1930).

But neither external remittances nor protective irrigation works could contain the steadily mounting debt of rural areas and the increasing control over agrarian production by merchants and money-lenders as the nineteenth century ended. The commercial forces unleashed by the British themselves and the merchant class the British originally fostered threatened the very colonial interests that had first given them purchase in Punjab's rural economy. Fearing rural unrest and loss of army recruits (the British clearly apprehended that their most successful recruiting came from locales in which smallholders working marginal plots predominated) and distrusting what they often now saw as the parasitical moneylender, the British colonial administration passed legislation (the Land Alienation Act of 1900) that prevented cultivators from alienating their land or mortgaging it for extended periods, except to other cultivators. The act phrased this defense of petty commodity production in caste terms: It divided Punjabis into traditional agricultural "tribes" and traditional nonagricultural "tribes," and disallowed commerce in land between them. But whatever its cultural phrasing, its economic intent was clear: The colonial state had intervened to protect a rural production system of its own making. The "natural" rationalization of peasant production by merchant capital—"natural" given the conditions British colonialism on the cheap had constructed—was aborted so that other colonial interests, which were also valued by colonial underdevelopment—namely, cheap military recruits and inexpensive rural policing–could be maintained.

State support for petty commodity production and the limitation of rural indebtedness (or at least its consequences in terms of land sales and mortgages) did not maximize export crop production or government revenues, however. The colonial government had already taken steps to implement these interests in other ways. These ways, part of a new colonialism of development, would increasingly immiserate the central Punjab smallholders and eventually bring them into confrontation with a government that could no longer afford to protect them against new market forces.

STATE CAPITALISM AND THE CANAL COLONIES

Beginning in the 1880s and continuing into the 1920s the colonial government undertook massive capital investment in raising the agricultural productivity of the Punjab to increase land revenue and export income. This rise in the organic composition of capital took the form of immense irrigation works, which by the 1920s irrigated over 10 million acres (Punjab Board of Economic Inquiry, 1928: pub. 52) of formerly desert lands. Under this emergent state capitalism, the British settled cultivators from the overpopulated central Punjab as tenants of the state on consolidated plots of 25 acres. Larger plots of 50 to several hundred acres were sold to what the British called "yeomen" and "capitalists." Although the early canal colonies, as these irrigation settlements came to be called, were mainly settled with peasant proprietors, the government increasingly turned to land auctions as a source of quick returns on its investment.

Colonial transformation of agrarian production paid other major dividends: It resettled populations from the central Punjab; it provided lands that could be awarded to Indian soldiers; it provided much greater amounts of export crops like wheat and cotton, as the export figures in Table 4.2 indicate; and it enhanced government revenue greatly, both through the reclamation of wastelands and through irrigation charges. The budget of the Punjab government became increasingly dependent on irrigation receipts. The contribution of irrigation revenues to total government receipts rose from 15 percent in 1913-1914 to nearly 40 percent by 1925-1926. During the same period land revenue receipts contributed slightly less than 30 percent of total government revenues and remained basically unchanged from their contribution before World War I (Punjab Board of Economic Inquiry, 1928: pub. 52).

As the costs of government rose, the flow of capital into irrigation under government initiative continued. Much as the early colonialism on the cheap precipitated British colonialism into a domino game of conquest, the new colonialism of development required a constant refloating and reinvestment of capital. By the 1920s, however, the physical limits on the extension of irrigation were evidently reached (within the context of then current technology and available capital) because the acreage under government canals remained fairly steady compared to its steep ascent earlier. Thus, from 1888 to 1902 the irrigated acreage under government canals increased by over 100 percent; from 1902 to 1916, the increase was well over 60 percent; but from 1916 until the end of the 1920s, the irrigated acreage leveled off and even in the peak year of 1923 represented less than a 20 percent increase (Punjab Board of Economic Inquiry, 1928: pub. 52). In the late 1920s and early 1930s, the colonial government brought more land under canal irrigation, mainly because it reduced irrigation charges during the Great Depression and thereby created more demand among cultivators. But as I shall indicate later, the agrarian system and colonial administration had already undergone a crisis in part precipitated by the lack of new canal colonies in the late teens and twenties.

TABLE 4.2 Wheat Exports from the Punjab and Selected Punjab Regions

	Net Exports* (in thousands of maunds) from:		
Average for Years	*Punjab*	*Cis-Sutlej Region (central Punjab)+*	*Sutlej-Jhelum Region (canal colonies)+*
1890-1894	8126	3821	3185
1895-1899	6392	954	3617
1900-1904	15339	2850	10947
(1901 missing)			
1905-1909	23218	6172	15796
1910-1914	26370	6835	18214
(1912 missing)			
1915-1919	19435	5375	13252
1920-1922	12908	1003	13372

SOURCE: annual publication of *Internal Trade of the Punjab.* Lahore: Civil and Military Gazette Press. In an austerity move, the government ceased publication after 1922.
* The figure for net exports from the Punjab was calculated by subtracting wheat imports into the Punjab from the Punjab's wheat exports. Net exports from the Cis-Sutlej and Sutlej-Jhelum regions was calculated by subtracting imports into these regions from outside the Punjab and other Punjab regions from exports going from these regions to places outside the Punjab and to other Punjab regions. These calculations are required because trade statistics were reported by the Government of the Punjab in the form of figures for rail freight coming into and out of the Punjab and moving between several regions.
+ The regions used by the Government of the Punjab for the collection of trade statistics are not identical with those referred to as the central Punjab (region B) and the canal colonies (region D) in the text. These figures, however, show the increasing transfer of export wheat production to the Sutlej-Jhelum area, which contained all of the canal colonies and only a small part of the central region.

Early in the twentieth century, a new region consisting of the canal colonies appears in the Punjab and grows ever larger until about 1920. It became the premier locale for the production of government revenue and export crops (see Table 4.3). Yet the older agrarian system, which prevailed under the colonialism of underdevelopment, still endured under the protection of the colonial government's legislation. The contradictions inherent in the two forms of British colonialism would come to be expressed in a growing inequality and competition between the two Punjab regions that embodied these separate colonialisms: the canal colonies and the central Punjab.

Unequal exchange. The British irrigation works were major capital investments in the means of production, and they markedly increased the efficiency of production. By comparison to the central Punjab petty commodity producer, canal cultivators worked fewer hours, needed less bullock labor, and allocated much less land to fodder crops (see Tables 4.4, 4.5, and 4.6); these figures from the 1930s are the earliest available, but there is no reason to think much changed from the 1920s). The difference in human and animal labor expenditure and in cropping pattern mainly arose from the technical requirements of the well irrigation on which most central Punjab smallholders depended. Drawing water from a well was time-consuming labor for humans and animals; it added further labor time for the upkeep of bullocks and for the cultivation of their food. No wonder that the central Punjab smallholder had to work harder to maintain his family holding—in fact, more than 12 hours a day per adult.

As the canal region came to replace the central Punjab as the major exporter of wheat (see Table 4.2) early in the twentieth century, the smallholders of the latter region increasingly suffered from unequal competition and then finally from unequal exchange. Table 4.7 shows that even assuming the most adverse circumstances for the canal cultivator (namely, that he was only a sharecropper) and the most advantageous conditions for the central Punjab smallholder (that he owned all his cultivated land) the canal cultivator received on average a higher return for his labor than the peasant proprietor received for his labor and land ownership. The net return per acre was also higher on the canal-irrigated lands, as shown in Table 4.8, in spite of the fact that central Punjab peasants often earned a higher return on the well-irrigated portions of their lands. Their problem was that from one-third to one-half of their holdings was unirrigated and brought a quite

TABLE 4.3 Punjab Regions in 1921-1922

Characteristic	Southeastern Region	Central Region	Southwestern Region	Canal Region
Canal irrigation, percentage	.1313	.1528	.1197	.6294
Wheat acreage, percentage of cultivated land	.1256	.2501	.3765	.4022
Cotton acreage, percentage of cultivated land	.0393	.0278	.0275	.0883

SOURCE: Computed from Government of India, Punjab District Gazetteers.
NOTES: *Southeastern region*: Same as in Table 4.1 except for deletion of Delhi District and Kalsia Native State. *Central region*: Same as in Table 4.1. *Southwestern region*: Same as in Table 4.1 except for deletion of Districts of Lahore, Gujranwala, Shahpur, Multan, and Montgomery. *Canal region*: Districts of Lahore, Gujranwala, Shahpur, Jhang, Montgomery, Lyallpur, and Sheikhupura.

inferior return compared to the fully irrigated holding of the canal cultivator.

Another indication of this unequal competition was the rise in wage rates in the canal colonies relative to those in the central Punjab. Table 4.9 shows that a day's labor in the canal region was worth a good deal more than the same labor in the central Punjab, and was even worth more at times than the prorated return earned by the smallholder working his own lands. This difference in wage rates does not seem attributable to a difference in market involvement. That is, the subsistence sector does not appear to have supplemented the wages of the central Punjab laborer more than the canal cultivator. Table 4.10 indicates that smallholders from the central region depended on the cash market for a greater percentage of their household expenditures than did the canal colony sharecropper.

The existing data on household income also show that in most years the canal colony sharecropper was better off than the peasant proprietor of the central Punjab (see Table, 4.10), and the same is true for household savings. (This difference results in part from caste-distinctive consumption patterns; canal sharecroppers came from lower castes and for this reason ate less *ghi* and milk than did peasant proprietors; alternatively, it may have been the greater amounts of wheat—a high status grain—available for the sharecroppers' consumption that made expenditures on dairy products unnecessary.) When prices were high, as they were throughout the period of World War I until the late 1920s, the balance of farm income weighed most heavily in favor of the canal sharecropper.

The greatly increased export of wheat from the Punjab, for which the canal colonies were mainly responsible, produced a world determination of prices. Instead of local scarcity and supply determining wheat prices or even demand and supply within India, Britain's needs, which in turn were influenced by the availability and price of American and Canadian wheat, became a major determinant. Wheat prices stayed up at "famine level" for the first quarter of the twentieth century, no matter how good the agricultural season had been. The price of other foodstuffs tended to follow the upward course of wheat. Increasing commodity prices helped the canal cultivator who sold more in the market than he bought, but put the smallholder of the central Punjab, whose condition was often the reverse, at a disadvantage (Brij Narain, 1926).

The central Punjab peasant smallholders tried to cope with this competition and market disadvantage by increasing their labor input on the family farms. They were forced into a condition of increasing self-

TABLE 4.4 Percentage of Cultivated Land Given to Fodder Crops

	1936-1937	1937-1938	1938-1939	1939-1940	1940-1941	1941-1942	Average
Peasant proprietors (well irrigation)							
dry land	28	27	26	30	28	27	28
irrigated land	28	25	38	28	20	22	27
Canal cultivators	14	13	14	13	NA	11	13

SOURCE: Punjab Board of Economic Inquiry, *Farm Accounts in the Punjab*, publications nos. 63 (1939), 66 (1940), 75 (1941), 78 (1943), 85 (1945), and 89 (1946).

TABLE 4.5 Labor-Days per Worker on Cultivation and Upkeep of Livestock

	1937-1938	1938-1939	1939-1940	1940-1941	1941-1942	Average
Peasant proprietor	370	328	317	345	339	340
Peasant proprietor, central Punjab	NA	412	387	381	370	388
Canal cultivator	215	261	239	271	345* (280)	247+

SOURCE: See Table 4.
* The figure given in the sources appears to be an error. The figure in parentheses is the average labor-days expended by canal tenants on the government farm in 1941-1942.
+ Excluding 1941-1942.

TABLE 4.6 Labor-Days per Bullock

	1937-1938	1938-1939	1939-1940	1940-1941	1941-1942	Average
On peasant proprietor holdings	168	166	160	161	152	161
On peasant proprietor holdings in central Punjab	NA	176	161	170	159	167
On canal cultivator holdings	104	112	113	128	120	115

SOURCE: See Table 4.5.

TABLE 4.7 Annual Return* per Worker and per Holding
(in rupees)

	1936-1937	1937-1938	1938-1939	1939-1940	1940-1941	1941-1942	*Average*
Return per worker:							
Peasant proprietor[+]	177	137	124	181	179	255	175
Canal cultivator[S]	123	112	123	233	175	342	185
Return per holding (cultivated acreage):							
Peasant proprietor[+]	218	152	151	198	216	313	208
Canal cultivator[S]	98	90	114	218	173	298	165

SOURCE: See Table 4.4.
* Based on cost estimates for all inputs, depreciation, and crop outruns.
Because not all of these inputs and outruns were bought and sold in the market, these figures must be treated with caution.
[+] Assuming that all land was owned by the peasant proprietor. In reality some proportion was rented.
[S] Assuming that the canal cultivator owned none of the land and received only a tenant's share. These two assumptions thus hypothetically differentiate peasant proprietors from canal cultivators as greatly as possible.

exploitation. Central Punjab cultivators could not simply revert to subsistence cultivation because debt compromised their ability to withdraw from the market.

By the early twentieth century these stresses led to an odd labor and class situation in the central Punjab: Smallholders spread widely the one factor of production they could expand—labor—by becoming sharecroppers and periodic wage laborers in addition to working their own plots. Families with insufficient labor rented out their lands to families with excess workers (see Kessinger, 1974: 114-115; Calvert, 1925). Workers who could not be accommodated in this fashion went off as wage labor emigrants. Thus, from 1901 to 1911, net outmigration from the central Punjab region increased from 1.52 percent to 4.72 percent—the highest of any Punjab region. Such accommodations helped maintain the rural system of petty commodity production, but it led many cultivating families in central Punjab into situationally combining petty proprietorship, sharecropping, and wage labor. This

TABLE 4.8 Net Returns per Acre on Punjab Holdings (in rupees)

Year	Canal-Irrigated Total	Well-Irrigated Total	Well-Irrigated Dry Lands	Well-Irrigated Lands
1927-1928	24	—	—	—
1928-1929	34	32 (36)*	—	—
1929-1930	24	18 (24)	—	—
1930-1931	8	8 (11)	—	—
1931-1932	15	11 (12)	—	—
1932-1933	19	21 (26)	—	—
1933-1934	17	10 (9)	—	—
1934-1935	22	16 (19)	9	21
1935-1936	28	15 (19)	3	12
1936-1937	25	—	12	33
1937-1938	24	—	7	25
1938-1939	27	—	4	29
1939-1940	38	25	9	35
1940-1941	29	24	11	32
1941-1942	51	35	14	53
Average	26 (21)[+]	20 (20)[+]	9	30

SOURCE: Punjab Board of Economic Inquiry, Farm Accounts in the Punjab.
* Figures in parenthesis represent the return per acre on well-irrigated holdings in the central Punjab.
[+] These averages represent the return per acre on canal-irrigated holdings and central Punjab well-irrigated holdings from 1928-1929 to 1935-1936.

amalgam of labor processes defies rigid Marxist class categories but probably reflects common conditions in colonial situations.

The unequal competition between the canal colonies and the central Punjab soon gave way to unequal exchange between them. As the canal region came to dominate the production of export wheat and cotton in the early twentieth century, the southeastern Punjab began to specialize in gram and barley production for export to the canal colonies. Gram and barley represented cheaper foodstuffs, which fed the canal cultivators while they sold their wheat. The central Punjab stood midway between the southeast and the canal regions in crop specialization. It had always combined wheat and gram production. As the canals competed successfully in wheat, from 1900 on the central Punjab was forced to specialize more and more in gram, which was primarily grown on unirrigated land. But its production of this crop soon came under competition from the increased gram cultivation of the southeastern region and the still-unirrigated lands within the canal districts (all relevant data are in Table 4.11).[1] Here again the market dedication forced upon the central region by early British colonialism was, under

TABLE 4.9a Regional Daily Wage Rates of Unskilled Workers
(most common rate,* in annas)

Region	1909	1912	1917	1922	1927	1932	1937	
A	3.70	4.10	4.70	6.40	6.80	6.40	4.00	Southeastern
B	5.91	6.17	7.92	11.67	10.50	11.67	6.00	Central
C	4.55	5.35	6.11	8.89	8.66	8.89	6.00	Southwestern
D	6.60	7.00	8.00	14.83	12.00	12.80	8.20	Canal colonies

SOURCE: Reports on Wages in the Punjab, Government of the Punjab.
* When two rates are listed as most common, an average of them is taken.

TABLE 4.9b Comparison of Daily Wages of Laborers with Per
Diem Return on Cultivation per Family
Worker* (in annas)

	1936-1937	1937-1938	1938-1939	1939-1940	1941-1942
Wages					
Canal wage	5.17	4.17	4.83	5.50	6.58
Central Punjab wage	—	—	4.00	4.00	5.08
Average wage in regions other than canal	4.67	3.67	3.83	4.83	
Return to cultivator in:					
Canal	2.83	2.58	4.50	9.58	14.75
Central Punjab	—	—	1.83	7.17	4.83
Other well-irrigation regions	4.00	1.92	1.50	4.42	4.83

SOURCE: Punjab Board of Economic Inquiry nos. 53, 66, 75, 78, 85.
* The figures for return per family worker equals net income from cultivation after paying
for all rented land, hired labor, and cost of manure. It does not include rental of land
owned, outside wages earned by family workers, or interest on capital.

the changed colonial conditions of the twentieth century, becoming an
increasing liability.

Not only unequal competition but also unequal exchange came to
afflict the central Punjab smallholders as they specialized in gram as a
cash crop. If they grew gram on unirrigated land for sale and ate the
wheat grown on their irrigated acreage, smallholders thereby recognized the advantage enjoyed by the canal colonies in wheat production.
But they then fell into competition over gram production with the
southeastern region and, perhaps more importantly, reduced the cash
income generated by their agriculture. Net returns per acre for dry
lands were always less than half and usually under one-third of the net
return to well-irrigated holdings, as Table 4.8 indicates. The strategy of

TABLE 4.10 Comparison of Family Budgets of Well-Irrigators (peasant proprietors) and Canal Tenants

	1936-1937		1937-1938		1938-1939		1939-1940		1940-1941		1941-1942		1942-1943	
	C	W	C	W	C	W	C	W	C	W	C	W	C	W
Total income	454	520	430	530	330	514	559	453	589	452	898	652	2045	13
Total expenses	446	451	433	436	337	420	296	515	366	402	372	483	706	7
Savings	8	69	(3)	95	(7)	93	263	(62)	223	50	526	169	1339	6
Percentage of maintenance from farm	49	45	56	50	47	46	56	38	56	51	69	48	49	—
Percentage of food from farm	74	76	75	77	71	76	78	64	78	69	83	74	71	—

SOURCE: Punjab Board of Economic Inquiry, Family Budgets of Punjab Cultivators.

growing gram as a cash crop on irrigated land was even less satisfactory. Although this strategy recognized the superiority in wheat production of the canal colonies and did not lead to competition in this crop, and although this strategy gave the central Punjab a competitive advantage over the southeast in gram production (where it was mainly an unirrigated crop), it led to an unequal exchange between the central Punjab and the canal colonies. Central Punjab gram purchased by canal cultivators allowed more wheat to be exported. Because the outrun of gram was less per acre than of wheat and yet the price was less, and because the amount of labor that a central Punjab cultivator invested in the production of a *maund* (about 80 lbs.) of gram greatly exceeded the equivalent investment by the canal cultivator in an equal volume of wheat, there was a flow of value—an unequal exchange—in favor of the canal colonies (see Tables 4.5 and 4.12).

Agrarian protest. The deteriorating market position of petty commodity producers in the central Punjab reached a crisis point of contradiction after World War I. Government policies had unintentionally helped precipitate problems that brought the agrarian system to this difficult juncture. After the war, the many soldiers demobilized from the British Indian army became so many more mouths to feed from a family income that no longer included military remittances. The fiscal difficulties of the colonial government in the 1920s dictated economies that reduced the size of the peace-time army to below what it

TABLE 4.11a Gram Exports from the Central Punjab to the Canal Colonies[+] (in thousands of maunds)

Period	Amount	Proportion of Total Gram Export from Central Punjab
1900-1904*	190	34.86
1905-1909	245	25.02
1910-1914*	860	59.97
1915-1919	551	50.88
1920-1922	760	64.85

SOURCE: Government of the Punjab, *River and Rail-Borne Trade of the Punjab,* 1900-1922.
*One year missing.
[+]See definition of trade regions in Table 4.3.

TABLE 4.11b Gram Acreage by Region (thousands of acres) and Percentage of All Cultivated Land in Gram

Region	1902	1912	1922	1932	
A	339	1140	1724	1478	Southeastern
percentage	.0511	.1261	.2069	.1815	
B	694	1806	1994	1691	Central
percentage	.0908	.1390	.1725	.1359	
C	305	453	517	767	Southwestern
percentage	.0260	.0449	.0578	.0705	
D	9	564	1517	1079	Canal colonies
percentage	.0244	.0908	.1942	.1342	
Total	1347	3963	5752	5015	Punjab
percentage	.0498	.0963	.1472	.1815	

had been before World War I. A similar loss of external remittances resulted from the many Punjabi workers who had been repatriated to India from North America and Southeast Asia before and during the war. These sources of income disappeared at the same time that new canal properties ceased to be available. There were no new government irrigation works underway, and, in any case, the last canal lands had been auctioned to large landlords to raise revenue for government— again, a policy that government followed for financial reasons.

There were internal forces threatening the agrarian system of production and labor in the central Punjab, some of which were also the unintended consequences of state actions. The Land Alienation Act had curtailed the dominance of merchant capital over peasant small-

TABLE 4.12a Wheat and Gram Prices
(in rupees per maund)

	Wheat	Gram
1861-1870	2.058	1.907
1871-1880	2.081	1.751
1881-1890	2.101	1.595
1891-1900	2.727	2.268
1901-1905	2.510	1.945
1906-1910	3.376	2.769
1911-1915	3.609	2.871
1916-1920	4.982	4.409
1921-1925	4.53	3.54
1926-1930	3.51	3.45

SOURCE: Board of Economic Inquiry, pub. nos. 7, 52.

TABLE 4.12b Outrun of Wheat and Gram
(in tons per acre)

	Wheat	Gram
1906-1916	.3254	.2678
1917-1926	.3275	.2260

SOURCE: Board of Economic Inquiry, Punjab, pub. no. 52.

TABLE 4.12c: Return per Maund of Wheat and Gram
(in rupees*)

	Return		Market Price	
Period	Wheat	Gram	Wheat	Gram
1927/8-1931/2	1.73	1.33	3.07	3.11

SOURCE: Board of Economic Inquiry, pub. no. 33.
*Gram and wheat grown on canal-irrigated land.

holdings. But it had only transferred rural debt bondage to a new type of moneylender, the rich farmer, who stepped in to supply the same credit and extract the same concessions as had the traditional nonagricultural "tribes" excoriated by the British. Besides the effects of moneylending, several other factors conspired to further class differentiation among rural cultivators. The war accelerated the rise in wheat prices set in motion by export production. Those central Punjab cultivators who managed to raise more for sale in the market than they bought amassed capital. During World War I, most of this capital had been secreted away from British war drives and other "voluntary" contributions, but in the 1920s it reappeared en masse and was used to buy out the smallholder. Land prices had also risen steeply. The start-up capital required to engage in petty commodity cultivation in the many cases where men inherited no or insufficient land therefore increased.[2] Table 4.13 shows the meteoric rise in land prices.

In the early 1920s this crisis erupted into the longest and largest rural protest against British colonialism that had been seen since the mutiny of 1857-1859. Ostensibly against British intervention in the Sikh religion, it fused class and religious protest against colonial rule (see Mohinder Singh, 1978; Gulati, 1978). The British were surprised by this rural upheaval because the urban lower-middle class backing the nascent nationalist movement in other regions of India was not very political in the Punjab. They were dismayed that a province whose productivity they had invested in so heavily and whose people they had favored so selectively in military service should now become so untrue to their (British-given) "salt." The British did not see that these two benefits of colonial domination represented two quite different—and contradictory—forms of colonialism, and they did not see that their own state policies intentionally or unintentionally maximized the good fortune of the canal colonies at the expense of central Punjab smallholdings. The two agrarian regions remained locked in an unequal competition so long as the state could maintain these two contradictory forms of colonialism. But the patches that the state had applied, like the Land Alienation Act, or that central Punjab smallholders had utilized, like army service or emigration, to dam the destructive forces flowing from the canal colonies could only be maintained in the post-war world with great difficulty and through serendipitous changes in the world capitalist system and the Indian political order.

By the mid-1920s the protest movement had been contained by suppression and cooptation. The petty commodity class in central Punjab was buried under a deluge of mortgages and land sales (see Table 4.14) that concentrated agricultural wealth in a growing class of rich landlords. Formerly independent smallholders became sharecrop-

TABLE 4.13 Sale Price of Land Per Cultivated Acre
(in rupees)

	For Five-year Period Ending in:						
	1901	1906	1911	1916	1921	1926	1931
Land price	81	79	114	166	258	400	392

SOURCE: Punjab Board of Economic Inquiry, pub. no. 52.

TABLE 4.14a Land Sales (thousands of acres)

Region	1905	1910	1915	1920	1925	1930	
			(for preceding five-year period)				
A	177	155	193	142	174	154	Southeastern
B	453	496	601	524	682	810	Central
C	400	365	422	386	455	569	Southwestern
D	47	78	187	139	207	153	Canal colonies
Total	1077	1094	1403	1191	1581	1686	Punjab

TABLE 4.14b Area Sold (thousands of acres)

Region	1905	1910	1915	1920	1925	1930	
			(for preceding five-year period)				
A	2412	2243	4841	1300	1596	922	Southeast
B	4766	3739	4338	5609	7376	11166	Central
C	3635	2959	2027	1864	2076	2191	Southwest
D	538	2071	5331	4863	8761	9360	Canal colonies
Total	11351	11012	16537	13636	23639	23639	Punjab

SOURCE: Computed from Government of India, Punjab District Gazetteers.

pers and tenants-at-will. The Great Depression saved the central Punjab cultivator from complete destruction, as it brought back low commodity prices, cheaper land, and greater removal of the Indian economy from the world capitalist system. Independence in 1947 and the trauma of partition also helped preserve the Punjab smallholder because it removed the canal colonies to Pakistan and replaced the unequal competition and exchange between the two regions with an impenetrable international boundary. With heavy government investment in new irrigation works and tube-well construction and with new opportunities for labor migration to Britain, the central Punjab became the center of a novel capitalist agriculture in independent India, based on the same sort of capital investment in transforming agrarian means of production that earlier and on a smaller scale had characterized the canal colonies.

CONCLUSION: CONTRADICTION AND RESISTENCE IN THE PUNJAB

Critics of world-systems and dependency theory have strongly attacked the "functionalist theory of imperialism" they believe these approaches espouse (see Banaji, 1977; Brenner, 1976; Skocpol, 1977; Kahn, 1980; Trimberger, 1979; Mouzelis, 1980). The neo-Marxist notion that the requirements of core capitalism deformed systems of production and labor in semiperipheral and peripheral societies is at the heart of this functionalism. This "development of underdevelopment" supposes that the apparent preservation of precapitalist forms outside the core results from their unequal incorporation into the world capitalist system. Core capitalism conserves these forms to meet its needs for accumulation; they are, in fact, necessary and ineluctable outcomes of capitalist penetration. By this view, neo-Marxists amend Marx's expectation that capitalism would transform systems of production and labor everywhere according to its own laws.

Critics of the neo-Marxist "functionalist theory of imperialism" recognize that Third World countries are not fully capitalist. But they interpret this empirical situation as reflecting the failure of capitalist penetration or its historical limitation rather than taking it that capitalism has had its unimpeded way in these nations. They therefore adhere to Marx's conception of a juggernaut capitalism that crushes all precapitalist forms in its expansion over the globe. To explain why capitalism has yet to fully transform labor and production in all societies, they generally offer a notion of indigenous "resistance." Rey, for example, ascribes the maintenance of precapitalist forms to an active struggle against them, and Banaji argues that capitalism will operate within the systems of exploitation "as it finds them" in precapitalist societies until it has had time to crystallize a fully capitalist structure (for Rey, see Kahn 1980: 205; Banaji, 1977). Alavi (1980) makes much the same point when he charts the various stages by which British colonialism transformed feudal landlord-tenant relations in India into wholly capitalist ones. Like the neo-Marxists, these critics argue against using typological characteristics to determine what a system of production is—as, for example, taking the presence of wage labor as definitive of capitalist relations. Capitalist relations can infuse a system of production no matter what its superficial forms appear to be. Unlike the neo-Marxists, however, these critics suggest that noncapitalist forms of labor exploitation are not necessary to capitalism; they are only compatible with capitalism as it works ultimately to transform the system into its own image.

Where does this indigenous resistance to capitalist penetration come from? Banaji and Alavi evidently presume that this resistance arises from an inherent conservatism or cultural chauvinism in precapitalist societies; it takes time for capitalism to wear down the natural defenses of indigenous societies. This explanation of resistance falls into the same

functionalism afflicting neo-Marxist underdevelopment theories because it takes the preservation of precapitalist forms as sufficient proof
that resistance exists—or, in other words, that the preservation of
precapitalist forms is always a functional outcome of the natural
antipathy of precapitalist systems to capitalism.

Kahn's (1980) analysis of petty commodity production among the
Minangkabau of Sumatra avoids this functionalism by portraying the
rise of indigenous resistance to capitalism as much more historically
complex. Rather than simply being a product of cultural conservatism,
Sumatran petty commodity production arose in adaptation to conditions created by the world capitalist market. It is therefore fit into the
world economic order, but its precapitalist form is not necessary to that
world order. Kahn suggests other forms of Sumatran production
(including a fully capitalist one) that the world system could equally
well incorporate. Therefore, the preservation of petty commodity
production in the face of capitalist penetration of Indonesia cannot be
assumed; it must be explained. Its persistence is due to class "forces
which oppose the complete capitalisation of the Indonesian economy"
(Kahn, 1980: 210). The peasant producers who are actively engaged in
petty commodity production form one of the classes resisting its
destruction. But there are also merchants who profit from the
maintenance of this form of production. Thus, for Kahn, resistance in
this case depends also on "the benefits which accrue to certain fractions
of the bourgeoisie" (Kahn, 1980: 205). In the struggle between classes
and class fractions within the capitalist world system, the preservation
of noncapitalist relations can betoken the political and economic
supremacy of localized classes, whose interests are best served by
incomplete capitalization—or so Kahn argues.

The dynamic of resistance in the Punjab does not easily reduce to the
class forces that Kahn posits for Indonesia. To be sure, the culminating
agrarian protest of the central Punjab peasantry was resistance by a
class that had been called into existence by the world economy and
British colonialism. It was ultimately ineffective, however. Both the
initial preservation of this class of petty commodity producers and the
economic pressures against which it resisted and protested were
outcomes of the colonial state's policies and the contradictory means of
exploiting Indian labor and production that the state followed. The
contradictory policies of British Indian colonialism undoubtedly favored different segments of the home bourgeoisie; but like their effects
on the Indian bourgeoisie, this seems often to be an unintended
consequence of policies whose ultimate determinant was the solvency of

the colonial state, the balance of payments in Britain and India, and the relative valuation of their currencies.

Although it may be lobbied by various classes and physically resisted by others, the colonial state stands above and acts independently of any particular class. This partial autonomy exists because the state must often undertake functions that no single capitalist or capitalist fraction would do, as, for example, the construction of the railroads or the irrigation works; because the state must often adjudicate the conflicting interests of capitalists or capitalist fractions, whose pursuit of self-interest threatens the entire system, as in the regulation of merchant capital under the Land Alienation Act; and because the state also is directly subject to the world economic order, as in the devaluation of the rupee and its consequences for government finances. Furthermore, the state has its own imperatives, such as the recruitment of an indigenous army with which to defend India cheaply, that dictate state policy. Resistance arises because the colonial state fails to balance the several conflicting ways of exploiting labor and production in order to satisfy the goal of solvency and the contradictory imperatives of military security, government revenue, and social stability. Such contradictory state imperatives not only worked upon India, but also on the home country. For example, the fiscal difficulties of the government of India in the 1920s required tariffs against manufactured imports that deeply hurt the Lancashire cotton industry (Dewey, 1978). As with Lancashire capitalists, and so too with petty commodity production in central Punjab, the state is hoist on its own petard as the forms of production on which it earlier depended resist those that the state later unfurls.

Colonial state policy often results from the contest between factions with different political philosophies within the administration itself. However, the degree to which or in what fashion these internal disputations are apologia for class interests (as Kahn would lead us to expect) is moot; it cannot be assumed. For example, the major directive behind the utilitarian political philosophy that led the British to establish peasant proprietorship in the central Punjab was the hope of increased land revenue. Setting aside large landholders and prebendaries and equalizing tenants and peasant proprietors, within the limits of British military power, the colonial state operated as a class in pursuit of its own interests with an internal class of literati—its Indian administrative cadre—to define those interests and implement them.

Resistance, in the Punjab at least, is resistance against the state and against the intentional or unintentional outcomes of its contradictory colonial policies. The colonial state makes noncapitalist forms of production and labor, suffers them to exist so long as they answer state imperatives, and then actively tries to break them down or passively stands by while they undergo stress when other systems promise to meet such imperatives better.

NOTES

1. The railways built to the canal colonies for moving wheat exports gave the impetus for growing gram on nearby dry lands.

2. Compare Kahn (1980) for the opposite condition, that is, where capital demands do not increase and therefore wage labor, rather than being a permanent class condition, is only a temporary stage in the acquisition of sufficient capital to become a petty commodity producer in one's own right. Friedmann (1978) similarly argues that the sons of early twentieth-century American farm families labored only to amass enough capital to become independent proprietors themselves.

REFERENCES

ALAVI, H. (1980) "India: transition from feudalism to capitalism." Journal of Contemporary Asia 10: 359-399.

AMIN, S. (1976) Unequal Development. New York: Monthly Review Press.

BANAJI, J. (1977) "Modes of production in a materialist conception of history." Capital and Class 3: 1-44.

BRENNER, R. (1976) "Agrarian class structure and economic development in pre-industrial Europe." Past and Present 70: 30-74.

BRIJ NARAIN. (1926) Eighty Years of Punjab Food Prices, 1841-1920. Punjab Board of Economic Inquiry, Rural Section publication 13, Lahore.

CALVERT, H. (1925) The Size and Distribution of Agricultural Holdings in the Punjab. Punjab Board of Economic Inquiry, Rural Section publication 4, Lahore.

DEWEY, C. (1978) "The end of the imperialism of free trade: the eclipse of the Lancashire lobby and the concession of fiscal autonomy to India," pp. 35-67 in C. Dewey and A.G. Hopkins (eds.) The Imperial Impact: Studies in the Economic History of Africa and India. London: Athlone.

FRIEDMANN, H. (1978) "World market, state, and family farm: social bases of household production in the era of wage labor." Comparative Studies in Society and History 20: 545-586.

FRYKENBERG, R. (1965) Guntur District 1788-1848. London: Oxford.

Government of India (1922) Census of India, 1922: Punjab.

——— (1912) Census of India, 1911: Punjab.

——— (1902) Census of India, 1901: Punjab.

——— (1870) Punjab District Gazetteers.

Government of Punjab (1890-1922) Internal Trade of the Punjab. Lahore: Civil and Military Gazette.

——— (1910) Report on Wages in the Punjab.

GULATI, K. C. (1974) The Akalis Past and Present. New Delhi: Ashajanak.

KAHN, J. (1980) "Minangkabau Social Formations," in Indonesian Peasants and the World Economy. Cambridge: Cambridge University Press.

———— (n.d.) "Mercantilism and the emergence of servile labor in colonial Indonesia."

KESSINGER, T. (1974) Vilyatpur 1848-1968. Berkeley: University of California Press.

MOHINDER SINGH (1978) The Akali Movement. Delhi: Macmillan.

MOUZELIS, N. (1980) "Modernisation, underdevelopment, uneven development: prospects for a theory of Third-World formations." Journal of Peasant Studies 7: 353-374.

PAUSTIAN, P. (1930) Canal Irrigation in the Punjab. New York: Columbia University Press.

Punjab Board of Economic Inquiry (1932-1933). Household Accounts in the Punjab. Lahore: Civil and Military Press.

———— (1928) Farm Accounts in the Punjab. Lahore: Civil and Military Press.

RAJ, K.N. (1973) "The politics and economics of intermediate regimes." Economic and Political Weekly VIII 27, 7:1189-1198.

SKOCPOL, T. (1977) "Wallerstein's world capitalist system: a theoretical and historical critique." American Journal of Sociology 82: 1075-1089.

STOKES, E. (1978) The Peasant and the Raj. London: Cambridge University Press.

TOMLINSON, B.R. (1979) The Political Economy of the Raj 1914-1947. London: Cambridge University Press.

TRIMBERGER, E. K. (1979) "World Systems Analysis: The Problem of Unequal Development." Theory and Society 8: 127-137.

WASHBROOK, D.A. (1976) The Emergence of Provincial Politics: The Madras Presidency 1870-1920. London: Cambridge University Press.

WOLF, E. (1982) Europe and the People Without History. Berkeley: University of California Press.

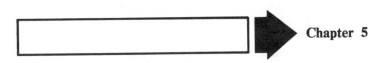

Chapter 5

LABOR AND INTERNATIONAL CAPITAL IN THE MAKING OF A PERIPHERAL SOCIAL FORMATION:
ECONOMIC TRANSFORMATIONS IN GUATEMALA, 1850-1980

Carol A. Smith
Duke University

Scholars who have attempted to analyze labor in relation to the world-capitalist economy have developed two different ways of doing so. World-system theorists define labor in terms of the commodities it produces and their exchange value in the global economy, and on that basis describe it as core, peripheral, or marginal (Wallerstein, 1974, Chase-Dunn, this volume). Orthodox Marxists define labor in terms of the general organization of the economic units utilizing it, and on that basis describe it as subject to capitalist or noncapitalist relations of production (Kay, 1975, Bunker, this volume). By either scheme one could classify any social formation, such as Guatemala's, as more or less peripheral or more or less capitalist. And by either scheme one could then advance certain ideas about the internal dynamics of the social formation, based on a number of principles thought to apply universally to economies whose labor is utilized in particular ways.

AUTHOR'S NOTE: This chapter was produced (and reproduced) when I was a fellow in the Latin American Program of The Wilson Center, Washington, D.C.; I am grateful for their support. I would like to thank Arif Dirlik for stimulating discussions that helped me sharpen the arguments presented here and for helpful comments on a first draft of this chapter.

Scholars taking either position assume that they are not only opposed to one another in their analysis of the internal dynamics of economic systems, but that they are also opposed to standard economic views on labor and the nature of peripheral economies. In fact, both stances share certain fundamental assumptions with each other and with the standard views: that a universal scheme can be applied to particular social formations at any point in time; that a certain convergence in social formations is taking place due to the worldwide spread of capitalism; and that analysis of any social formation or region requires mainly that one determine the degree to which labor is subject to a number of principles (whether through the organization of labor or through the kinds of commodities produced by labor).

Social and labor historians, who have elaborated a critique more than an alternative position on labor in the world economy, reject all of the above assumptions.[1] They assume no universal teleology, and posit instead a unique determination for each social formation based on particular combinations of labor processes, each of which is historically determined. Such an approach is much more attractive from the perspective of process and dialectics, but those concerned with the general laws of economic systems find other faults in it. David Harvey (1982), for example, suggests that much labor history suffers from a different kind of teleology, that of unprincipled historicism—an approach that basically eschews the problem of explanation. If one's task is merely that of tracing how everything influenced everything else (dialectically, of course), one ultimately explains nothing.

As I take the problems associated with each approach seriously, I see no easy solution to this impasse. Yet some way out is needed, and my efforts in this chapter will be directed toward that end. My first suggestion is that we recognize each position to have legitimate claims: The global economy, although nothing more than the separate components which make it up, does act as a *system* to influence each of its component parts and thus must be treated as a system in one's analysis; yet, relations of production organizing labor also affect local social formations and are not simply given by position in the world economy; and the political histories of each particular laboring group in a peripheral economy determines the kind of capitalism that will take root as much as the more general global or capitalist dynamics. My second suggestion is that we consider how labor processes influence *one another* in a local system. In the case I consider, the relevant types of production are peasant, petty commodity, and capitalist production. I treat these as interacting *forms* of production rather than as articulated *modes* of production. And I treat them in two contexts: that of

Guatemala, a social formation in which the state plays a critical role in the expansion and development of certain means to deploy labor; and that of the global economy from about 1850 to the present.[2] My final suggestion is that we deal with history and the concrete by examining political struggles over the organization of labor as they take place in particular contexts created by varied class interests and alliances. Unless we ask specific questions about why peripheral capitalist social formations have diverged from one another in ways that cannot be accounted for simply by space and time, we will only describe and never explain their variation. Looking at class formation and alliance in political struggles over the organization of labor provides a specific focus for asking questions about histories that are otherwise endlessly diverse.[3]

I pay particular attention to petty commodity production in this case study, not only because it is historically important in Guatemala, but because it is the form of production least understood in theoretical terms. As a type of production process, petty commodity production can take various forms: the form of classic urban artisanry; the form of rural (peasant) production of both food and nonfood items for market sale; and the form of small urban enterprise (the "informal" sector) that operates in close association with capitalist forms of enterprise. Petty commodity production, assumed never to be an independent mode of production, associates with several "dominant" ways of organizing labor: slave, feudal, and capitalist.[4] Students of petty commodity production rarely consider how other ways of organizing labor (slave, feudal, or capitalist), each of which operates in a distinctive economic environment, shape the operation of petty commodity production. They dodge the question by assuming that petty commodity production functions to meet certain needs of the economic processes located in the dominant mode of production that cannot be or are not being filled by the basic labor process in the dominant mode.[5] Yet this assumption raises other issues, such as what one means by mode of production, by location of labor processes, and by the domination of one economic system over another. If one rejects the assumption that petty commodity production is spawned by certain needs of the dominant economy and asserts, in contrast, that this labor process arises in order to fit the needs of social groups in an economy that does not fit those groups into the dominant labor process, one faces further questions. The most important of these is how petty commodity production itself might affect or condition the operation of the so-called dominant modes of production. I will attempt to address, if not fully answer, all of these questions here.

In order to avoid certain assumptions embedded in describing labor organized by different modes of production (especially as these have been codified by Althusser and Balibar, 1972), I take a somewhat different approach. I describe different "forms" of production in an economy, by which I mean the relationship between forces and relations of production, as these are influenced and changed not only by their own internal dialectics but also through association with other forms of production in the same social context. This allows me to describe different forms of petty commodity production (or of capitalism) without considering all but one form as deviations from the ideal type. When dealing with a particular form of production, I will concentrate upon the labor processes within it, specifically the social and economic conditions under which labor operates. My aim in focussing on the organization of labor in a social formation is not to reduce social relationships to economic ones but, on the contrary, to suggest that one must deal with labor relations in a *total* social context that does not separate the parts or layers of the context in an arbitrary and hierarchical manner. In dealing with forms of production, I shall attempt to specify how units of production operate and reproduce themselves *and* to observe relevant elements of the social context that permit or encourage them to operate the way they do.[6] In other words, I do not assume that forms of production underlie or create their own social context, only that they require certain contexts to exist. At the same time, I do not intend at this point to offer wholly novel definitions of the three forms of production with which I deal.

I assume the distinguishing characteristics of labor organization in peasant, petty commodity, and capitalist production to be the following. Under peasant production, workers produce most of what they consume and they control their own means of production; they are also forced to turn over some portion of their product to nonproducers through extra-economic means of compulsion, and they are rarely free to change place or occupation.[7] Under petty commodity production, workers also produce goods and services with means of production they control; but they produce in order to sell, engaging in free and competitive markets for subsistence goods, for their commodities, and for their factors of production; in addition, petty commodity producers are free to change place or occupation.[8] Under capitalism, workers are free of means of production and free to change both place and occupation; they subsist on commodities purchased through a market, paid for exclusively from wages earned from working in capitalist enterprises, where the aim of the enterprise is to valorize labor on an increasing basis and where labor is directly controlled by capital in the production process.[9] These are the "classic" forms. Needless to say, I do not believe one encounters a classic form of production very often in the concrete world.

At present Guatemala has few pure examples of any of the types of production described above. The predominant worker is a petty commodity producer who earns additional income either as a peasant or as a wage-earner. Such mixed activity has been present for more than a century. But the importance of each type of activity has changed in this century, and along with it the *nature* of each form of production has changed (see Table 5.1).

In the following brief account I depict how the changing organization of labor transformed the nature not only of each labor process but also of the entire production system of which they formed a part. I consider both global economic forces and local political struggles, paying more attention to the latter than the former only because the impact of global forces is better known, not because global forces have been less important.

* * *

At independence from Spain in 1821, Guatemalan labor consisted of peasants and of petty commodity producers. The latter were primarily traditional urban artisans. Most peasants paid the tribute that distin-

TABLE 5.1 Changing Attributes of Labor in Production: Guatemala

Classic Attributes of Labor in:	1850	1920	1980
Peasant production			
Subject to direct forms of tribute exaction	(+)	–	–
Self-sufficient in most domestic goods	(+)	–	–
Engaged primarily in agriculture	+	(+)	–
No access to free market in land	+	+	–
No access to free market in labor	+	+	(+)
Petty commodity production			
Produces commodities for market sale	(+)	+	+
In competition with equivalent producers	–	+	+
Free to buy and sell to anyone	–	+	+
Access to open markets in factors of production	–	–	+
Free to change place and occupation	–	–	(+)
Capitalist production (agriculture)			
Can purchase goods needed for reproduction	(+)	+	+
Free to find employment anywhere	–	(+)	+
Organized and controlled by capital	–	–	(+)
Formally protected by state and unions	–	–	(+)
Subsists entirely from wages (free of property)	–	–	–

guishes peasants from "primitive" producers directly to the state in the form of taxes and tithes; few peasants worked on estates to support a landlord class.[10] (Thus nonproducers consisted almost entirely of Spanish colonial authorities.) Some peasants also exchanged goods in marketplaces, but the marketplaces were mostly located in urban centers, under the direct control of state representatives. Through market exchange, in fact, colonial authorities extracted additional surplus through further taxes, price fixing, and regulation of the urban monopolists who controlled various goods needed by peasants. A peasant (and at this time most peasants were socially recognized as Mayan Indians) could not easily change community or ethnic identification—which essentially defined his or her peasant status as producer of basic foodstuffs and payer of tribute. Peasants were tied to particular communities not only through sentiment but through legal restrictions upon their movements. Neither labor nor land were market commodities in this period. The colonial state regulated access to each directly.

Urban artisans, most of whom were non-Indian (Ladino) in social identity, produced most of the commodities exchanged in colonial Guatemala.[11] These artisans had few of the attributes of modern petty commodity producers because of the poor development of national markets, especially markets in factors of production. No labor market existed. Most artisans were born to their trades in that they followed the occupations of their parents, from whom they acquired their skills. In consequence, artisans lived in communities that were ethnically distinct, endogamous, and held monopolies on particular skills or markets. Limited markets existed for other factors, in that artisans purchased raw materials and they sold finished goods to clients mostly for cash. But the state regulated market exchanges strictly, pushing artisans to form ties of personal dependency in order to obtain supplies and dispose of products. Undeveloped markets maintained undeveloped forces of production. The means of production owned by artisans were rudimentary in the extreme: needles for tailors, simple adzes for carpenters, and so forth. Artisans produced goods for peasants as well as for elites (nonproducers), but mainly produced for the urban classes. People of the same class and ethnicity, often women, handled marketplace exchanges with peasants, by which both artisans and the elites were fed.

At this point the distinction between rural peasant and urban artisan was not yet blurred. Some rural Indians did market some commodities, but most produced rather than purchased their raw materials. (Rural carpenters, for example, cut their own trees for lumber.) Peasants, moreover, did not usually sell their finished goods but turned them over to the Spanish authorities or traders through the *repartimiento* system.[12]

Thus we have no difficulty considering such people peasants, given the circumstances under which they worked. It is somewhat more difficult to classify the urban artisans of this period. Clearly artisans produced and purveyed those few commodities that existed in the economy. But they did so under state regulation of their enterprises. Market conditions were such that Guatemala's artisans more closely resembled peasants in the conditions under which they worked—political regulation of their economic lives—than they resembled modern artisans or petty commodity producers. At the same time, the urban artisans of colonial Guatemala were the direct antecedents of modern artisans or the informal sector in twentieth-century Guatemala. If we place them within the context of both history and process, then, we must consider the urban artisans of colonial Guatemala as representative of the kind of petty commodity production most likely to exist in a social formation that supports no capitalist enterprise.

The working conditions for peasants and artisans changed in Guatemala only after prolonged class struggle. The social classes of Guatemala grouped around conservative and liberal ideologies after independence, a typical pattern in Latin America. The usual alignment had those Spanish settlers who lacked the privileges of the Spanish bureaucracy (i.e., *criollos*) on one side, wishing to destroy the restrictions preventing capitalist enterprise; and it had the urban artisans, Church people, and Spanish authorities on the other side, wishing to preserve them. Peasants in Latin America were usually an inert mass, unable to articulate a distinct set of interests in the struggle. But in Guatemala, peasants played a more significant role in the battle that ensued, and articulated an interest that was neither liberal nor conservative. Moreover, they won national power for a brief period through supporting a guerrilla movement against the state, led by Rafael Carrera—an expeasant and pig merchant who was to become "president-for-life" in Guatemala (Ingersoll, 1972). Carrera and his regime cannot be categorized as either liberal or conservative. Some of his conservative policies helped protect peasant communities from many aspects of rampant, early capitalism; but some of his liberal policies helped open up Indian communities, allowing much greater freedom of movement and commerce than had been possible earlier (Woodward, 1976). In both these respects, Carrera represented peasant class interests (Miceli, 1974). By 1871, when Liberals finally captured state power in Guatemala, a very strong peasant class had formed that on the one hand took over much of the domestic economic activity formerly monopolized by urban artisans, but on the other hand retained considerable ability to protect their basic means of production (land)

and the political autonomy of their communities. The formation of this relatively self-conscious peasant (Indian) class—a rare event in nineteenth-century Latin America—would affect labor history in Guatemala far into the future.

To explain why a relatively strong peasantry emerged in Guatemala is too complex a task to be attempted here (see Smith 1984b), but several points about it call for comment. First, Guatemala City was the seat of imperial power for all of Central America during the colonial period—in part, because most surviving Indians lived in Guatemala. The majority of Spanish settlers lived either in Guatemala City or as far away from that city (and its control over them) as they could get— which put most of them outside the boundaries of the new Guatemalan nation at the time of independence (Woodward, 1976). Thus, Guatemala's Ladinos (both artisans and *criollos*) were few and concentrated in the national capital, distant from where the bulk of peasants lived. Second, few Guatemalan peasants lived on the most suitable land for the production of commodities in demand by the world economy: The Church owned most of it (MacLeod, 1973). Finally, no one worried very much about the existence of a strong peasant class in Guatemala. At the time it emerged, it did not appear to be a tremendous obstacle to the development of the export-oriented agrarian economy that was wanted at the time. Peasants could be tapped for cheap plantation labor and they could also supply the plantation labor force with cheap commodities (McCreery, 1976). Thus international capital, supplied and put into operation mainly by Germans, could take land from the Church, seasonal labor from nearby peasant communities, and infrastructural support from the Guatemalan state to make a tidy profit on the production of coffee for world export—without destroying a land-based peasantry.

The development of coffee and later banana exports (as well as the development of a liberal capitalist ideology) in Guatemala followed a general trend in the world periphery, a trend put into motion by the tremendous expansion of the world market in the late nineteenth century. But it is important to note that different places produced for the world market the same commodities, such as coffee, in quite varied ways, and this created major differences in peripheral economies. In the same period, Costa Rica's small farmers produced coffee mostly with family labor; El Salvador's large plantations produced coffee with wage labor that was almost completely landless by the turn of the century; but Guatemala's large plantations produced coffee mainly with seasonal labor levied by the state from peasant communities that held onto much of their own land (Cardoso, 1975).

The failure of Guatemala's Liberals to separate most peasants from their property meant that capitalist agriculture, indeed capitalism in general, took a very distinctive form in Guatemala. One reason is obvious enough. Guatemala's incipient capitalists were not spurred to capital investment because labor power had not become a real cost to them. Another reason is less obvious. Because plantations had to be supplied with commodities, and Guatemala did not have enough urban centers and artisans to supply them, petty commodity production spread from urban places to rural areas, assisted by a rural marketing system run by peasant traders (Smith, 1978). Thus petty commodity production and trade opened up to everyone in Guatemala. This provided a niche for peasants living on shrinking plots of land, giving them an alternative to wage labor on plantations. Such an alternative did not present itself to peasants elsewhere in Central America even though coffee was grown for export throughout the region. Elsewhere trade and artisanal production remained concentrated in urban centers and an increasingly land-short peasantry had to turn to wage labor rather than to petty commodity production and trade. The political strength of Guatemala's peasants, gained in earlier political struggles, explains the difference.

If we compare Guatemala's extant production systems at two points in time (see Table 5.1)—one before the expansion of coffee production (1850) and one after coffee production had reached one of its highest levels (1920)[13]—we see certain complementary patterns. The first period shows no capitalist enterprise,[14] a "classic" peasantry, and a few protected artisans. The only opening for capitalist development was that both artisans and peasants produced for the domestic market some commodities that could be used to feed a specialized labor force. Even here, however, the development was weak. With the expansion of coffee plantations we find considerable loosening of the system—wrought by political struggle rather than by direct economic impulse. Yet petty commodity production rather than capitalist agriculture took up most of the slack given by the declining self-sufficiency of the peasantry. Labor was legally free to find employment anywhere, but most free labor went into small-scale domestic production; plantations continued to rely on the state to obtain labor. And the development of a competitive market for domestic commodities was not matched by the development of a competitive market in the commodities needed to *produce* commodities. Even though people could buy and sell land, land did not have a price determined by its market value; even though producers could find raw materials and means of production in the marketplace, they assured supplies only by developing relationships of clientage; and even though plantations paid wages to some workers, a given wage rate did not call forth labor in the quantities needed. In short, none of the institutional bases for the real subsumption of labor by capital existed in Guatemala fifty years after export production as the world-capitalist market had come to dominate Guatemala's economy.

The second major political battle to ensue in Guatemala had less to do with the struggle between labor and capital and more to do with different capitalist and labor interests. Once again the battle was stimulated by a general global trend following World War II, when Guatemalan capitalists diversified and began the process of import-substitution industrialization. The class alliances in this struggle were somewhat different from before (see Jonas, 1974; Wasserstrom, 1975). On one side lined up the entrenched coffee interests (Guatemala's oligarchy) and the few successful urban businessmen with protected monopolies; this group wanted to retain the extant distribution of property and an authoritarian state regime. The other side consisted of full-time wage workers (a very small but politically active bunch) and most elements of the petite bourgeoisie (professionals and urban businessmen without protected monopolies); this group wanted some of the benefits of "real" capitalism in Guatemala, including liberal democracy, trade unions, and the incorporation of Indian peasants into national life. (Very few Indians wanted to be incorporated, however, and to the extent that they took a position in this struggle it was with the old regime.) The new capitalists won briefly in 1944, with the election of Arbenz and then Arevalo; but the old capitalists won ultimately with the military overthrow of the elected regimes in 1954. The old capitalists still hold power today. The price they had to pay to win was increasing U.S. control over internal affairs in Guatemala.

No higher rationality given by the needs of the world economy can explain why the old capitalists won in Guatemala. The United States played a major role in helping them win—that much is clear. But we cannot conclude from this that the general interests of United States or core capital simply asserted itself over Guatemalan or peripheral capital. In 1954 U.S. capital had specific interests to defend in Guatemala, to be sure. But in the same year it had quite different interests in Iran, Vietnam, and elsewhere, even though the U.S. government pursued political policies in those places similar to the ones it pursued in Guatemala. It seems clear that U.S. capital had much more to gain from the progressive developments taking place in Guatemala under Arbenz and Arevalo than from protecting the traditional order in Guatemala. Later, under the Alliance for Progress, the United States actively promulgated more progressive policies for capital in Latin America, favoring regimes such as those it had earlier toppled. That the U.S. government did not recognize the value of "progressive" regimes for capital in 1954 should come as no great surprise. We cannot assume that capitalists always recognize or follow their economic interests in political struggles, especially when they must work through an agent, the state, which represents not only varied interests within a divided class, but also represents other classes and its own perpetuation as an agent.

Let us now consider how other groups involved in Guatemala's political struggles of 1944-1954 fared. Guatemala's Indian peasants, often described as losers in this struggle because of the value many people attach to national integration, were big winners from the perspective of what they wanted. Whether what they *wanted*— continued political autonomy, expanded commercial freedom, and growth of the domestic economy based on plantation exports—was what they *needed* to guarantee their continued reproduction along these lines is a different issue, one that the present situation throws into question. The big losers were the few remaining successful urban monopolists in the provincial towns of Guatemala. Many of them left those towns for Guatemala City, swelling the growth of the informal economy there as well as the size of one of the world's most primate cities (Roberts, 1973). They were replaced in the provinces by former peasants, mostly Indian, who gave up little in the way of ethnic identity or community solidarity to become successful in expanding petty commodity production and exchange in rural areas.

Because traditional groups won, trends established in the late nineteenth century intensified rather than changed. Plantation agriculture expanded and diversified (into cotton, cattle, and sugar, as well as coffee), but changed neither its market nor its ownership. Traditional oligarchs and multinationals invested in capital-intensive industry in Guatemala City, but they did not form a new industrial class in Guatemala that could represent distinct progressive interests. Petty commodity production grew enormously in Guatemala City, but its apparent novelty as an "informal" sector was misleading; it represented only an extension of earlier patterns first developed in rural areas. The most important legacy of the 1944-1954 struggles was the removal of the last formal barriers to the free movement of labor and capital. The state no longer used force to bring labor to the plantations and it encouraged capital investment from any and all quarters. In addition, the growth of a few "real" capitalist enterprises in Guatemala City promoted the growth of a "real" urban working class in that city, although most members of the proletariat tried to maintain sources of income in addition to wages (Roberts, 1973). Indians gained political equality with Ladinos—more in the letter than in the operation of the law—and for the first time became fully free to change place and occupation. But while political and legal conditions now existed for the expansion of "real" capitalism—one that would really subsume labor—capitalism in Guatemala remained stunted.

In order to understand the present organization of labor in Guatemala, we must look more closely at developments in petty commodity production—or the informal economy as it is sometimes called. Most scholars describe the informal economy as a novel form, basically urban, directly conjoined to capital-intensive industry in the world periphery (see Leys, 1973; Hart, 1973; Bromley and Gerry, 1979). On these grounds yet other scholars (e.g., Portes, 1981) explain it as a phenomenon spawned by the needs of capitalist expansion in the world periphery. The Guatemalan case suggests that all of these assumptions need reexamination. I have shown above that small-scale urban producers and traders have always existed in Guatemala. What is new about the present small-scale producers and traders is that their activities take place in an intensely competitive environment. Urban artisans existed long before any kind of capitalism existed in Guatemala, but they operated under state protection over limited monopolies. When the state stopped protecting small artisans, many more people entered commercial activities and through unrelenting price and service competition drove down the prices of domestic goods to make them much more important in the reproduction of all economic life in Guatemala. An especially interesting feature of the transformation in Guatemala is that it began in *rural* areas and thus involved former *peasants*, rather than in *urban* areas to involve former *artisans*. This demonstrates, rather conclusively, that there is nothing especially urban about the phenomenon. The social preconditions for an informal economy, in fact, can spread from rural areas to urban centers rather than vice versa.

The more important issue is the extent to which we can say that expanded capitalist production encourages expanded petty commodity production. An association clearly exists. Harriet Friedmann (1980), for example, observes that the same economic (i.e., market) conditions needed for capitalist forms of enterprise are also needed for petty commodity production (in its classic form). In particular, one needs integrated and competitive markets for most factors of production for either form of production. (One needs a market in labor only for the capitalist form of production.) Hence it is not surprising that the social preconditions favoring the expansion of capitalism also encourage classic petty commodity production. *Before* the market conditions exist for capitalism, one would find another type of petty commodity production, such as the type I described above: traditional urban artisanry, highly constrained through political means. Yet given the very existence of traditional artisanry, the connection between capitalism and petty commodity production is somewhat misleading. The linking mechanism is merely that of a competitive factor market, that market affecting the mode of operation of *all* forms of production within it. Thus one finds not only traditional artisans becoming petty commodity producers, one also finds traditional peasants becoming petty commodity producers—when the market conditions necessary for capitalism exist within a particular social formation. Those market conditions do not leave noncapitalist forms of production unaffected, but that is not to say that they force the growth of classic capitalism.

The real question thus becomes the degree to which petty commodity production arises to meet certain needs of early capitalism. The situation in Guatemala suggests quite the opposite. To the extent that petty commodity production exists and expands, it directly *competes with* expanded capitalist forms of production. It may, to be sure, deliver cheap commodities to capitalist workers and capitalist enterprises. But while capitalists will always seek the cheapest raw materials and labor from whatever source, they do not do so deliberately at their own expense. If there is one unfailing tendency or "need" of capitalism for its expanded reproduction it is to *replace* all prior forms of production—whether it can do so at high or low cost. Yet capitalists cannot always have it the way they want it. Capitalists in peripheral formations such as Guatemala do not invest in capital-intensive industry, thus marginalizing an enormous Indian workforce, because they are racists, because they are dazzled by high technology, or even because they want to create a large reserve army of unemployed. They do so because it is the only arena of production in which *they* can compete, given the existence of well-developed petty commodity production. At the same time, however, if capitalists face a consistently narrow market for their goods and have continuous difficulty obtaining the cheap labor they need for expanded reproduction, they will often try to do something about it—through political means.

Let us now turn to the situation and options for capital in Guatemala in the present period to see how this might be played out. By the late 1970s Guatemala's traditional peasantry had vanished. In my 1978 survey of 3000 highland Indian households (who once constituted the traditional peasantry) I found *no* household that was not heavily dependent upon market activity of some sort for reproduction (Smith, 1984a). Perhaps more surprising, I found that less than half of the households depended to any significant extent upon agricultural activities of any sort (whether as farmers or as agricultural workers). Virtually all Indian households did carry out some agricultural activities; but it was a rare household that could provide for more than half its food needs from its own land. As is heavily emphasized in the literature on Guatemala (cf. Jonas, 1974), many households made up the difference between production and need with seasonal wage labor on export-oriented plantations. But my data show that the proportion (if not the actual number) of such families had dropped significantly over time.[15] Most households engaged in petty commodity production. Considering only heads of households, 41 percent found employment primarily in self-controlled manufacturing activity of some kind and 17 percent in trade.[16] When one considers the occupations of all Indian workers in my sample (men, women, and children), the number of people in these two categories rises from 58 percent to 69 percent. All of these people, of course, are classic petty commodity producers.

I have less complete data on urban Guatemala and on plantation agriculture. But most scholars of the country agree that in the late 1970s an enormous informal sector existed in Guatemala City (Roberts, 1973), that capital-intensive industry flourished only briefly and then began to flounder as it reached its market limit (Williams, 1978), and that plantation agriculture continued to expand (CSUCA, 1978). Thus we have what *appears* to be the classic pattern of development in the periphery: capitalist enterprise growing at the expense of a traditional peasantry, but failing to absorb it, and peasants becoming redundant labor and thus finding ways to survive in the cities as part of the informal sector and in the countryside by balancing petty commodity production and wage work.

Before endorsing this picture, however, let us examine more closely the conditions of labor in the three forms of production under consideration here (see Table 5.1). As noted above, the peasant form of production had disappeared by 1980. A very sticky market in labor remained as a last vestige of the peasant form of production. Different Indian communities paid different wage rates to labor, and this situation did not move "surplus" labor to areas of scarcity (Smith 1983). This very same condition remained a barrier to the full development of petty commodity production in the countryside. Former peasants did not move freely between communities to engage in the most lucrative forms of production. Most of them took up the predominant activity of their community; and although new activities were constantly being added to each community's repertoire, one's position in a *community of producers*—if one remained an Indian—clearly constrained individual enterprise. This was not the situation in urban areas, where "community" among petty commodity producers no longer existed. The particular barrier involved here was the ethnic one—a barrier no longer legally enforced (the state, in fact, now actively encouraged ethnic assimilation) but one that persisted anyway.

Now let us examine the condition of labor upon which capitalist agriculture continued to rely. Even in 1978 Guatemala had relatively few full-time wage workers in agriculture: Most plantation workers engaged in other forms of production. Partly in consequence, plantation agriculture remained undercapitalized, workers rather than machines controlled the pace and organization of production, the state did not enforce minimum wage standards or allow trade union activity, and very few workers could subsist entirely on their wages. In other words, labor was subsumed by capital in a formal rather than real sense.[17] The position of capital in urban industry was somewhat better. Here higher wages allowed for full-time workers, machines controlled production, and limited trade union activity took place.[18] Yet the only kind of enterprise that could support this form of production required huge infusions of capital, most of it from external investors (multinationals) and most of it oriented toward an external rather than domestic market. In other words, we find an implanted form of capitalism in Guatemala, not a native one—a form of capitalism with very limited growth potential. Why do we find such limited capitalist development in Guatemala? My explanation, it should be clear by now, is the existence of other thriving forms of production in the economy, especially that of petty commodity production and the informal sector.

It could be argued that petty commodity production expanded so hugely in Guatemala in the period following World War II because no alternative source of employment existed for now redundant labor—and, in fact, this is the usual interpretation of the matter. Two kinds of evidence belie this interpretation and support my view, however. First, wages and income levels of families in the informal sector (both rural and urban) have been *higher* than those in the formal wage sector (for documentation see Smith, 1983, 1984a). This is not a unique finding, as a recent study comparing average informal incomes to those employed as blue collar labor in Columbia documents (Lopez et al., 1982). Second, a consistent body of evidence, for Guatemala anyway, indicates that capitalist enterprise in the last decade has faced an increasing shortage of labor—especially agricultural labor.[19] This should come as no surprise, given the higher incomes to be garnered in petty production and trade than in agricultural labor. One might ask why, if labor is short, capitalists do not increase the wages they offer. But this question assumes that the economic power of capitalist producers in Guatemala is so great that raising wages would offer no problem to them. It is indeed possible that Guatemalan plantations could offer higher wages without folding, but I believe they could not do so without a major transformation in the organization of production requiring a large investment of capital. And the market for agricultural commodities such as coffee and cotton is uncertain enough at present that it does not draw the kind of capital investment needed.

The present economic situation in Guatemala, then, is one in which the vast majority of expeasants find employment in petty production and trade rather than in capitalist enterprise. Most capitalist production in Guatemala, in consequence, is poorly developed and weak. Coffee production, for example, shows a very low level of technical and labor efficiency—one of the lowest levels in Latin America (Villacorta, 1976); industrial production is not much better (World Bank, 1978). I do not believe this is true because Guatemalan capitalists constitute an especially backward, retrograde group. I suggest it is true because they have faced strong resistence to their efforts to transform the Guatemalan economy over a long period of time. The economic difficulties this has created in recent years, exacerbated by the downturn in the global economy as well as by economic difficulties stemming from other sources in other parts of Central America, has led to another major political struggle in Guatemala, perhaps the most significant in its history.

The present political struggle in Guatemala, as I interpret it, centers once again around labor. But for the first time since the development of export production on a major scale, Mayan Indians—Guatemala's former peasants—are in the forefront of the struggle. Those who know little more about the economic life of Guatemala's Indians than that they make up the bulk of its plantation labor force have argued that revolution broke out in Guatemala in 1978-1979 because Indian workers and peasants finally reached an economic breaking point. From what I know about the economic adaptations of Guatemala's Indians, I believe the opposite to be the case: Guatemala's capitalist class finally reached an economic breaking point. There was no danger of Guatemala's capitalists disappearing as a class or as a political force in Guatemala; but unless they could release a significant amount of labor from the Indian countryside—which they believed was rightfully theirs to exploit—they would not be able to take advantage of the new opportunities that were beginning to surface in the 1970s.

Scholars agree about most of the following facts in the unfolding of Guatemala's revolution. Major oil and mineral deposits were discovered in a remote area of Guatemala in the 1970s. The act of violence most people use to date the onset of the present struggle—the Panzos massacre—occurred in 1978 in the oil-mineral area. The massacre, like the many others following it, was carried out by the state against unarmed, nonpoliticized, rural people, located either in zones planned for future capitalist development or in zones thought to have considerable potential commercial development. Also targeted was anyone perceived to be Indian, especially an Indian traditionalist in a position of leadership (Davis and Hodson, 1982). Little direct military action was taken against guerrilla organizations, extant in the area from the early 1970s on, but small in numbers until the massacres began. The plantation area, where guerrilla recruitment was most successful, felt little military pressure. The military objective of the state seemed to most observers to be that of terrorizing the entire indigenous population, especially those in the zones noted above.

Various interpretations of these facts exist. My own is that the Guatemalan state, representing Guatemala's capitalist class, has declared war on what it perceives to be the bases of "peasant" resistance to the capitalist development of Guatemala. As Guatemala's capitalists see it, these bases are the following: peasant economic self-sufficiency, based on their continued ownership of land in the highlands; peasant community solidarity (especially in Indian areas), which assists peasant resistance to certain kinds of outside influences, such as those promulgated by the state; Indian ethnic identity per se, which leads to satisfaction with a noncommercial way of life and a reluctance to leave local communities for work; and certain external influences, especially by Catholic missionaries, that help create dissatisfaction with the "appropriate" economic and political roles for Indian peasants. As I see it, the Guatemalan capitalists are partly right and partly wrong about the bases for peasant (Indian) resistance to the capitalist development of their country. Nonetheless, I suspect that the present course of action, especially that taking place today, could eventually break Indian resistance to the state, unless organized resistance against the state grows stronger.

Yet I do not believe the present struggle is one in which the capitalist development of Guatemala will necessarily be strengthened. For one thing, the struggle will destroy much of Guatemala's labor force (as well as its capital). For another, the present capitalist class of Guatemala runs a significant risk of losing its present position in the economy altogether—to be replaced by another dominant class carrying out a socialist form of production. Finally, present political and economic tactics will not necessary eradicate petty commodity production in Guatemala, and its competition with capitalist enterprise. In any event, the eventual development of capitalism in Guatemala will depend upon the outcome of political struggles and will not simply emanate from global tendencies or from the unfolding of the laws of motion of capitalism—although the political struggles that take place have been and will be significantly affected by such.

* * *

This short chapter provides scant evidence to support its many assertions about the social and economic forces involved in the making of modern Guatemala. But its goal was not to convince the skeptical reader about the particulars of one peripheral country. It was to suggest an approach to the analysis of peripheral social formations, shaped by a multitude of forces in which no single force dominates, but shaped nonetheless in patterned, explicable ways. To the extent that the approach points to certain general principles that can be applied to the analysis of variation in the economies of peripheral social formations, explaining their diversity without resort to an unordered welter of possible influences, it has been successful. Labor and the forms of production it creates lie at the center of the analysis. Labor and labor processes are given form by local class interests that are shaped by the *totality* of social life in a particular historical context; they are also given form by external economic and social processes, which impinge upon local interests in significant ways. If we are to account for variation as well as for similarity in the world-system periphery, we cannot neglect either side of the picture. If we are certain that material conditions affect the way in which people live and act politically, we must consider the interaction of labor and politics in concrete material contexts. And if we are concerned to understand the world in order to help change it, we must make the analysis of class relations and class struggle central to the enterprise.

NOTES

1. Because social and labor historians usually deal with political and economic struggles in highly localized contexts, few of them deal directly with world-system theory. Most of them have been critical of the more orthodox Marxist approaches, which they find neglectful of social context and social consciousness (the classic study being Thompson, 1966). I am assuming here that they would be equally if not more critical of world-system theory, if they were concerned about it.

2. This chapter cannot present the data that ground my analysis. For documentation, the interested reader should consult the various papers of mine listed in the reference section.

3. Many others have raised some of these same problems (e.g., Martinez Alier, 1977; Mintz, 1977; and Kahn, 1980), but few have suggested how we might resolve them in a consistent way.

4. For this reason, Hindess and Hirst (1975), who attempt an analysis of all precapitalist modes of production, neglect petty commodity production altogether. Most other orthodox scholars, however, usually accord petty commodity production the status of "mode" even though they consider it incapable of "dominance."

5. For examples of this kind of reasoning see Meillassoux (1972), Hindess and Hirst (1975), and Portes (1981).

6. Harriet Friedmann (1980) suggested using form of production as I use it here in order to understand how different *economic* contexts shape particular labor and market processes. I take the approach she developed one step further, suggesting that it is a way of seeing how a total *social* context shapes labor processes and the overall organization of production in particular economies.

7. My definition of the classic peasant here is mostly taken from Wolf (1966). I add the observation that few classic peasants are mobile, or free to change place and occupation. Differences in this last characteristic, rather than in the nature of what they produce, strike me as the most important feature distinguishing peasants from petty commodity producers.

8. My definition of the "classic" petty commodity producer is taken from Kahn (1980). By Kahn's definition, similar to that of most others, traditional urban artisans would not be petty commodity producers; this leaves an important form of labor organization out of most classificatory schemes.

9. I have taken, somewhat arbitrarily, the conditions of labor under capitalism from Harvey (1982) and Burawoy (this volume). I admit to choosing those characteristics that most differentiate labor under capitalist forms of production from labor under noncapitalist forms of production.

10. A few large estates, owned mostly by the Church, did exist in Guatemala (MacLeod, 1973). Most of Central America's large estates, however, were located in areas that became other countries (e.g., El Salvador). Those goods produced in Guatemala for the world commodity market in the colonial period were mostly produced by Indian peasants who directly controlled the means and conditions of production.

11. The following description of Guatemala's traditional artisans rests on two sources: Lutz's (1976) discussion of urban life in the colonial city of Santiago de Guatemala; and extrapolations from more recent descriptions of artisans in neighboring San Cristobal de las Casas (Chiapas, Mexico) before traditional monopolies over certain urban products by Ladino artisans were broken by actions of the state (Siverts 1969).

12. Guatemala's *repartimiento* system was one in which Spanish merchants were assigned the commercial distribution of certain products produced and consumed by

Indians; Indians were required by law to produce certain goods for these merchants and to purchase other goods purveyed by the merchants (MacLeod 1973). Thus commercial activity was strongly developed among Guatemala's peasants from a very early period; yet it was higly constrained commercial activity, which did little to alter the relationship between peasants, artisans, and the Spanish bureaucracy in the colonial period.

13. Coffee earned more than 75 percent of Guatemala's foreign exchange between 1880 and 1950. In 1920, coffee was in its heyday, having reached an areal extension and level of production it was not to exceed until the 1970s (Torres Rivas, 1971).

14. Some people might consider Guatemala's cochineal farms of this era a form of capitalist enterprise, since they produced a commodity for the world market—even though with coerced rather than free labor. Obviously that is not the position espoused here. It is nonetheless relevant to note that relatively little production for the world market—even of cochineal—existed in Guatemala as late as 1850.

15. My data consist of the following: interviews with municipal authorities, conducted in 1968-1969 and 1977-1978 about the percentage of people working seasonally on plantations in those years; and interviews with hamlet residents about the number of people migrating from the community in various years (using presidents then in power in Guatemala to fix time periods). For further discussion of the evidence, see Smith (1984a, 1984b).

16. Of the people engaged in manufacturing, slightly less than half were wage earners for small local enterprises; none of the enterprises had more than 10 wage workers in them and the vast majority had no more than 1 or 2. Very few traders used wage labor to conduct their activities.

17. The distinction between formal and real subsumption of labor in capitalism was made by Marx (1976: Appendix) to show that the "laws of motion" of capitalism could not come into play until certain conditions had been reached in making a commodity of labor power.

18. Following Harvey (1982) and Burawoy (this volume), I assume that in protecting the *economic* interests of the working class, trade unions make workers *more* dependent upon capital than they are when engaged in noncapitalist forms of production to supplement their livelihood. In that sense, then, higher wages and trade unions deepen capitalist control over labor.

19. I should warn the reader that my view about decreasing numbers of peasants available for plantation labor is not widely held. I should also note that few people have data on the organization of "peasant" production in highland Guatemala in more than one or two communities. In this respect, my data on production in Indian Guatemala is relatively unique. I attribute the general view that Indians constitute and have constituted an unending source of labor to the plantations to the following unquestioned (and wrong) assumptions: (1) Guatemalan Indians are classic peasants; (2) classic peasants farm; (3) Indian farm production has decreased dramatically on a per capita basis in recent years; and (4) most highland Indians have no other economic resources.

REFERENCES

ALTHUSSER, L. and E. BALIBAR (1970) Reading Capital. London: Schocken Books.
BROMLEY, R.J. and C. GERRY (1979) "Who are the casual poor?" in R.J. Bromley and C. Gerry (eds.) Casual Work and Poverty in Third World Cities. New York: John Wiley.

CARDOSO, C.F.S. (1975) "Historica económica del café en Centroamerica." Estudios Sociales Centroamericanos 10: 9-55.

CSUCA [Consejo Superior Universitario Centroamericano] (1978) Estructura Agraria, Dinámica de Población y Desarrollo Capitalista en Centroamerica. San José, Costa Rica: EDUCA.

DAVIS, S. and J. HODSON (1982) Witnesses to Political Violence in Guatemala. Boston: Oxfam America

FRIEDMANN, H. (1980) "Household production and the national economy: concepts for the analysis of agrarian formations." Journal of Peasant Studies 7: 158-84.

HART, K. (1973) "Informal income opportunities and urban employment in Ghana." Journal of Modern African Studies 11: 61-89.

HARVEY, D. (1982) The Limits to Capital. Chicago: University of Chicago Press.

HINDESS, B. and P. HIRST (1975) Precapitalist Modes of Production. London: Routledge & Kegan Paul.

INGERSOLL, H. (1972) "The war of the mountain: a study of reactionary peasant insurgency in Guatemala, 1837-1873." Ph.D. dissertation, University of Maryland.

JONAS, S. (1974) "Guatemala: land of eternal struggle," pp. 89-219 in R. Chilcote and J. Edelstein (eds.) Latin America: The Struggle with Dependency and Beyond. New York: John Wiley.

KAHN, J. (1980) Minangkabau Social Formations: Indonesian Peasants and the World-Economy. London: Cambridge University Press.

KAY, G. (1975) Development and Underdevelopment: A Marxist Analysis. New York: St. Martin's.

LEYS, C. (1973) "Interpreting African underdevelopment: reflections on the ILO report on employment, incomes and equality in Kenya." African Affairs 72: 419-29.

LOPEZ, H., M. LUZ, and O. SIERRA (1982) "El empleo en el sector informal: El caso de Colombia." Center for Economic Research, University of Antioquia, April. (unpublished)

LUTZ, C. (1976) "Santiago de Guatemala, 1541-1773: the socio-demographic history of a Spanish American colonial city." Ph.D. dissertation, University of Wisconsin.

MacLEOD, M. J. (1973) Spanish Central America: A Socioeconomic History, 1520-1720. Berkeley: University of California Press.

MARTINEZ ALIER, J. (1977) "Relations of production in Andean haciendas: Peru," pp. 141-164 in K. Duncan and I. Rutledge (eds.) Land and Labour in Latin America. Cambridge: Cambridge University Press.

MARX, K. (1976) Results of the Immediate Process of Production (Appendix to Capital, Vol. 1). New York: Viking.

McCREERY, D. (1976) "Coffee and class: the structure of development in liberal Guatemala." Hispanic American Historical Review 56: 438-60.

MEILLASSOUX, C. (1972) "From reproduction to production." Economy and Society 1: 93-105.

MICELI, K. (1974) "Rafael Carrera: defender and promoter of peasant interests in Guatemala, 1837-1848." The Americas 31: 72-95.

MINTZ, S. (1977) "The so-called world system: local initiative and local response." Dialectical Anthropology 2, 4: 253-270.

PORTES, A. (1981) "Unequal exchange and the urban informal sector," pp. 67-106 in A. Portes and J. Walton (eds.) Labor, Class, and the International System. New York: Academic Press.

ROBERTS, B. (1973) Organizing Strangers. Austin: University of Texas Press.

SIVERTS, H. (1969) "Ethnic stability and boundary dynamics in southern Mexico," in F. Barth (ed.) Ethnic Groups and Boundaries. Boston: Little, Brown.

SMITH, C. A. (1984a) "Does a commodity economy enrich the few while ruining the masses?" Journal of Peasant Studies 11, 3.

——— (1984b) "Local history in global context: social and economic transitions in western Guatemala." Comparative Studies in Society and History 26, 2.

——— (1983) Regional analysis in world-system perspective: a critique of three structural theories of uneven development," in Sutti Ortiz, (ed.) Economic Anthropology: Topics and Theories. New York: University Press of America.

——— (1978) "Beyond dependency theory: national and regional patterns of underdevelopment in Guatemala." American Ethnologist 5: 574-617.

THOMPSON, E.P. (1966) The Making of the English Working Class. New York: Random House.

TORRES RIVAS, E. (1971) Interpretación del Desarrollo Social Centroamericano. San José, Costa Rica: EDUCA.

VILLACORTA, M.E. (1976) Recursos Económicos de Guatemala. Guatemala: Editorial Universitaria.

WALLERSTEIN, I. (1974) The Modern World-System, Vol. 1. New York: Academic Press.

WASSERSTROM, R. (1975) "Revolution in Guatemala: peasants and politics under the Arbenz government." Comparative Studies in Society and History 17: 443-478

WILLIAMS, R. (1978) "The Central American common market: unequal benefits and uneven development." Ph.D. dissertation, Stanford University.

WOLF, E. (1966) Peasants. Englewood Cliffs, NJ: Prentice-Hall.

WOODWARD, R. (1976) Central America: A Nation Divided. New York: Oxford University Press.

World Bank (1978) Guatemala: Economic and Social Position and Prospects. Washington, DC: World Bank.

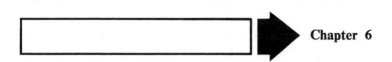

Chapter 6

CYCLES, TRENDS, OR TRANSFORMATIONS?
BLACK LABOR MIGRATION TO
THE SOUTH AFRICAN GOLD MINES

William G. Martin
State University of New York
at Binghamton

Season after season, year after year, black workers have trekked to and from the great gold mines of South Africa. As one of the most prominent and consistent features of the landscape of southern Africa, this century-long movement has been studied in great detail. Yet the shape and flow of the migratory stream has changed radically in recent years, upsetting widely shared conceptions of the processes of migration. One needs to mention but two of these changes to indicate the extent of the reversal of past patterns. Real wages that were constant for over half a century tripled in the 1970s, while the proportion of foreign labor—often over 75 percent throughout the post-World War II period—is now less than half of the labor force.

Such radical developments have had a considerable impact upon foreign migrants, their families, and their governments. For families in rural areas with a long tradition of migration, the curtailment of migrant contracts has severely reduced not just money incomes but even agricultural production, which has often depended upon resources

AUTHOR'S NOTE: This chapter has benefitted from comments by Giovanni Arrighi, Mark Beittel, and members of the Fernand Braudel Center's Research Working Group on Southern Africa and the World-Economy, and I gratefully acknowledge their assistance.

purchased with miner's wages. Unemployment has mushroomed in these rural areas because agriculture has proven unable to absorb returning migrants. At the national level, state revenues and foreign exchange associated with the migrant flow have been similarly affected.

This transformation of migration patterns has occurred in conjunction with an increasing political and military confrontation between South Africa and the independent African states surrounding the apartheid regime. Regional economic relations—highly interdependent and dominated by South Africa—have become a major arena of conflict. Migrant flows have, of course, been one of the most important networks binding the region together. The decision by the Chamber of Mines to "internalize" its supplies, in the face of the victories of liberation movements in Angola, Mozambique, and Zimbabwe (among other factors), is but one example of how decisions made in South Africa can severely affect its peripheral neighbors.

In this atmosphere the search for an understanding of migration trends has become ever more urgent. Supplier states, organized into the regional Southern Africa Development Co-ordinating Conference (SADCC), have undertaken individual country studies. International agencies such as the International Labour Office (ILO), as well as individual social scientists, have been no less active. Almost all of these studies assume that the new migration trends of the 1970's represent a secular trend—that is, the demand for foreign migrants will steadily decline from, or at best hold at, current levels. As one recent ILO study concluded,

> Compared with an average number of 450,000 African gold-miners today, of whom the proportion from outside South Africa has deliberately been pushed below 50 percent, it seems probable that by the end of the century fewer than 150,000 will be employed in the gold mines [Stahl and Bohning, 1981: 151].

And as another study concluded regarding the proportion of foreign labor over time,

> It seems unlikely that the demand for migrant African labour will return to past levels. . . . the demand will most likely continue to subside [Stahl, 1981: 42].

Such projections may well hold over the short term, say for the next five to ten years. Yet an acquaintance with historical trends in the directions and characteristics of migrant flows makes such projections over a longer period—say, ten to twenty years from now—decidedly less certain. Changes in the proportion of foreign migrants to South African workers, for example, are hardly without precedent, having occurred in the interwar period. Production and employment levels, and the predictions regarding them, have fluctuated as well. Throughout the 1920s and again in the 1960's and early 1970s, for example, both the South African government and mining officials predicted the demise of the gold mines—just prior to periods of increased profitability.

This chapter was in fact prompted by an acute awareness of the notorious inaccuracy of past attempts to project the prospects of the gold mining industry and patterns of migration. If intelligent choices for the future are to be made, it seems imperative that we begin to grasp which features of gold mining and migration have been cyclical, which secular, and which have undergone qualitative transformations and thus broken with past trends.

Current studies on gold mining and labor migration offer little guidance toward these ends, although both have been the subject of substantial literatures. Migration in southern Africa has in particular been extensively examined, as the works by Wolpe (1972), Meillasoux (1975), Burawoy (1976), and Bohning (1981) attest. Such works tell us much, for example, of how migration benefits mining capital and of how it is morally and politically undesirable. Yet we actually understand very little of how the processes that regulate migration and mining together have changed and fluctuated over time. Thus while migration's effects are almost universally condemned, the recent changes in migration patterns caught almost all concerned actors by surprise. Little guidance existed as to how the structures of migration are organized and operate over time and space.

Rather than putting the blame on haphazard research practices, it would seem that an indictment of existing paradigms is in order. This chapter shifts the ground of discussion by locating migration and mining within a world-historical perspective. This is turn focuses attention directly upon the problem of historical change by insisting on the importance of long-term cycles and trends on the one hand, and the interpenetration of social and economic processes across national boundaries on the other.

To uncover the full character and determinants of the migration/mining network is a subject fit for a major research project. My goal is necessarily much more modest. Two nodes of the migration network are examined: the mining production process, and household complexes in sending areas. Both mining production and migrant households englobe distinctive economic and social relationships; and although highly interdependent, each struggles for survival against different sets of forces. Also, it is argued, these two modes only become explicable if we grasp the world-economic character of the network itself.

GOLD MINING AS A PRODUCTION PROCESS IN THE WORLD-ECONOMY

Far from being a commodity whose output is ensured by a stable price and market, gold has undergone major fluctuations in both price and output throughout the history of the modern world-economy. A cursory glance at data on long cycles, usually based on commodity price movements (Research Working Group on Cyclical Rhythms and Secular Trends, 1979), and on gold prices and output (Vilar, 1969) would suggest that gold prices bear a generally inverse relationship to periods of "stagnation" and "expansion" of the world-economy. This in itself is hardly surprising. When gold serves formally as the international monetary equivalent, its value as expressed against major currencies could be expected to rise in periods of stagnation as world prices fall and to decline in periods of expansion as prices increase. Readjustments of an official gold price, moreover, would tend to accentuate this pattern, as international gold prices have been readjusted in periods of stagnation and hegemonic rivalry.

The response of gold production to price movements is less clear. It does however seem evident that over the long term increases in the price of gold during periods of stagnation have led to increased prospecting, and only later the development of new mines. Thus, for example, the nineteenth century discoveries in California (1848) and Australia (1851) came at the end of a long period of declining prices. In a similar manner the discovery of new fields in South Africa—as well as Alaska (1881), Colorado (1890), Mexico (1894), and the Klondike (1894)—were made late in the 1873-1896 depression and were only fully developed in the succeeding phase of expansion (Blainey, 1970).

As we move towards the more reliable data of the twentieth century there is evidence to suggest that these types of movements have been in force. As Figure 6.1 illustrates, gold production increased significantly during the late phase of interwar depression, following the upward adjustments in the international price of gold in 1925 and 1931. Production fell during the war years, only reaching prewar peaks in the mid-1960s. Whether and to what extent recent price increases will lead to a sustained rise in output remains to be seen.

The price South African producers have received for their gold in last century has closely paralleled international price movements. Marked changes in the prices of gold have tended to occur in periods of depression, with the price remaining relatively stable during expansionary phases of the world-economy. This holds true even if we take into account the specificities of South African price movements and currency devaluations. In large part this is attributable to South Africa's consistent links with both the world-economy economy and the hegemonic power in the interstate system: A high degree of participation in the world-economy has kept South Africa generally open to the influence of international price movements, while South Africa's close links with the British banking system prior to World War II, and with the U.S. hegemonic order after the war, have also kept South African financial development in step with the world monetary system.

Price movements have not, however, been directly and immediately translated into increased production levels at the South African mines. This clearly separates the South African case from most of the rest of the world's gold producers. As Figure 6.2 indicates, the most rapid increases in output were around the periods of 1880 to World War I and from 1950 to the mid-1960s. The first expansion of this phenomenon would seem to lie in the well-known, short-term tendency of producers to increase total production in periods of adverse prices in order to maximize aggregate revenue. (This strategy is rarely sustained over the long term.) In South africa this device has been structured by institutional factors at the level of both mining capital and the state. As Hirsch (1968) demonstrates, the historical level of such intervention is much greater in South Africa than for any other major Western gold producer.

Both mining capital and the state have been concerned throughout this century to maintain short term stability and long-term growth of the gold mining industry. Toward this end the welter of taxes, lease payments, tariffs, and freight charges attributable to state policies have been designed such that the state vigorously skims profits from individual mines during periods of high profitability and relaxes its demands during periods of declining profits. As Figures 6.3 and 6.4 show in different ways, government revenue from the mines has in fact increased as gold prices have risen in periods of economic stagnation in the world-economy. Underlying and complicating these practices has been the principle of "mining to the average grade."

Simply stated, "mining to the average grade" involves exploiting the average value of the ore reserve in any mine, including the *lowest* grade of ore that can be profitably treated (Hirsch, 1968: 445-446). This

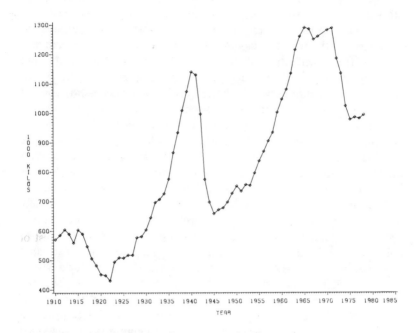

SOURCES: U.S. Federal Reserve (1943) for 1910-1927; United Nations (1948, 1955, 1959, 1967, 1971, 1979/1980) for the rest.

Figure 6.1 Global Gold Production (USSR and China excluded)

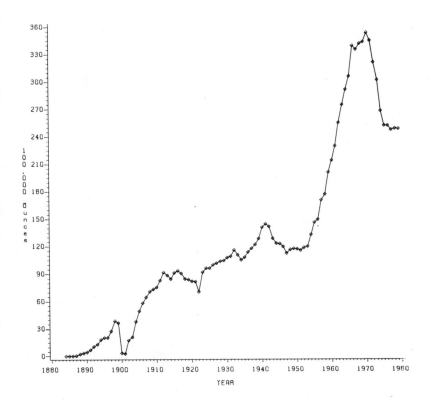

SOURCES: Frankel (1967) for 1887-1965; South Africa (1980) for the rest.

Figure 6.2 South African Gold Production

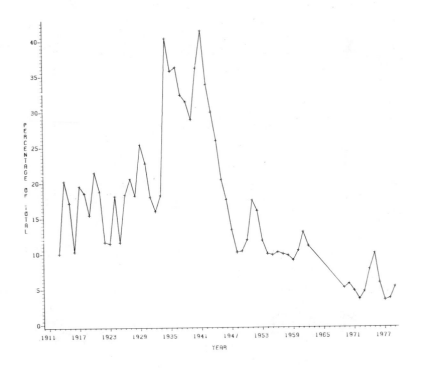

SOURCES: South Africa (1960) for 1912-1955; South Africa (1964) for 1956-63; South Africa (1980) for the rest.

Figure 6.3 Percentage of State Revenue from Mining

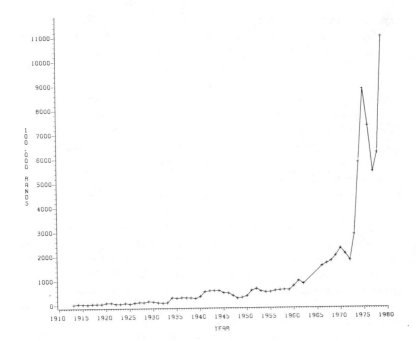

SOURCES: South Africa (1960) for 1912-55; South Africa (1964) for 1956-63; South Africa (1980) for the rest.

Figure 6.4 State Revenue from Mining

practice, enforced by law, results in lengthening the life of the mines, as the calculation of the "average grade of ore" changes as working costs and output prices fluctuate. Given the structure of tax and lease liabilities, considerable inducements exist for producers to mine lower grades of ore than would otherwise be considered most rewarding. High profit mines, for example, pay taxes considerably in excess of rates applicable to both non-mining companies and low-profit mines.

These types of intervention in the market have served to mitigate economic fluctuations in the gold mining sector, but they have have not eliminated them. Over the long run the divergence between working costs and gold prices has led to periods of intense pressure on the continued viability of the mining sector. The two most notable instances were in the late 1910s to the mid-1920s and during the post-World War II period, particularly in the mid-1960s to the early 1970s. This becomes evident if we calculate the "real" price of gold in South Africa or, more simply stated, the purchasing power of gold.

As Figure 6.5 illustrates, both periods represented the culmination of a movement of steadily increasing factor costs over and above changes in the price of gold. Even increased government subsidies and assistance, and a decrease in development work, could not offset what appeared at the time to be a secular trend in the decline of the gold mining industry. One result in both cases was that the government attempted to stimulate other sectors: In the first period a policy of import substitution was instituted to promote manufacturing for the internal market; in the second the government turned its attention to increasing manufacturing exports.

For mining capital the prospects and options were more difficult. In the first "crisis" period mining capital turned toward reducing the one cost directly under its control, namely labor power. The mining labor force in the early 1920s was composed of an army of unskilled, migrant black workers and a comparatively small artisanal and supervisory group of white workers. As has been documented by others (e.g., Johnstone, 1976), mining capital sought to reduce working costs by increasing the proportion of black to white workers and reorganizing the labor process. The result was the white workers' militant 1922 Rand Revolt, immortalized by the banner of "Workers of the World Unite and Fight for a White South Africa."

Although the Rand Revolt was bloodily repressed by mining capital and the state, the ensuing political strength of white miners was to structure the character of the labor force until the present day. At the point of production, job segregation and the ratio of black to white workers were relatively fixed. At the more important level of the state, a

SOURCES: South Africa (1960) for 1910-1959; South Africa (1964) for 1960-1963; South Africa (1980) for the rest.
NOTE: Real price = gold price index/wholesale price index.

Figure 6.5 Real Rand Gold Prices (1938 = 100)

repressive corporatist policy toward white labor was instituted after 1924, aggressively incorporating into the state apparatuses the interests and institutions of white labor. The strictly repressive policy toward black workers continued as in previous decades. The rising international price of gold, a major devaluation in the South African pound (precursor of the current rand), and falling factor costs during the 1930s also played a large role in mitigating the price pressures of the early 1920s.

By the time of the second "scissors" crisis in the mid-1960s several of the structural characteristics of mining production, as outlined above, had changed. Intensified prospecting after the 1933 rise in the international price of gold had led to the postwar development of new mines East and West of the Rand, and in the Orange Free State. The gold-bearing ore of the new mines was much richer, although it required mining to much greater depths. Yet once again factor costs mounted in relation to the gold price: Between 1936 and 1969 the retail price index rose 195 percent while the price received for gold rose only 86 percent. Under these conditions many of the older and less profitable mines faced closure. In 1963 the government began to subsidize marginal producers; by 1969, 19 of the 49 producing gold mines were receiving state assistance (Wilson, 1972: 40). Attempts by the South African state to force a rise in international price of gold in 1968 and 1969 were also defeated (Strange, 1976: 300-319). Although marginal mines produced a small proportion of total output (Hirsch, 1969: 450), they were considerable employers of labor. Reduction of the wage bill—28 percent of total revenue in 1969 (Wilson, 1972: 160)—presented one alternative to the mines, as in the early 1920s. Black wages were however already at historical minimums; the defeat of African trade unions in the late 1940s had been sustained throughout the 1950s and 1960s. Attempts to reorganize the labor process in order to extend the use of black labor did occur in the early to mid-1960s. They were nevertheless largely defeated by militant action on the part of white miners. Since then rapidly increasing prices for gold and major devaluations of the rand have once again mitigated the "price squeeze."

FLUCTUATIONS IN LEVELS AND SOURCES OF LABOR SUPPLY

A formal economic analysis of mining is of only limited assistance to the analyst of migration. One might expect that increased prices, and thus profitability, would correspond to increased production levels.

This as I have argued is not necessarily the case at any one moment: *Extraction* of ore, and thus indirectly employment levels, cannot be assumed to correlate with price levels, as producers and the state may decide to vary the "average grade" over the short term. This occurs even if we account for changes in the capital-labor ratio and productivity, both of which increased for example with the development of the new mines in the post-World War II period. (The major area open to further mechanization, stoping work—the breaking and handling of the rock face—has consistently resisted mechanization; see Spandau, 1980.)

Over the long term, however, even institutional manipulations bow to market forces. As Figure 6.6 shows, total employment figures from 1911 to 1980 reveal that employment remained roughly steady in the 1910s and 1920s, rose in the 1930s, fell during World War II, rose in the 1950s, stabilized in the 1960s, and rose again in the mid- and late 1970s. If we look at foreign black labor as a percentage of total black labor (Figure 6.7), and interesting picture emerges. From well over half the labor force in the 1910s and 1920s, foreign labor either falls below or hovers around 50 percent during the 1930s. Recovery occurs throughout the post-World War II period, with the 1906 peak of 77 percent being reached and maintained in the early 1970s. From an 80 percent high in 1973, foreign African labor falls off rapidly to well below half of the labor force after 1976. Fluctuations in foreign migrant supplies thus appear to have four distinct phases: high levels in the early twentieth century; lower levels in the late interwar period; high levels after World War II; and finally much lower levels after early 1970s.

Do the above statistical trends represent a cycle? Could, for example, new mining development and increased production levels lead over the long term to yet once again an increased demand for labor, including foreign labor? Such a formulation would only hold if the social and economic relationships that constitute the migration network could be demonstrated to correspond to such trends. To what extent is this the case?

Determination of the factors influencing migrant labor supplies requires a different set of analytical tools than those applied to mining capital. Neither the rationality behind reproduction, nor the forces determining participation in the market, are at all comparable between migrants and business enterprises. These different premises of social action direct attention toward those social institutions that encapsulate and regulate an individual's participation in the migratory stream, and reproduce such participation over general life spans. This institution is the "household." By utilizing the concept of the household we are able

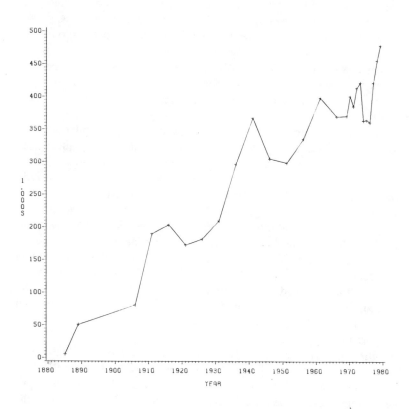

SOURCE: C. W. Stahl (1982).

Figure 6.6 Total Black Employment on the Gold Mines

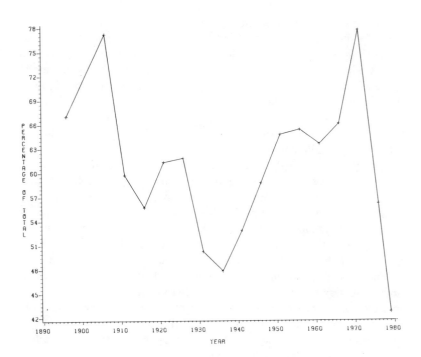

SOURCES: Wilson (1972) for 1896; Stahl (1981) for the rest.

Figure 6.7 Foreign Labor Supply to South African Chamber of Mines

to locate the specific social conditions and processes that demarcate migrant labor from other forms of labor market participation.

The introduction of the concept of the household to the study of the development of South Africa's labor force and migration is particularly illuminating. Behind this century-long movement of men from rural areas to the mines stood the development of a particular household structure—one set apart from those supplying and reproducing labor to other peripheral production processes in the region (such as commercial white agriculture or independent black cash-crop production). Each of these household types emerged with South Africa's incorporation into the world-economy and the destruction of precapitalist modes of production. And each was marked by a specific matrix of productive activities, the allocation of tasks by age and gender, and gender hierarchy. I have delineated the historical development of these contradictory labor force/household structures at greater length elsewhere (Martin, forthcoming). For our purposes here, what is important to stress is that the development of the migrant labor force corresponded to the emergence of a particular kind of household structure in the countryside. Mining was as dependent on its links to this household as members of the household were dependent upon income from mining.

The most obvious characteristic of the labor-exporting or migrant household was of course the absence of adult males. This entailed far more, however, than simply the export of "surplus" labor. Household production on the land typically rested on a transition to labor-saving crops (as in cassava in southern Mozambique and a maize monoculture in parts of South Africa), the increasing importance of female and child labor, and the organization of gender and age hierarchies in order to coalesce and to reproduce specific household relationships. The pooling of resources from the participation of household members in both agriculture and mining was necessary to sustain and reproduce such households; often even the supply and replacement of agricultural implements and cattle came through migrant earnings.

Until the mid-1970s the mining labor force predominantly came from areas where the conditions supporting such a labor-exporting household existed, however tenuously. The rise and decline of the South African percentage of the mining labor force during the interwar and post-World War II period indicates this most clearly. By the interwar period production for self-use or for the market in the Reserve areas of South Africa already was below levels necessary for the reproduction of the residents of these areas.[1] With the arrival of the difficult years between the wars these areas were especially susceptible to intensified recruitment drives on the part of mining capital. By the post-World

War II period production for self-use had fallen off dramatically as overcrowding on the land increased and more profitable employment opportunities developed in urban areas. The development of a wage labor force for core industrial production processes in South Africa was especially crucial: Wage disparities between the mining sector and the manufacturing sector widened rapidly. While black mining wage rates were 85 percent of manufacturing wage rates in 1936, by 1971 black miners received but 33 percent of black wage rates in manufacturing.[2] During the post-World War II boom black labor would increasingly displace white workers in industrial production processes, especially as the labor process was reorganized.

One of the results of these developments within South Africa was that the mines increased their recruiting efforts outside South Africa as their operations expanded after World War II. Households in these areas were still able to combine resources from agricultural production with migrant remittances. Thus although the geographical sources of labor shifted over the whole time period under examination here, the type of household structure that supplied "cheap labor" remained quite similar.

Much of this changed in the mid-1970s. A return to a high proportion of South African miners in the last ten years has represented a qualitative transformation in the social basis of the labor force. The increasing proportion of South African miners came from households quite unlike those that had earlier been sustained, and structured by, the combination of money wages and rural subsistence. Crucial to the mines' efforts to move in this direction was an explicit recognition that higher wages were necessary to attract *South African* labor—thus the historic rise in wage rates during the 1970s, with black mining wages reaching 70 percent of manufacturing wages in 1978 (see note 2). Increasing unemployment in other sectors of the South African economy also assisted the mines in their recruiting campaign. Thus while mining wages have always been higher than those offered in contiguous countries, the more recent expansion of the South African proportion of the labor force rests upon wage structures necessary to provide a substantial proportion of the expenditures of a black household that lacks any significant input from agricultural production even when resident in rural areas. Simply stated, to attract black South African labor in the 1970s forced the mines to raise black wage rates.

REPRISE: CYCLICAL, SECULAR, OR TRANSFORMATIONAL CHANGES?

This chapter opened by questioning current predictions of declining prospects in the gold mining sector of South Africa, especially those predictions concerned with employment and foreign migrant labor. It was proposed that an historical analysis, within a world-historical framework, was necessary to understand the past, present, and future trajectories of gold mining and migrant labor. It should be evident by this point that it is not difficult to construct a prima facie case against the argument of a demise of the gold mines and their demand for labor. No secular trend of declining profitability or production is evident if one closely examines the long-term operations of the mines. In a similar vein it is easy to challenge claims that employment, and the foreign migrant component of it, necessarily face a long decline. Can we not however proceed beyond simply ruling out current predictions?

An answer to this question requires the amplification and reorganization of above discussions. I will accordingly treat this query by briefly examining two sets of relationships: (1) the relationship between mining capital and the forces of the world-economy, and (2) the relationship between capital and labor. Both are considerably shaped by political factors.

For the mining sector, much depends on price and production movements on both the input and output sides. As shown above, these elements exhibit both cyclical and secular characteristics. If we assume that the floating price of gold internationally has approached its value vis-à-vis other commodities, and that further major devaluations of the rand are unlikely, then the potential revenue expected from mining operations should not vary substantially in the near future—at least not to the extent of the big upward movements of the 1970s and early 1980s. Here again it is assumed that the major price adjustments characteristic of periods of global stagnation and breaks in hegemonic orders have run their course (Arrighi, 1982). We should not forget of course the substantial transformation of the gold price in the last ten years.

Set against these prospects are increasing difficulties with factor costs. Unlike previous stagnation phases, the present period of depression has not seen major deflationary movements in cost of the mines' inputs—a fact largely attributable to the oligopolistic organization of the world market under the post-World War II free enterprise system. This factor alone, even disregarding the emergence of a long-term period of expansion and its attendant price inflation, suggests that the divergence between working costs and revenue returns may close more quickly than in previous periods. No longer would the gold price adjustments of a phase of depression be matched by decreased factor costs. If an upturn and increased inflation were to occur simultaneously a "cost squeeze" of serious dimensions could well emerge, even beyond that which could be solved by increasing the average grade of the ore mined.

It is against this background of structural economic trends that employment and migration must be placed, and the question of the relationship between labor and capital over the long term must be analyzed. There is little doubt that mining capital, especially those producers operating the richest and newest mines such as Anglo-American, would prefer to stabilize skill levels and workplace unrest by offering wages comparable to those in other sectors of the South African economy. Faced with intractable cost pressures, however, the mines could be expected to attempt to reduce working costs. As in previous periods the costs most directly under mining capital's control remain those associated with the purchase of labor-power.

There are two main tactics by which reductions in the cost of labor-power could be attempted. The first tactic would be to reorganize the labor process in order to eliminate the job reservation system that allocates a fixed proportion of positions and skills to white miners. Previous attempts to proceed along these lines have not been very successful as has been noted above: A Pyrrhic victory was achieved in the early 1920s, while white miners successfully resisted such tactics in the mid-1960s.

The conditions that underpinned white miners' strength in these previous encounters with mining capital have however been qualitatively transformed. First of all, white labor's workplace bargaining power has declined precipitously, as black miners have increasingly become responsible for most of the tasks associated directly with the actual mining process. Second, the political and marketplace bargaining power of white workers and their unions has also declined. No longer do white workers organized into craft unions represent an important social basis of the regime, as is evident in the ruling party's willingness to accept capital's opening up of skilled positions and union representation to black workers. Should confrontation between capital and white labor occur, it is reasonably clear that the state cannot be expected to automatically intervene on the side of white labor.

The second avenue open to mining capital in reducing labor costs would be to hold down or even reduce real black wages. To some extent this is already occuring, as the price of gold has not risen as sharply in the last several years as it did in the late 1970s, limiting the rate of increase of black wages. The changed household structure underpinning a good segment of black South African participation in the mining labor force presents however several countervailing factors. Most, if not all, of black miners' households no longer have any appreciable resources to mix with returns from mining, or to fall back upon in difficult times. This represents a significant alteration in the nature of the class confronting mining capital. Thus as migrants have increasingly become dependent upon returns from mining, the capital-labor relation has become increasingly polarized. This has had concomitant ideological and cultural implications, many of which have strengthened the cohesion and militancy of black labor. All of these factors, when added to black miners' increased workplace bargaining power, severely restrict a turn by capital to an attack on the wage front. Nowhere was this more evident than in the compound rebellions of the last ten years, which have led to the recognition of black trade unions. The latter reflects the broader strategy of industrial capital, and less directly of the state, of moving from a strictly repressive policy toward black labor to a repressive *corporatist* policy, whereby black trade unions would be recognized in return for their integration with the labor-regulating institutions of the state.

The existence of powerful black trade unions in a period of cost pressures would have the effect of providing the mines with stronger incentives for returning to the use of foreign migrant labor. Such a labor supply could, as we have seen, potentially be obtained at significantly lower costs due to the different household structures involved. The political advantage of once again segmenting the mining labor force from the South African labor market would also be considerable due to foreign workers' geographical and political distance from the South African polity. An increasingly foreign labor force would be far less secure in its trade union and political rights than one composed of black South Africans.

Which strategy mining capital might pursue is still open to debate, although it would appear that the reorganization of the labor process is far more likely to be rigorously developed than is a serious attack on black wages. Mining capital is undoubtedly aware that the latter course would be immediately translated into a very intense level of class conflict. It is entirely possible that mining capital—hitherto treated as one monopolistic bloc—may split apart over which strategy to pursue, or whether to follow both. Mining groups working low-grade mines, especially those without strong ties to industrial capital, may well decide to choose the low-wage option, employing greater quantities of rural and foreign labor. This would put them at direct odds with the developing tactics of groups such as Anglo-American, which not only exploit newer, higher grade mines (and are thus less susceptible overall to price pressures), but also run vast industrial enterprises whose labor/capital relations are increasingly based along "corporatist" lines. It is not too difficult to perceive a definitive splintering apart of the indomitable Transvaal Chamber of Mines over these issues.

A central objection to the above trends and scenarios must be recognized. It is often noted that the increasing unemployment level in South Africa would mitigate against such a move toward the use of foreign labor. This argument however seems open to question. There is no direct connection between unemployment in general and the mines' options in moving toward foreign sources of labor. The state would have to intervene politically in the labor market to direct mining capital's recruitment efforts. Yet in a period where the mines' existence or even profits were threatened, the state would be at least as equally concerned with retaining the tax and foreign exchange earnings that flow forth from mining production.

It has so far been possible to rule out many future possibilities on the basis of the evaluation of past and present trends. The task of estimating the likelihood of any of the remaining scenarios rests upon judging the long-term cyclical movements associated with gold mining as a production process in the world-economy, the impact of the structural transformations of the labor force, and contemporary political considerations. I am not so confident or foolish as to make detailed predictions of the future course of events. Which of the remaining courses will be pursued remains a subject of debate, and a subject of controversy among the classes concerned.

There remains one final question that should be noted given the situation in southern Africa today: What might the above mean for the regional political situation? If an increased demand for foreign labor were to arise, it would clearly enhance the bargaining power of the supplier countries vis-à-vis mining capital. Schemes such as those constructed by the ILO to wrest concessions from the mines would have increased chances of success. An even more intriguing question over the long run would be, What policies could we expect under a majority rule government in South Africa? It is evident that many of the strictly economic factors affecting mining production, such as those emanating from the mines' integration into the world-economy, would remain the same. How these would be handled under a radically altered relationship between labor, capital, and the state remains a subject for only the most bold speculations.

NOTES

1. The exact dating of the decline of agricultural production in the Reserves remains a matter of some debate. See Simkins (1981).
2. Calculated from figures in C. W. Stahl (1981: 23). Wage data for South Africa are by and large not very reliable.

REFERENCES

ARRIGHI, G. (1982) "A crisis of hegemony," in S. Amin et al. (eds.) Dynamics of Global Crisis. New York: Monthly Review Press.
BLAINEY, G. (1970) "A theory of mineral discovery: Australia in the nineteenth century," Economics History Review 23, 2: 293-313.
BOHNING, R. W. ed. (1981) Black Migration to South Africa. Geneva: International Labour Office.
BURAWOY, M. (1976) "The functions and reproduction of migrant labor: comparative material from South Africa and the United States," American Journal of Sociology 81, 5: 1050-1087.
FRANKEL, S. H. (1967) Investment and the Return to Equity Capital in the South African Gold Mines, 1887-1965. Cambridge, MA: Harvard University Press.
HIRSCH, F. (1968) "Influences on gold production," IMF Staff Papers 25, 3: 405-490.
JOHNSTONE, F. (1976) Race, Class and Gold. London: Routledge & Kegan Paul.
MARTIN, W. G. (forthcoming) "Beyond the peasant to proletarian debate: an outline of African household formation in South Africa during the long twentieth century," in Joan Smith et al. (eds.) Households and the World-Economy. Beverly Hills: Sage.
MEILLASSOUX, C. (1975) Femmes, greniers et capitaux. Paris: Maspero.
Research Working Group on Cyclical Rhythms and Secular Trends (1979) "Cyclical rhythms and secular trends of the capitalist world-economy: some premises, hypotheses and questions," Review 2, 4: 483-500.
SIMKINS, C. (1981) "Agricultural production in the African reserves of South Africa, 1918-1969," Journal of Southern African Studies 7, 2: 256-283.
South Africa (1980) South African Statistics 1980. Pretoria: Government Printer.
———(1964) Statistical Yearbook 1964. Pretoria: Government Printer.
———(1960) Union Statistics for Fifty Years. Pretoria: Government Printer.
SPANDAU, A. (1980) "Mechanization and labour policies on South African mines," South African Journal of Economics 48, 2: 167-180.
STAHL, C. W. (1981) "Migrant labour supplies, past, present and future; with special reference to the gold mining industry," pp. 7-44 in W. R. Bohning (ed.) Black Migration to South Africa. Geneva: International Labor Office.
———and R. W. BOHNING (1981) "Reducing dependence on migration in southern Africa," pp. 113-178 in R. W. Bohning (ed.) Black Migration to South Africa. Geneva: International Labour Office.
STRANGE, S. (1976) "South Africa against the Oligarchy," pp. 300-319 in A. Shonfield (ed.) International Economic Relations of the Western World 1959-1971: Vol. 2, International Monetary Relations. London: Oxford University Press.
United Nations (various) Statistical Yearbook. New York: United Nations.
VILAR, P. (1969) A History of Gold and Money, 1450-1920. London: New Left Books.

WILSON, F. (1976) Labour in the South African Gold Mines 1911-1969. London: Cambridge University Press.

WOLPE, H. (1972) "Capitalism and cheap labour-power in South Africa: from segregation to apartheid," Economy and Society 1, 4: 425-456.

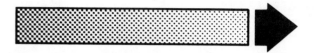

PART 3

WORKING CLASS CULTURE, ORGANIZATION, AND PROTEST

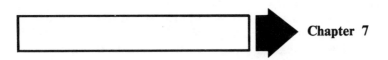

Chapter 7

LABOR MOVEMENTS AND CAPITAL MIGRATION:
THE UNITED STATES AND WESTERN EUROPE IN WORLD-HISTORICAL PERSPECTIVE

Giovanni Arrighi
Beverly J. Silver
State University of New York, Binghamton

It is our thesis that the U.S. labor movement in the 1930s and 1940s has "shown the future" to the European labor movement of the late 1960s and 1970s; and that the structural link between the two movements is the transnational expansion of U.S. capital in the post-World War II period.

Our argument is divided into four parts. In the first part, "Divergent Patterns of the Interwar Labor Movement," after a brief comparative survey of the vitality and effectiveness of the labor movements in the United States and Europe in the interwar years, we conclude that the labor movement in the United States at the time showed both an unprecedented and largely unparalleled strength. In "The Rise of Workplace Bargaining Power" we develop a dual hypothesis to explain the main source of this strength; that is, the relatively more advanced stage of two processes in the United States that strengthened labor's

AUTHORS' NOTE: In revising this chapter we have benefited greatly from discussions (individually and collectively) with members of the World Labor Research Working Group at the Fernand Braudel Center, SUNY at Binghamton, and from the comments and criticisms of P. Anderson, T. Hopkins, P. Katzenstein, P. Lange, W. Martin, and S. Tarrow.

bargaining power vis-à-vis capital. These are, very briefly, first, the development of "labor's workplace bargaining power" arising from capitalist transformations in industrial organization and labor process that increase capital's vulnerability to workers' direct action at the point of production. The second process, partly related to the first, is the relative exhaustion of reserves of partially proletarianized or nonproletarianized labor available for mobilization, either to increase competition in the ranks of labor or to form part of antilabor political coalitions.

In "The Containment of Workplace Bargaining Power," the third part, we trace how this strength of U.S. labor has been contained (although not rolled back) in the postwar period as the result of the institutionalization of new forms of labor control, on the one hand, and the transnational expansion of U.S. capital, on the other hand. Finally, we show how the experience of the labor movement in postwar Europe has been analogous to the trajectory of the U.S. labor movement from the 1920s through the 1950s in the section on "Convergent Patterns of the Postwar Labor Movement." The structural link between the two periods and movements is the transnational expansion of U.S. capital that has speeded and facilitated the transformations in industrial organization and labor process in postwar Europe that underlay the emergence of labor's structural strength in the United States in the interwar period. Thus, while on one side of the coin we find the containment of the postwar labor movement in the United States, on the other side is the more than compensatory strengthening of the movement in Europe.

DIVERGENT PATTERNS OF THE INTERWAR LABOR MOVEMENT

One of the most significant phenomena of the interwar years was the unprecedented vitality and effectiveness revealed by the U.S. labor movement in the mass production industries during the 1936-1937 strike wave. Unlike previous experiences of strike waves during periods of mass unemployment, and unlike what was happening elsewhere at the time, workers' direct action at the point of production wrested significant and long-lasting concessions from employers and the state.

One of the first of such actions to be successful began at a Firestone tire plant in Akron, Ohio, on January 29, 1936. A small group of workers secretly planned a sit-down strike to protest the imposition of industrywide layoffs and the extension of the workday. Within 10 days, sit-down strikes spread to Goodrich and Goodyear, and the industry was forced to concede to workers' demands (Green, 1980: 153).

The most dramatic sit-down strike began when workers occupied General Motors' Fisher Body Plants No. 1 and and No. 2 in Flint, Michigan, on December 30, 1936. The outcome of this struggle had an electrifying impact on the labor movement as the newly organized UAW-CIO triumphed over the nation's largest industrial corporation, whose vast financial resources and "colossal supersystem of spies" had previously succeeded in keeping GM an open-shop sanctuary (Dubofsky and Van Tine, 1977: 256, quoting the LaFollette Report).

When General Motors was forced to capitulate and signed a contract with the UAW on March 12, 1937, the wave of sit-downs turned into a flood. In March 1937, "167,210 people engaged in 170 occupations of their employers' property. Within a year, 400,000 workers engaged in a total of 477 sitdown strikes" (Green, 1980: 157). And if we include conventional strikes, the total number of strikers increased from 2.1 million in 1936 to 4.7 million in 1937 (Green, 1980: 158).

This flood of strikes resulted in a significant number of victories for labor. According to Fine (1969: 332) "substantial gains" were achieved in over 50 percent of the 1937 sit-downs, and compromises worked out in another 30 percent. In the face of this militancy and apparent labor strength, U.S. Steel gave up without a fight and agreed to bargain with the Steel Workers Organizing Committee (SWOC) rather than risk a long-term strike at a time when the international demand for steel was finally rising (Green, 1980: 159).

In no other major capitalist country at this time did the labor movement show a similar vitality and effectiveness. The 1920s and early 1930s had been a period of retreat and eventual defeat of organized labor everywhere. In summing up a worldwide survey of labor movements (including those in the United States) in the interwar years, Demarco et al. (1966: 3) observe that "lorsque la grande dépression économique . . . commence a se manifester, la période pendant laquelle, aprés la première guerre mondiale, la puissance des organizations ouvières a atteint son point culminant, est déjà assez éloignée."

In France the defeat had been immediate: The disastrous general strike of 1920 led to a CGT membership decline from 2 million to 1 million in a single year and to ideological and organizational divisions that left labor powerless in the face of French employers' intransigence and refusal to recognize the legitimacy of unions. In Italy, the strike wave of 1919-1920 (the so-called Biennio Rosso) obtained concessions unprecedented in any capitalist country: the eight-hour day with greatly increased wages: cost of living allowances; unemployment insurance and paid holidays; and factory committees of elected workers with technical and financial control over production. However, these gains were short-lived: Two years later, when Mussolini became Prime Minister, membership in the Confederation of Labor had fallen from 2.2 million to 400,000; and, by 1924, the organization ceased to exist and was replaced by government controlled syndicates that lasted until the overthrow of Fascism twenty years later.

In Germany, union membership and strike activity began to decline rapidly after 1924. The fading of the movement, however, did not lead to an immediate collapse of the political power of the unions and the SPD. Between the end of the hyperinflation of 1923 and the onset of the depression in 1929, they managed to enact into law an advanced social welfare system and to establish a comprehensive framework for collective bargaining. The SPD was actually in government at the time of the world crash of 1929. Unemployment, which had already been high since 1923 (fluctuating around 10 percent), shot up from 9.3 percent in 1929 to 15.3 percent in 1930 and to 30.1 percent in 1932. The SPD proved totally unable to cope with the situation, lacking the power and the determination either to pursue antideflationary policies or to revive the labor movement to meet the growing National Socialist threat. Strike activity fell to its lowest point since World War I, while the labor vote increasingly shifted toward the KPD, thereby deepening the divisions within organized labor. When the Nazis came to power in 1933, the dissolution of workers' organizations met with practically no resistance. As Galenson (1976: 152-153) remarks, "What many had believed to be the most solidly built labor movement in the world simply ceased to exist."

In Britain, the decline of the organized power of labor followed a far less dramatic but in some ways analogous pattern. The intense strike wave of 1919-1920 ended with the liquidation of the triple alliance of business, trade union leaders, and government that, during the war, had attempted to produce consensual policies in order to keep inflation under control and to allow maximum production of armaments. Thereafter, unemployment rose sharply (from approximately 2-3 percent in 1919-1920 to about 15 percent in 1921-1922, and then remaining at 10 percent from 1923-1929), union membership declined (from over 6 million in 1919-1920 to 4.3 million in 1922-1923, and to 3.7 million in 1928-1929), while strike activity fell drastically. The defeat of labor was comprehensive and was confirmed by the result of the General Strike of 1926. Yet, as in Germany, the extent of the labor movement's defeat in Britain was partly obscured by the continuing electoral strength of its parliamentary arm, the Labour Party, which formed short-lived minority governments in 1924 and again in 1929. In Britain too, therefore, a working class party was in government at the time of the world economic crash. The impact was less severe than in Germany, but the inability of the Labour Party to cope with the new situation was as great as that of the German SPD. Antideflationary policies were not pursued, and the movement was not revived. Instead, the Labour Party leadership split, strike activity fell to the lowest postwar levels, and electoral protest turned against the Labour Party in favor of the Conservatives. Unlike the German SPD, however, the Labour Party refused to join in responsibility for the wage cuts and the decrease in unemployment pay, but fought against them both, thereby preserving the unity of organized labor notwithstanding the leadership split (Abendroth, 1972: 96-97).

The trajectory of the U.S. labor movement in the 1920s was not too dissimilar from that of the European labor movement. The defeat of the 1919 strike wave had been accompanied by the definitive disappearance of what little had been so far generated in terms of working class political organization: the Socialist Party and the IWW, a small but powerful syndicalist organization. As in Britain, the defeat ended with the final liquidation of the tripartite arrangements between business, union leaders, and government set up during the war to regulate labor-capital relations. Thereafter, corporations succeeded in rolling back trade unionism through a combination of repressive and cooptive measures called welfare capitalism. While ruthlessly repressing strikes and labor organizations (with the assistance of federal, state, and local governments and the courts), the large corporations offered their workers rising real wages (albeit at a rate much lower than productivity increases), company unions and limited schemes of union-management cooperation, consumer credit, fringe benefits, pension funds, profit-sharing schemes, and various other enticements designed to buy labor loyalty and industrial peace.

While the material benefits of welfare capitalism were limited to workers in the oligopolized sectors of the economy, the spread of welfare capitalism's ideology was more pervasive: The existence of a harmony of interests between labor and capital was proclaimed. Independent labor organizations were deemed unnecessary as each business would take paternalistic responsibility for the welfare of its own workers.

The success of this strategy in rolling back labor militancy and organization was evidenced by the rapid decline of strike activity and union membership in the 1920s. However, the ability of welfare capitalists to buy labor peace depended on the prosperity of their industry. Thus, within a couple of years after the crash, welfare capitalism was completely abandoned. In October 1931 Ford abandoned the seven-dollar day, and by November 1932 the minimum was driven down to four dollars. By 1932 business had ceased to talk about caring for its own and had begun to call for federal relief. As the material benefits of welfare capitalism withered then disappeared, the system of labor control in corporate industry broke down.

Initially, the response of U.S. labor to widespread unemployment was similar to that of European labor: a further decline in strike activity and union membership, on the one hand, and an electoral shift, on the other. Soon after, however, the response began to differ sharply. The electoral shift toward the Democratic Party in 1932 was followed by the strike wave of 1933-1934, which led to virtual civil wars in Toledo, Minneapolis, and San Francisco. Capital won this first round of struggles, which by and large did not involve the most advanced mass production industries. However, by 1936-1937 labor was once again on the offensive, leading to the victories outlined at the beginning of this chapter.

The vitality and effectiveness of the U.S. labor movement of the 1930s had virtually no parallel in Europe with the only significant exception of Sweden. As we have seen, the Italian and German movements succumbed to Fascist repression and did not reemerge until the end of World War II. The British movement preserved its unity and organizational strength but remained passive and largely powerless throughout the 1930s. At first sight, the French labor movement provides a close parallel to the U.S. experience. The experiences of labor in the two countries during the 1920s seem similar: early defeat of the postwar strike wave, rollback of unionization, and industrial peace in a context of relative full employment and improving living conditions for industrial wage workers. The responses to the world economic crisis of the 1930s, whose effects were felt in France with some delay, also seem similar. The electoral successes of FDR in 1932 and 1936 were matched by the electoral successes of the SFIO in 1932 and the victory of the Popular Front in 1936. In addition, although no French strike wave matched the American wave of 1933-1934, the victory of the Popular Front in May 1936 brought in its wake a major upsurge of workers' militancy.

Five days after the election a strike wave began, and within a month or so as many as one million workers were on strike demanding union recognition, wage increases, and improved working conditions. Three-quarters of the strikes involved sit-ins where workers refused to work or leave the plant until their demands were met. Incredibly rapid negotiations summoned by Prime Minister Blum led to the Matignon agreement, which granted an average increase in wages of 12 percent, promised the right to organize and protection of union members against victimization, and set the principle of "immediate conclusion" of collective bargaining agreements. In line with these undertakings, the Blum government rushed through the Chamber a new labor legislation that established the 40-hour week, guaranteed paid holidays for the first time in French history, specified in detail matters to be covered by collective agreements and defined arrangements for employee representation at the workplace (Kendall, 1975: 43-44).

"All in all," Kendall (1975: 44) concludes, "the social legislation of the Popular Front represented a major milestone in French history, only to be compared with that of the British Labour Government in 1945-51 or the Roosevelt New Deal in the USA." The analogies with the New Deal are undoubtedly considerable. In both instances, a government elected with the decisive contribution of the labor vote was induced by an outbreak of labor militancy in the midst of a depression to enact social and industrial legislation highly favorable to labor. Even the effect on unionization was similar, as the tremendous upsurge in American labor unionization after Roosevelt's 1936 reelection was matched by an increase in French union membership from 700,000 in 1934 to over 5 million in 1937, most of the increase having occurred between May and December 1936.

Yet, the differences between the two movements and their outcomes is even more striking. In the first place, the French explosion of conflict was more directly linked to political events and tendencies than was the American upsurge. Important elements of the rank and file saw factory occupation as a springboard of socialist revolution in France, and the PCF (which had played no role in bringing about the explosion) played a key role in bringing it to an end in order not to compromise the possibility of Franco-Soviet rapprochement (Kendall, 1975: 44). In the second place, and partly related to this first characteristic, the French wave of social and industrial conflict as well as its effects were very short-lived. The American upsurge of the 1930s started off a sequence of moves and countermoves: The first FDR victory and the 1933-1934 strike wave, then the Wagner Act, a second FDR electoral victory and the 1936-1937 strike wave, consolidation of union power and union cooperation with government and business, renewed workers' militancy during the war, and so on. These constituted stages in a long drawn out process, which as we shall see was to transform completely labor-capital relations in the United States. By contrast, within six months of its beginning, the French movement had collapsed and the hardening of attitudes on the part of employers met with no resistance whatsoever: Inside the plants, union organization was quickly undermined and management prerogatives reestablished; outside the plants, a reinvigorated employers' organization effectively sabotaged union endeavors to set up a national network of collective bargaining agreements. Within a year, the Popular Front government had gone out of office; within two years, the wage boost that followed Matignon had been completely wiped out by rising prices; within three years, CGT membership had fallen to around a quarter of the 5 million claimed for 1936, and by 1940 the CGT claimed only 800,000 members (Kendall, 1975: 45-8). By then France was at war and, as Kendall (1975: 48) remarks

> [the] draconian measures taken by the government against its political opponents . . . the serf-like regulations with which it surrounded workers in the war production industries, did much to undermine the will to resist. Long before the Vichy regime assumed power, fascism was being prepared in the guise of resistance to Hitler.

Once we recognize these other aspects of the Popular Front episode, we soon realize that the strongest analogies are not with the American New Deal experience but rather with the Italian experience of the Biennio Rosso. In both instances we have an intense movement of strikes and factory occupations, spontaneous in its form of organization but highly politicized in its objectives, which obtained remarkable successes in a very short time but collapsed immediately afterwards, losing all that it had won in an equally short time. French workers' militancy under the Popular Front has therefore to be considered an "Indian summer" of the political confrontation between labor and capital that characterized the immediate post-World War I years, rather than an unprecedented show of strength *in a period of economic depression* which, in our view, is what the U.S. labor movement of the 1930s was.

From this point of view the labor movement in Sweden is the only one in Europe to show long-term strength in the interwar period. This experience was exceptional in two related ways. In the first place, it was the only movement of those examined here not to be defeated in the 1920s. During the decade, unionization continued to increase, the electoral strength of the SPD fluctuated but remained considerable, and strike activity declined after 1923 but remained relatively high (Korpi, 1980: chap. 3; Sjoberg, 1966). In the second place, it was the only labor movement that in the 1930s (besides responding to unemployment with a combination of electoral protest and increased strike activity as the

U.S. and French labor movements did) produced a working class party with enough power and determination to pursue a viable policy of full employment and national recovery.

THE RISE OF WORKPLACE BARGAINING POWER

Summing up this quick survey of labor movements in various national contexts in the interwar years, we may say that if we were to order them in terms of their *long-term* vitality and effectiveness, the movements in the United States and Sweden would come out on top of the list (albeit for different reasons), the movements in continental Europe at the bottom, and the movement in Britain somewhere in between. This "ranking" is broadly consistent with the relationship of forces between labor and capital in the different national locales as can be gauged from trends in wages and productivity.

Using data provided in Phelps, Brown, and Browne (1968: 436-452) and leaving aside France and Italy for which no comparable data are given, we have calculated that in the period 1913-1938 as a whole labor productivity (as measured by real income per occupied person) grew roughly at the same rate in the United States, the United Kingdom, and Germany—that is, at an average (compounded) annual rate of 0.9 percent, 0.9 percent, and 1.0 percent respectively. In contrast, real wages (as measured by average annual wage earnings in real terms) grew at average (compounded) annual rates of 1.7 percent in the United States, of 1.1 percent in the United Kingdom, and of 0.9 percent in Germany. As for Sweden, its rate of growth of real wages (1.6 percent) was almost as high as that in the United States, but its rate of growth of productivity (1.2 percent) was higher than in the other three countries. If we take the period 1934-1948—the period of establishment and consolidation of a social-democratic regime in Sweden and of sustained industrial strife in the United States—we still find trends more favorable to labor in the United States than in Sweden: While productivity grew faster in the United States (3.0 percent) than in Sweden (2.7 percent), real wages continued to grow faster than productivity in the United States (3.4 percent) but slightly slower than productivity in Sweden (2.4 percent).

We may conclude therefore that the United States and Sweden were the two main exceptions to the general rule of decline and eventual powerlessness of labor movements in the course of the interwar depression; and that, if the movement in Sweden was most successful in attaining and consolidating political (i.e., state) power, the movement in the United States was the most successful in counteracting the tendency toward intensified capitalist exploitation. The question now arises as to how we can account for the strength of the U.S. labor movement—a strength that was without precedent in a period of mass unemployment and largely without parallel at the time.

To begin with, it should be obvious from our survey that this strength cannot be traced to superior organization or ideological mobilization. The more ideologically oriented movements were (such as the movements in continental Europe), the weaker they turned out to be in the end, notwithstanding their successes in the short run. Moreover, of the three movements with strong union organization, one (the German) was totally destroyed, one (the British) was moderately successful in preserving its organizational strength but little else, and only one (the Swedish) was able to further strengthen its position. In any event, from both points of view, the labor movement in the United States had traditionally lagged behind the labor movement in Europe, and trends in the 1920s had further reduced (both absolutely and relatively) its organizational and ideological strength.

Nor can the vitality and effectiveness of the labor movement in the United States and Sweden simply be traced to "favorable" political conjunctures created by the disarray in which ruling elites and dominant classes were thrown by the deepening worldwide depression. The labor movement in all the countries examined in this chapter, except Italy, faced "favorable" political conjunctures at one point or another during the Great Depression: in Germany and the United Kingdom in 1929-1930; in France in 1936-1937; in Sweden throughout the decade. Yet, only in Sweden and the United States did the labor movement show any capacity to sustain and take advantage of such conjunctures. Elsewhere the labor movement was thrown by the deepening depression, or by its own contradictions, into an even greater disarray than the dominant classes.

Furthermore, favorable political conjunctures are often symptoms of the existence of a strong labor movement as much as they are preconditions for the emergence of the latter. In the case of Sweden, the favorable political conjuncture can at least in part be accounted for by the strategies and values of the movement's institutional leadership. The remarkable ideological cohesion of union and party leaders and their close organic relationship with industrial workers through powerful industrial rather than craft unions, which had characterized the labor movement in Sweden since the beginning of the century, put the Social Democratic party in a particularly strong position in dealing with a weak and divided bourgeois political front in the course of the interwar crisis. Also, the innovative strategies and policies pursued in the crisis itself ("precocious Keynesianism" and political alliance with organized independent farmers) were undoubtedly crucial in the establishment of organized labor's national hegemony and in the further isolation of bourgeois political forces (cf. Buci-Glucksmann and Therborn, 1981).

Even in the case of the United States, where the labor movement was almost completely acephalous, it is more useful to see the New Deal labor policies as a response to the intensity and character of the labor movement itself rather than the other way around. The Wagner Act was in large part a response to the disruption caused by the 1933-1934 strike wave. Given the strength of labor at the point of production and the impotence of capital in the face of the economic crisis (and the consequent decline of business prestige), unionization appeared to be an eventual certainty. The question remaining was not whether it would happen, but rather was how much disruption of the national economy the battle would entail and whether the instability of industrial relations would jeopardize all efforts aimed at economic recovery. Thus when the House Committee considering the Wagner Act came out in strong support of the bill, it emphasized "the intent . . . to promote industrial peace" (Millis and Brown, 1950: 28). According to Brody (1980: 144), "[the] new direction of labor legislation actually reflected a massive shift in American opinion. The most that can be said for the New Deal administration was that it followed in the wake of this change."

If Sweden illustrates the importance of innovative and nonsectarian leadership in determining the outcome of labor-capital conflicts in a given national context, the United States illustrates the historical possibility of a strong labor movement developing and effectively impinging upon the political context even in the absence of ideological commitments and centralized political direction. The question still remains as to what the source of the strength of this movement was, if it cannot be traced to ideology and organization or indeed (since we are dealing with a movement unfolding in a period of supernormal unemployment) to market power.

It is our hypothesis that the main source of strength of the industrial workers in the mass production industries that spearheaded the movement in the United States since the middle 1930s was what we shall call labor's workplace bargaining power—the bargaining power of workers when they are expending their labor-power within the course of the capitalist labor process. In general terms, the very transformations in industrial organization and labor process (typically, growing technical division of labor and mechanization) that undermine the marketplace bargaining power of labor (as embodied, for example, in the skills of the craft-workers) simultaneously enhance labor's workplace bargaining power (see Arrighi, 1982: 82-91).

Thus, with specific reference to the historical instance under examination, continuous flow production and the assembly line, while increasing labor-market competition through its homogenization/deskilling of industrial work roles and while subjecting the mass of workers to the dictates of the system of machines, also increased the vulnerability of capital to workers' direct action at the point of production. Likewise, while the increasing concentration, centralization, and integration of capital gave the corporations formidable material resources with which to confront and oppose workers' struggles, these processes also increased the damage that could be done to an entire corporation by a strike in one of its key plants and the disruption that could be caused in the national economy by a strike in a key corporation or industry.

The limits of the assembly lines' technical control of the workforce became apparent during the 1936-1937 sitdown strike wave. It was demonstrated that a relatively small number of activists could bring an entire plant's production to a halt. As Edwards (1979: 128) puts it, "[technical] control linked the entire plant's workforce, and when the line stopped, every worker necessarily joined the strike." This type of direct action was most potent in industries such as meat-packing, electrical products production, and auto manufacturing where assembly line methods had been extensively developed. However, even in the steel industry, as one steelworker quoted by Montgomery (1979: 156) observes, "bringing the workflow to a crunching halt is both easy and commonplace for those who are familiar with the intricacies of their machinery."

The Flint sit-down strike that paralyzed GM's Flint Fischer Body plant was planned and executed by a "militant minority" of autoworkers who by "unexpectedly stopping the assembly line and sitting down inside the plant . . . catalyzed pro-union sentiment among the vast majority of apathetic workers" (Dubofsky and Van Tine, 1977: 255). Just as a militant minority could stop production in an entire plant, so if that plant was a key link in an integrated corporate empire, its occupation could paralyze the corporation. Such was the case when a group of union members stopped production and occupied one of the most critical plants in GM's entire empire: the Flint plant, which produced the bulk of Chevrolet engines. With these occupations autoworkers succeeded in crippling General Motors' car production and the corporation's rate of output decreased from 50,000 cars per month in December to only 125 for the first week of February. GM was not only losing money but even possibly a "permanent share of the market to its competitors" (Dubofsky and Van Tine, 1977: 268-269). With the federal and state governments unwilling to smash the strikes with military force, GM was forced to abandon its uncompromisingly antiunion stance and negotiate a contract with the UAW covering workers in 20 plants in order to end the strike and resume production.

It might well be asked why this strong workplace bargaining power manifested itself so dramatically only in the United States, and even there not earlier than the middle 1930s. There are various reasons. In the first place, European capital had either experienced little centralization, or more centralization than concentration (Sweden, as we shall see, being the main exception). In the second place, technical division of labor and mechanization in their new Taylorist and Fordist forms were lagging far behind trends in the United States. This is particularly true of the auto industry, the emerging "leading sector" of the world-economy:

> The adoption of what the Germans liked to call *der Fordismus* entailed a heavy investment in fixed plant and special-purpose machinery, while yielding large economies of scale. It was thus beyond the means of all but the biggest producers. Here the fragmentation of the European industry was a serious handicap. In contrast to the United States . . . Europe had no giants on the morrow of the war. There were 96 motor car factories in Britain in 1922, 150 in France in 1921, more than 200 in Germany in 1925 [Landes, 1969: 445].

Concentration did proceed quickly in the 1930s, yet mass production techniques continued, with few exceptions, to fall well short of U.S. standards (see Landes, 1969: 445-451). It follows that, generally speaking, labor in Europe had not experienced a development of its workplace bargaining power comparable to that experienced by labor in the United States.

Last but not least, Europe, with the notable exception of Britain, was endowed with much larger reserves of partially proletarianized or nonproletarianized labor than the United States. These reserves have a double significance from the point of view of the containment and the counteracting of labor's workplace bargaining power: They tend to increase the competitive pressure within the ranks of labor in industry, thereby preventing workers from taking advantage of whatever workplace bargaining power they might possess; and they can be mobilized politically to legitimize repressive labor legislation. We shall deal with the former aspect first.

When capitalist transformations of the labor process have shifted the main basis and locus of labor's bargaining power from the marketplace (i.e., from skills embodied in workers' labor-power and what labor-power in general can earn outside of wage employment) to the workplace (i.e., to the damage labor occupying specific work-roles can inflict on capital after entering wage employment), the elimination of alternatives to wage employment tends to strengthen rather than weaken the bargaining power of labor in wage employment. For the competitive pressures within the ranks of labor come to depend mainly on the existence of workers (often part-time and part-lifetime wage workers) who are prepared to accept conditions of pay and work that would be unacceptable to full-lifetime wage workers.

Thus, it is no accident that the "take-off" of scientific management, continuous flow production, and the assembly line in important sectors of American industry at the beginning of the century occurred in conjunction with a massive importation from Europe (particularly Southern and Eastern Europe) of what in the European labor market literature are sometimes referred to as "peasant-workers" (cf. Sabel, 1982). These immigrants were in fact sojourners: They came to the United States with plans to stay temporarily to take advantage of higher wages paid in the United States with the goal of returning as soon as possible with some savings to invest in their home country. Their short-term and instrumental attitude toward work in the United States meant they were not only lacking in the kind of permanent commitment to their job that would justify sacrifice for a union; they were also far more likely to put up with conditions of work and pay with which a long-term labor force would not. As a result, their massive incorporation prior to World War I was exploited by employers as a means to introduce new methods of production that undermined the position of the more stable segments of the labor force.

World War I temporarily cut off new immigration from Europe, and the immigration legislation of 1923 introduced a strict quota system that gave priority to relatives of earlier immigrants. This legislation brought to an end the importation of peasant-workers and led to a process of settlement of ethnic communities. The second generation of earlier European immigrants, unlike their parents, had a strong identity as both permanent wage workers and citizens of the United States. They came to dominate the U.S. labor force in the 1930s, roughly at the time when corporations were induced by the economic crisis to liquidate welfarism. It is not by chance that their coming of age coincided with the strike waves of the middle 1930s and the great political awakening in the ethnic communities that led to Roosevelt's 1936 landslide victory (a self-granted "mandate to organize"). Freidlander (1975: 5), in his history of UAW Local 229, for example, observes that these second-generation workers "provided the early initiative, the first real base, and much of the structure of leadership" in the union struggles. More in general, Piore (1979: 156-157) maintains that

> the organization of labor both in the shop and at the polls can be understood in large measure as a part of the process through which ethnic communities coalesced and the second-generation communities expressed their resentment against the job characteristics that the parental communities, with a different motivation and a different attitude toward the labor market, had come to accept.

While large reserves of nonwage labor were still present in the U.S. South, their recruitment into northern industry as a means to undermine the established labor force became increasingly problematic in the 1930s and 1940s. Beginning with World War I, Southern blacks were recruited in large numbers by employers as strike-breakers and as cheaper workers to permanently displace more expensive white workers. Paternalism was also used to tie black workers to their employer and impede unionization. The most important example was in Detroit where Ford paternalistically cultivated the loyalty of the black community by hiring blacks for all categories of work at the River Rouge Plant (Bonacich, 1976: 40-42). The resulting loyalty of black workers at Ford was a significant factor in enabling that company to resist unionization four years longer than could its competitors.

However, the success of this type of strategy was short-lived both at Ford and in general. In the first place, black migration from the South fell sharply during the 1930s. For example, while Detroit's black population increased by 79,228 during the 1920s, it increased by only 29,053 during the 1930s (Geshwender, 1977: 59). (This is a significantly different pattern from the ethnic immigrants whose numbers tended to increase in bad times and to decrease in good times [Piore, 1979: 152].) Thus the great sit-down strike wave came at a time when the incorporation of new labor supplies had slowed considerably.

Second, Southern blacks never had the same kind of instrumental and temporary attitude toward life and work in the North that characterized the European peasant-workers. From the start they tended to view the move as more permanent and, while they kept ties with family in the South, they more quickly adopted a settled attitude that made them less amenable to doing the worst work for the least pay without complaint.

Finally, especially as the rapid incorporation of Southern black labor supplies resumed with World War II (Detroit's black population increased by over 150,000 during the 1940s), white workers did not hesitate to use their newly found workplace bargaining power in racist wildcat "hate strikes" protesting the employment/upgrading of black workers. In turn, black workers responded with their own wildcat strikes to protest discrimination (Geshwender, 1977: 34-37). In short, employer efforts to use the threat of displacement by black workers to increase productivity and docility backfired, provoking an upsurge in strike activity and unrest.

On the other side of the Atlantic, the slower pace of capitalist transformations of the labor process noticed above was matched, particularly in continental Europe, by a much greater availability of indigenous or foreign labor of the peasant-worker type. A very rough idea of the larger reserves of such labor still existing in continental Europe in the interwar period as compared with the United States, can be obtained by looking at the different proportions of the total labor force employed in agriculture. Around 1930, this proportion was slightly higher than 20 percent in the United States, approximately 30 percent in Germany, just over 35 percent in France, and over 45 percent in Italy (see U.S. Department of Commerce, 1949: 64; Mitchell, 1976: 657-666). These figures underestimate the difference between the two locales. For, while in continental Europe there were much larger (although impossible to document with comparable data) reserves of nonwage labor outside agriculture than in the United States, the agricultural labor force in the United States included large numbers of blacks whose competitive mobilization, as we have just seen, created more problems than it solved. In addition, the closing of the United States border to European immigration increased the availability of labor from Eastern and Southern Europe (where the reserves of nonwage labor were largest) for the more advanced continental European countries (Germany and France, in particular). In France, for example, the number of foreigners increased from 1,160,000 in 1911 to 2,700,000 in 1931 (Kindleberger, 1967: 176-177).

It follows that in continental Europe, not only was labor's workplace bargaining power far less developed than in the United States on account of the overall less advanced technical division of labor and mechanization. In addition, there were larger reserves of peasant-workers that could be mobilized economically to enhance competition within the ranks of labor in industry. As mentioned earlier, they could also be mobilized politically to legitimize antilabor repressive measures. A common scenario of the interwar years was indeed one of antilabor mobilization of nonproletarianized and semiproletarianized strata by nationalist and antisocialist political forces.

True, the same strata could also be, and were, mobilized by working class parties in revolutionary or reformist anticapitalist alliances. But such alliances were always extremely unstable because of the political "volatility" of nonwaged groups and strata—groups and strata that showed a marked propensity to side with labor or capital according to whichever happened to be imminently stronger. The sudden shifts in the political fortunes of working class parties in continental Europe (in Italy in the early 1920s, in Germany in the early 1920s and in the early 1930s, in France in the second half of the 1930s) and their eventual defeat and repression owed much to this political volatility of nonwaged strata in a situation of underlying structural weakness of labor.

The British and Swedish exceptions simply confirm the rule. In Britain, capitalist transformations of the labor process had not advanced further, and in many sectors had advanced less, than in the more developed continental European countries (Germany and France). In Britain too, therefore, labor's workplace bargaining power can be assumed to have been less developed than in the United States; and this, in turn, would account for the weakness of the labor movement in the United Kingdom relative to the movement in the United States. At the same time, however, reserves of nonwage labor had been even more completely exhausted in the United Kingdom than in the United States. The proportion of the total labor force employed in agriculture, which we have adopted as a rough indicator of reserves of nonwage labor, was in 1931 as low as 6 percent. Moreover, far from importing large quantities of foreign labor, in the decade 1920-1931 over 2 million people emigrated from the British Isles, mainly to the colonies. This relative absence of reserves of nonwage labor, and their further depletion by emigration, was probably the main structural factor limiting competitive pressures within the ranks of British labor in the interwar years, notwithstanding the high levels of unemployment that affected it throughout the period. Politically, it meant both the absence of a problem of alliances for the labor movement (a highly divisive issue for the movement on the continent) and the impossibility for antilabor political forces of legitimizing the kind of repressive policies that broke the back of the movement on the continent.

In Sweden a similar outcome was brought about by an altogether different combination of factors. Here reserves of nonwage labor were fairly substantial: According to our rough index, more or less at the same level as France. In contrast, technical division of labor and mechanization in industry were probably more advanced in Sweden than anywhere else in Europe. Large-scale production, innovation, and continuous rationalization of the labor process have been the main characteristics of Swedish capitalist development since the turn of the century—characteristics that are reflected in the extremely high rate of growth of labor productivity in the period 1913-1938 quoted earlier. As Buci-Glucksmann and Therborn remark (1981: 193), "On comprend dès lors qu'une classe ouvrière très concentrée, assez unifiée dans la métallurgie, s'organise très vite en syndicat industriel, sautant pratiquement l'étape préliminaire des syndicats de métiers et l'éparpillement ouvrier à la française."

If these presuppositions (relatively large internal reserves of nonwage labor combined with advanced technical division of labor and mechanization) are correct, then Swedish "exceptionalism" finds a further explanation at the structural level. For they imply that the labor movement in Sweden, as the movement in continental Europe, faced a problem of alliances (i.e., of neutralizing the threat of the antilabor economic and political mobilization of non- and semiproletarianized strata), but faced the problem from a position of structural strength (due to labor's high workplace bargaining power) unparalleled in continental Europe. This argument is not meant to belittle the role of the political intelligence of Swedish labor leadership in devising appropriate strategies for the attainment of state power emphasized earlier on. It is simply meant to put such intelligence in its structural and world-historical context, thereby showing what was common to the two strongest labor movements of the interwar period.

THE CONTAINMENT OF
WORKPLACE BARGAINING POWER

The tight wartime labor market magnified the structural strength of U.S. labor and gave a new sense of urgency to efforts to contain and control labor militancy. Over 4,000 work stoppages took place in 1941, involving more workers (2.4 million) than in any previous year except 1919 (Green, 1980: 176). Strikes in 1941 at Ford, Allis Chalmers, Vultee Aircraft, and Bethlehem Steel "brought these bitterly anti-union companies to the bargaining table" (Lichtenstein, 1977: 215). Despite the no-strike pledge made by the nation's major union leaders after Pearl Harbor, wildcat strikes spread. By 1944 as large a proportion of the workforce was taking part in work stoppages as at the height of the sit-down strikes seven years before. Almost all these strikes were unauthorized by the national union (Lichtenstein, 1977: 234; Montgomery, 1979: 166). After V-J Day the no-strike pledge lost all patriotic appeal, and by the end of January 1946 "the industrial core of the economy was virtually at a standstill as auto, steel and electrical workers were simultaneously on strike" (Davis, 1980: 72). The year of 1946 became a banner year for strikes, surpassing even the 1919 strike wave in all key indicators: the number of strikes, the number of strikers, and the number of man-days lost.

As U.S. entry into the war approached, the federal government's labor policy took a repressive turn signalled by the use of the Army to break a UAW strike at the North American Aviation Plant in Englewood, California, in June 1941. However, there were limits to what a purely repressive labor policy could accomplish given the combination of workers' strong workplace and strong marketplace bargaining power in most defense-related industries. In response, the federal government and employers elaborated new forms of labor control that cast further light on the, at best, ambiguous relationship between trade union organization and labor strength. For the war and postwar years saw the federal government and employers pursue a policy of strengthening trade union organization with the goal of weakening the power of the rank and file to disrupt production.

The tripartite War Labor Board (WLB), established after Pearl Harbor, implemented a combination of repressive and cooptive measures aimed at maintaining industrial peace while simultaneously restraining wages and increasing productivity. In exchange for full cooperation with the war effort (e.g., the no-strike pledge, acceptance of speed-ups and of WLB arbitration including the "Little Steel" wage-freeze formula), union leaders were offered dues check-off and "membership maintenance" clauses (the latter requiring workers who were union members at the signing of the contract to remain members for the duration of the contract).

The WLB used award of these clauses as a means to strengthen "responsible" union leaders and to punish "irresponsible" ones, and thereby pressured the union leadership to act as disciplinarians vis-à-vis the rank and file and to restrain all spontaneous or "unauthorized" strikes or other direct action. "Even a stoppage of a few hours, when engaged in deliberately by a union, was enough evidence of irresponsibility for the board to deny it the protection of the membership maintenance clause." On the other hand, where "the rank-and-file membership struck despite the opposition of the local and international union . . . the board ordered membership maintenance on the grounds that the leaders had shown responsibility and that they need[ed] the power to discipline irresponsible elements" (Seidman, 1953: 105).

At the same time, the War Labor Board's policy of awarding membership maintenance and dues check-off clauses was a key factor behind the wartime expansion of unions, and led to a decisive turning point in membership growth and financial stabilization as well as in the routinization of collective bargaining. During the period of U.S. involvement in World War II labor union membership increased from 10.5 million to 14.7 million (Green, 1980: 174-75), while the proportion of workers under collective bargaining agreements rose from 30 percent of those eligible in 1941 to 40 percent in the following year and to 48 percent by 1945 (Seidman, 1953: 107). By the end of the war, unions and collective bargaining were far too entrenched for employers to contemplate the kind of rollback of unionism that took place after World War I.

The "social contract" between unions and management in the oligopolized sectors of the economy that emerged from the long and bitter reconversion period strikes involved a trade-off that deepened the role of trade unions in labor control. Management agreed to accept the permanent existence of trade unions and their ensured stability through union shop and dues check-off clauses. Furthermore, employers agreed to raise real wages in step with increased productivity. In exchange unions agreed to a reassertion of managerial prerogatives: Topics such as pricing policy, the organization of production, investment decisions (including foreign investment and plant location), and the introduction of new technology were all placed outside the scope of collective bargaining. In addition unions accepted a role in the containment of shop-floor activity, in the disciplining of the rank and file, and in increasing productivity. As the "contractual net" progressively outlawed informal shop-floor activity, the grievance procedures expanded, bringing "responsible" union leadership into the plant. By the 1950s grievance arbitration, which had been a rarity in the 1930s, appeared in well over 90 percent of all union contracts (Brody, 1980: 202-203).

Promotion of responsible trade unionism was not an ideal solution to capital's problem of labor control. For one thing, it was a very expensive solution. Trade union leaders could only influence the rank and file away from wildcat militancy to the degree that they retained legitimacy in the eyes of the rank and file. However, in order to retain legitimacy (and justify restraint) the established leaders had to deliver tangible gains to the membership. These gains have come mostly in the form of rising real wages and fringe benefits. This inherent contradiction in the form of labor control has made the U.S. work force expensive, especially once the world market was reconstituted under U.S. hegemony and the world as a whole increasingly became the unit upon which capital based labor-cost comparisons.

This contradiction became a major underlying cause of the massive transnational expansion of U.S. capital in the postwar period. In turn, the latter also became an important ingredient in the system of labor control. With the establishment of a global free enterprise system under U.S. hegemony, capital was able to use its superior mobility as both a threat and reality to brake labor demands effectively. By contrast we can see that the breakup of the world market from the crash in 1929 to the return of currency convertibility in Europe in 1958 was an important factor behind the advance of labor and the vulnerability of capital during that period: Corporations had no international escape route.

Management has used the investment freedom it was granted in the social contract to expand the use of labor saving technology intranationally and direct investment internationally, while disinvesting in the geographical areas and economic sectors that had been the CIO strongholds in the 1940s. The rapid growth of U.S. multinationals has resulted in a fundamental restructuring of domestic employment opportunities as the former send production and assembly line jobs abroad while concentrating the corporate brain—managerial, technical, and financial work—in the United States (Portes and Walton, 1981: chap. 5).

The expansion of the new sectors of the economy was in large measure based on the incorporation of a new supply of relatively cheap labor (i.e., the massive entry of women into the postwar labor market). These new entries were by and large ignored by the AFL-CIO (Milkman, 1980). As a result—and in combination with the twin processes of capital mobility out of the unionized, basic industries and into these predominantly female and minority nonunionized sectors— the post-World War II social contract has come to cover a progressively shrinking proportion of the total labor force in the United States.

Since the 1970s we have witnessed a redoubling of U.S. capital's efforts to reduce costs and increase profits (e.g., intensified plant relocation and automation, a new anti-union offensive, rapid incorporation of illegal aliens into the labor force) in response to the intensification of global economic competition resulting from the very success of the Pax Americana in restoring the unity of the world market and reviving the economies of Western Europe and Japan. Competition, heightened by world recession, has "eroded the traditional ability of oligopolistic employers in the basic industries to pay higher labor costs and still maintain their anticipated profit margins" (Craypo 1981: 154). The social contract has become a "fetter on profit making": The real rate of return for all nonfinancial corporations in the United States fell from 15.5 percent in the period 1963-1966 to 12.7 percent during 1967-1970 to 10.1 percent in 1971-1974 and finally to 9.7 percent for the period through 1978 (Bluestone, 1982: 147).

Capital's efforts to restore profits has been hindered by a number of processes. For one thing, while there exists a large and vulnerable supply of illegal immigrant labor, the cheap labor status of both women and blacks has been relatively undermined since the late 1960s. Women's status as cheap labor was in large measure based on the ideology defining women as primarily wives and mothers; their presence in the paid labor force was viewed as only temporary and their role as only secondary breadwinners within the family. However, the massive and permanent incorporation of women into the paid labor force during the postwar period led to a growing contradiction between ideology and reality that exploded into the women's movement and demands for equal employment opportunities and equal pay for equal work (Kessler-Harris, 1980: 300-319), in turn signalling the fact that a renewed capitalist expansion based on women's cheaper labor status is, at best, problematic.

At the same time, according to Piore (1979: 160-161), the coming of age of the second-generation of Southern black migrants and their numerical dominance in the labor force in the 1960s has had an impact on the cheap labor status of blacks outside the unionized oligopolized sectors of the economy that is in many ways parallel to the political and labor market impact of the settling of the ethnic communities in the 1930s. "This parallel implies that one can interpret the racial conflicts that developed in the North in the 1960s as parallel to the Roosevelt electoral coalition and the industrial union movement in the 1930s" (Piore, 979: 161). Black youth, excluded from the CIO stronghold jobs that some of the earlier black migrants were able to corner, increasingly rebelled against the other job opportunities that were left to them.

> What the changes of the 1960s do seem to have done, and in a fairly forceful way, was to signal to employers that the black labor force is no longer a reliable source of labor for secondary jobs, and since the late 1960s, employers in the secondary labor market appear to have turned increasingly toward undocumented workers from the Caribbean and Latin America instead [Piore, 1979: 163].

In addition to these problems of labor supply, capital's efforts to resolve the squeeze on profits through the relocation of production to low-wage areas has been inhibited by the world monetary and political instability that has accompanied the crisis of U.S. world hegemony. The result has been to place a higher premium on efforts to reduce costs of production within the United States. The Reagan administration's attack on the welfare state and the dismantling of the social safety net—which put a floor under wages and unemployment—as well as the duration and severity of the economic downturn that has been provoked are other manifestations of the efforts to reduce costs and restore U.S. competitiveness.

Some success for these strategies might be claimed in the wake of the wave of contractual "givebacks" that spread throughout traditional union strongholds during 1982: auto, rubber, meatpacking, steel, farm implements, trucking, and airline industries (Davis, 1982: 19). However, management may be premature in celebrating a victory; as soon as the industry in question begins to recover, workers who consented to "givebacks" demand that contracts be reopened and wages raised (e.g., Chrysler). Clearly worker docility imposed only by permanent economic depression can not be a satisfactory long-term solution for capital.

Finally, it still remains to be seen to what extent the reorientation of investment away from the sectors of production in which workers demonstrated strong workplace bargaining power (WBP) in the 1930s and 1940s will reduce the level of WBP in the labor force as a whole. To a large part the answer to this question depends on the nature and extent of WBP contained in the new job categories in the new sectors of the economy. While computerization may be once again weakening the marketplace bargaining power of labor (as mechanization did in the 1920s) it may be endowing workers with even more vast powers to disrupt production and society.

In sum, once we take into account war and postwar developments, we can for analytical purposes subdivide the trajectory of the labor movement in the United States since the 1920s into four, partly overlapping, stages. The first stage, encompassing most of the interwar years up to the confrontation of the middle 1930s, is that of the *latent* development of the strength of labor—that is, a strength rooted in a high workplace bargaining power that is due to an advanced degree of technical division of labor and mechanization combined with a relative exhaustion of exploitable reserves of nonwage labor. The effect of this structural strength is to reduce the effectiveness of market mechanisms (viz. unemployment) and of openly repressive extraeconomic mechanisms in reproducing the subordination of labor in the capitalist labor process.

The second stage is that of the *overt* manifestation of such strength in a confrontation with capital precipitated by corporate and state policies inconsistent with the new structural strength of labor. It unfolds from the middle 1930s through the war years and the immediate postwar years, largely overlapping with the third stage. The latter—most clearly observable during the war up through the 1950s—is the stage of the strengthening and transformation of union organizational structures and of political reorientation of their leadership toward liberal-corporatist stances. These two stages, taken jointly, show that the strength of the movement did not depend on its commitment to a specifically working class ideology or on any preexisting organizational strength of labor unions.

The strengthening and transformation of union structures and the political reorientation of union leadership was closely connected with the new forms of labor control that emerged in response to the structural strength of the movement. The ineffectiveness of purely repressive policies, however pursued (administratively, economically, or technically), induced the state and corporate management to involve unions in a system of representative/bureaucratic control. Unions were recognized as legitimate representatives of workers (a recognition that greatly enhanced their power, not only in society at large, but also vis-à-vis the represented) in exchange for unions' recognition of managerial prerogatives as well as a union role in guaranteeing the performance and predictability of work. This exchange presupposed a relative strengthening of industrial unions vis-à-vis general and craft unions and, above all, a much greater presence of unions at the plant level where, together with management, they came to constitute a kind of "private government" or "internal state" (cf. Pizzorno, 1978; Burawoy, 1979).

The fourth stage—most clearly observable in the late 1950s and, above all, in the subsequent two decades—is that of the relative, but only relative, weakening of both unions' and workers' bargaining power connected with the "emigration" of capital. This emigration was greatly facilitated by the union recognition of managerial prerogatives (capital's freedom of movement, in particular) and their unqualified initial support for the transnational expansion of U.S. capital. This transnational expansion, in turn, greatly facilitated the . enforcement of bureaucratic/representative control for two related reasons. On the one hand, it allowed the transplantation of the deskilled segments of the labor process endowed with high workplace bargaining power to regions still endowed with reserves of competitive labor. On the other hand, it allowed, in the United States, a faster expansion than would otherwise have been possible of relatively skilled work roles. As a result of these two joint tendencies, the structure of wage employment in the United States has acquired a "service" and "middle class" bias that has strengthened the structural basis of representative/bureaucratic control, and even somewhat reduced the importance of the mediational role of labor unions.

This apparent relative decline of the strength of the labor movement in the United States since the late 1950s is only one side of the coin. The other side is the transformation and eventual strengthening of the labor movement elsewhere in the world, particularly in Western Europe, prompted by the establishment of the Pax Americana and the consequent transnational expansion of capital. To conclude this chapter, we shall now turn to a brief analysis of this transformation.

CONVERGENT PATTERNS OF THE POSTWAR LABOR MOVEMENT

The growing importance of nominally working class parties in Western Europe and their continuing absence in the United States has obscured the fact that the labor movement in Western Europe since World War II has followed a pattern in many ways analogous to that first established by the labor movement in the United States in the interwar, war, and immediate postwar years. The analogies have also been blurred by two other sets of factors. On the one hand, the world political-economic context has changed dramatically since World War II and, moreover, structural tendencies have developed unevenly in the different Western European national locales. On the other hand, preexisting labor organizations have responded differently to similar (national and worldwide) contextual tendencies. As Lange and Ross (1982) have shown with reference to France and Italy, contextual tendencies constrain but do not determine unions' policies; and these, in turn, can lead to divergent trajectories of the labor movement even in national locales initially characterized by very similar features.

However, if we focus on what we singled out at the end of the previous section as the most distinctive features of the labor movement in the United States, the analogies become strong enough to be clearly observable in spite of all the differences in national and world contexts and in the responses of labor organizations to those contexts. Except for Sweden, which in its own way anticipated many of the tendencies in question before World War II (see the part on "The Rise of Workplace Bargaining Power"), a succession of stages similar to that identified for the United States is observable in Western Europe. The first stage (latent development of the structural strength of labor) is entered by some countries during World War II or even earlier, while in other countries it becomes relevant only in the 1950s and 1960s. In all cases, however, the transition to the second stage (overt manifestation of the structural strength) is completed between 1968 and 1972 and is immediately followed by a rapid succession of the other two stages (strengthening/transformation of union structures and emigration of capital). Let us look at the broad outlines of this development.

In Italy and France, the transition to the postwar pattern has passed through the revival and final defeat of the highly politicized labor movement that had characterized the interwar years. The revival was based on the considerable political strength with which working class organizations (the Communist Parties in the first place) had emerged from the wars of national liberation from German occupation. Its demise followed the traditional pattern of a political mobilization of predominantly nonwage groups and strata in an antilabor social bloc that isolated the working class and weakened its organizations. The demise was then made permanent by widespread transformations in the labor process and in the industrial structure discussed below.

In Germany, the structure of work and occupations had been, to a large extent, already revolutionized during the war. Partly because of this previous restructuring and partly because of the political and economic circumstances faced by Germany at the end of the war (widespread destruction of industrial plants, high rates of unemployment, military occupation and partition, massive influx of refugees from Eastern Europe, etc.) there was no revival of the movement either in the old or in a new form. There was, however, a reconstruction "from above" by veterans of the Weimar era of union and party organizations along the lines of the Scandinavian tradition (industrial unions, political and ideological neutrality of unions, a reformist Social Democratic Party). The success of these new organizational structures was immediate:

> By 1949 the trade unions in the Western zone alone already equalled the strength achieved in the whole land area of Germany under the Weimar Republic. Union membership soon came to exceed that of the Weimer Republic by a wide margin. This success is the more remarkable when one takes account of the freeze on wages and hours maintained by the Allied Control Council from the inception of the

Occupation, which placed close limits on the scope for trade union action [Kendall, 1975: 112].

In the United Kingdom, there was no break with the past, only an increase in the political power of the labor movement with the victory of the Labour Party in the 1945 elections. As the Labour Party began to socialize the consumption and final distribution of national income, strike activity remained at relatively low levels while union membership continued to climb. The United Kingdom seemed to be approaching the Swedish model of political exchange—industrial peace in exchange for full employment and welfare benefits. However, unlike the Swedish model and the recently established German labor organizations, the control of the party and union bureaucracies over the rank and file remained slender. Craft unionism remained powerful and the authority exercised by the Trade Union Congress was minimal. In addition, "many national unions had little control at the enterprise level. Because of overlapping jurisdictions . . . a great deal of power devolved upon shop stewards, a disproportionate number of whom belonged to the Communist Party" (Galenson, 1976: 157-158).

Whatever the situation in the different countries, starting in the early 1950s a noticeable calm came to characterize labor-capital relations all over Western Europe. "By the early 1960s the Ross-Hartman thesis of the withering away of the strike came to be widely accepted" (Clarke, 1980: 15-16). No one expected that before the decade was over the longest (and most impervious to political and economic control) strike wave in European history would sweep the region. With the French explosion of 1968, the Italian *autunno caldo* of 1969 and the Belgian and German wildcat strike waves of the same year, the sharp rise of strike activity in Britain between 1968 and 1970, and the Kiruna strike of 1970 and the public service strikes of 1971 in Sweden, "it came to look as if, far from withering away, the strike was taking on a new and unexpected dimension" (Clarke, 1980: 15-16).

What was new in this strike wave, in quantitative terms, was not its intensity and spread: The number of days lost in strikes or the number of countries involved in the upsurge fell short of numbers attained in the 1919-1920 wave. It was rather its length and persistence throughout the 1970s notwithstanding steadily rising levels of unemployment, particularly after 1973. From this point of view, the only historical precedent was the long wave of industrial unrest that swept the United States with only short interruptions from the middle 1930s to the early 1950s.

The length and relative imperviousness to labor market conditions is not the only analogy between the two waves. Although influenced by political conjunctures, the European wave was certainly not determined by them: It developed under the most different political regimes (conservative in France, centrist in Italy, reformist in Britain and Germany); it has not been greatly affected by the repressive measures (relatively mild by historical standards) attempted by various governments; and, generally speaking, it has forced governments and employers to make important economic and normative concessions. (Interestingly enough, real earnings have tended to increase faster in high strike countries, which have also been high inflation and high unemployment countries. See Clarke, 1980: 21-22.) In a word, as in the United States in the 1930s and 1940s and unlike in most European experiences in the interwar years, the strength of the movement has determined political conjunctures more than it has itself been determined by them.

The strength of the movement depended even less on its commitment to a specifically working class ideology. The 1960s had uniformly been a period of ideological disengagement on the part of the labor movement in Western Europe. At the Bad Godesberg Congress held in 1959, the German SPD wrote Marxism out of the party's constitution and began to cultivate a new "People's Party" image designed to attract middle class and confessional groups hitherto outside its clientele. The communist parties of France and Italy (particularly the former) did not of course write Marxism out of their constitutions, but did make equal, if not greater, efforts to cultivate a "People's Party" image. At the same time, the confessional, ideological, and political divisions among unions that characterized Italy and France began to break down through processes of deconfessionalization, greater autonomy from political parties, and unity of action.

The workers' militancy of the late 1960s and early 1970s confirmed these tendencies:

> [U]nions and parties as organizational units should not be regarded as the actors in the political process of the 'new militancy'. The real actor has been the working-class rank-and-file in the different countries. Their politics has determined, however diffusely, the changes and differences of the organizations [Deppe et al., 1978: 195].

Whatever these changes—and we shall shortly refer to them—the workers emphasis was generally on unity of action in the workplace, irrespective of ideological and political allegiances:

> The militant rank-and-file attempt to preserve such freedom of action as they possess on the plant level by 'playing down' the political dimension of plant and union struggles. This leads to the seemingly paradoxical circumstance that the strikers become progressively more politically conscious but simultaneously refuse to conduct the strike down an overtly political line . . . a similar tactic is the attempt to fashion the union into a substitute or proto-party [Deppe et al., 1978: 185].

In the light of what we have been maintaining, there is no contradiction in the circumstance that workers became progressively more politically conscious but simultaneously refused to conduct strikes on overtly political lines. For workers were bound to realize purely on the basis of their daily experience that while their actions had important implications and feedbacks, their strength did not derive from organizations and ideologies external to their work situation and allegiance to such organizations and ideologies could become, as it had been in the past, a force divisive of their unity.

Their strength derived rather from the very organization of production in which they were embedded:

> The evolution in industrial organization makes firms more vulnerable to strike action. Products become increasingly complex, job-tasks are broken down to a much greater extent, stock levels are reduced, fixed capital resources play a greater part in overall costs, and if the work force downs tools, white-collar employees and management staff (whose number has increased) have still to be paid, while the firm's working capital and liquid assets are cut fine. This means that if one part of the plant is shut down, not only is actual production disrupted, but financial problems also ensue as the plant must still assume a whole series of costs. The combination of loss of production and continuing fixed costs effectively means that even small groups of workers wield considerable power [Dubois, 1978: 17].

Like the American workers in the mass production industries thirty years earlier, the European workers of the late 1960s and early 1970s were quick to learn the forms of action that would substantially disturb production activities without themselves incurring total loss of earnings: Shop-floor strikes spaced at regular intervals, coordinated sector-by-sector strikes, acts of industrial sabotage, sit-ins, obstruction of entry and exit of supplies to the plants, slowdowns, and the like.

This reduplication, in totally different world and national contexts, of the forms of struggle and of workers' strength that had characterized the labor movement in the United States in the late 1930s and early 1940s was no accident. For the Pax Americana had long-term effects on labor-capital relations in Europe that in many ways were diametrically opposed to its effects on labor-capital relations in the United States. As we have seen, in the United States the main effect has been one of containment of workers' bargaining power. In Western Europe, in contrast, it provided the means, the context, and the stimulus for the structural transformations that had engendered that power.

The means were provided by the Marshall Plan and subsequent aid that eased—and in some countries (Italy and France, in particular) directly affected—the transfer of U.S. mass production technology to European industries. It provided the context by reconstructing the world market and sponsoring a unified European market that made feasible the adoption of such technology in Europe. It also provided the stimulus for their adoption in the form of what later came to be known as the "American challenge": the expansion within the European borders of American transnational corporations producing with the most advanced techniques. As a result of these circumstances and of a highly competitive reaction on the part of Western European capital, der Fordismus was transplanted in Europe on an unprecedented scale that thoroughly revolutionized the technical and commodity structure of European capital.

Up through the middle 1960s, the tendency implicit in these transformations toward an increasing workplace bargaining power of labor was easily counteracted by the competitive mobilization of the large reserves of peasant-workers that still existed within Western Europe and were being supplemented by massive immigration of workers from Southern Europe as well as from French and British excolonies. But by the middle 1960s, the progressive exhaustion of internal supplies of peasant-workers and the decreasing competitiveness of external supplies, shifted relationships of forces in production in favor of labor. When employers, now under the full impact of the reestablishment of world market competition, responded to declining profitability by intensifying work, the great confrontation of the late 1960s was precipitated (cf. Soskice, 1978: 233).

To complete the analogy between the long American strike wave of the late 1930s and 1940s and the long European wave of the late 1960s and 1970s, we shall briefly mention that not only their forms of manifestation and their underlying causes but also their effects were similar. As hinted earlier on, the strikes of 1968-1970 consisted of a wave of plant-level disputes over which the trade unions had little or no control. For the lack of formal authority of unions inside plants had remained the weak link in the institutionalization of industrial conflict that had occurred throughout Western Europe in the 1960s. The effect of the strike wave was to lead to a reinforcement of this process:

> The unions, for their part, were to aim at taking over rank-and-file militancy so as to integrate it within their own strategy, and use the force behind it to increase their influence at the level where they were the least strong, i.e. at plant level. The phase of increased militancy was also to provide a lesson to the authorities and the employers; as they too were to hasten the institutionalization process, either taking a tough line by further restricting the right to strike . . . , by taking measures to reinforce the unions' role, or by launching a vast ideological offensive [Dubois, 1978: 29].

Generally speaking, repressive measures on the part of government or management were not effective. They were resorted to "as a kind of crash-barrier to be erected as a last resort if other institutionalized means failed to work" (Dubois, 1978: 29). Repression was therefore a palliative, the "mid-wife" of the constitution of unions and management into internal-state/private-government formations similar to those engendered by the U.S. strike wave of the late 1930s and 1940s:

> Institutional developments at plant level manifest themselves through various different changes, in that the individual firm becomes a scene of bargaining in its own right, the union is more and more often acknowledged its place in the plant, and the 'traditional' structures of management/work force co-operation . . . find themselves invested with a greater number of functions. The desired aim is therefore to institutionalize conflict by setting up machinery to allow for the exchange of views with *a priori* no discussion points excluded, and each side recognizing the other as a valid opposite number [Dubois, 1978: 30].

In this and in other ways (that we cannot discuss for lack of space) Western European unions—as American unions thirty years earlier— have been greatly strengthened by a movement that had initially developed outside or even against their influence. They have used this greater power simultaneously to strengthen the weak points and to curb the strong points of the labor movement.

As in the U.S. case, the containment of the structural strength of the labor movement and the institutionalization of new forms of labor control in Europe in the 1970s has been greatly facilitated by capital emigration. The early to middle 1970s have been characterized by a simultaneous fall in the net immigration of foreign labor into Western Europe and a tremendous increase in the transnational expansion of capital out of Western Europe, in particular toward more peripheral sites of production.

This increase was mainly due to a sustained take-off of the transnational expansion of capital from Germany, which throughout the 1960s had shown no tendency of this sort, and to an increase and reorientation of French direct investment abroad, hitherto sustained mainly by the colonial heritage. From this point of view, it is interesting to notice that the two European countries in which (as indicated in the second part of this chapter) labor's structural strength had developed earlier (Sweden and England), were also the countries in which labor immigration had been supplemented throughout the 1960s by relatively high levels of direct investment abroad. Equally significant is the fact that the country that in the 1970s has most lagged behind in the transnational expansion of capital (Italy) is also the country that has had the greatest problems in bringing labor unrest under control.

We may conclude that if, as we think, previous and present U.S. experience can be of any guide to an understanding of present and future Western European tendencies, we may expect the world labor movement to move in two partly contradictory directions. We may expect a partial containment (not a roll back) of the labor movement in Western Europe through the joint development of representative-bureaucratic forms of control and of the emigration of capital. But we should also expect that this relative weakening will be more than compensated for by the strengthening of the labor movement in the national locales where capital is emigrating. Is not that, after all, what we can already observe in countries like Spain, Greece, and to some extent even Brazil and South Africa—four of the most preferred destinations of the emigration of core capital in the 1960s and 1970s?

REFERENCES

ABENDROTH, W. (1972) A Short History of the European Working Class. New York: Monthly Review Press.

ARRIGHI, G. (1982) "A crisis of hegemony," in S. Amin et al. (eds.) Dynamics of Global Crisis. New York: Monthly Review Press.

BLUESTONE, B. and B. HARRISON (1982) The Deindustrialization of America. New York: Basic Books.

BONACICH, E. (1976) "Advanced capitalism and black/white race relations in the United States: a split labor market interpretation." American Sociological Review 41 (February).

BRODY, D. (1980) Workers in Industrial America. New York: Oxford University Press.
BUCI-GLUCKSMANN C. and G. THERBORN (1981) Le défi social-démocrate. Paris: Maspero.
BURAWOY, M. (1979) Manufacturing Consent. Chicago: University of Chicago Press.
CLARKE, R.O. (1980) "Labour-management disputes: a perspective." British Journal of Industrial Relations 18, 1 (March).
CRAYPO, C. (1981) "The decline of union bargaining power," in M. Carter and W. Leathy (eds.) New Directions in Labor Economics and Industrial Relations. Notre Dame, IA: University of Notre Dame Press.
CROUCH, C. and A. PIZZORNO, [eds.] (1978) The Resurgence of Class Conflict in Western Europe since 1968 (Vol. 2). New York: Holmes and Meier.
DAVIS, M. (1982) "The AFL-CIO's second century." New Left Review 136 (November-December)
————(1980) "The barren marriage of American Labour and the democratic party." New Left Review 124 (November-December).
DEMARCO, D., J. DHONT, and D. FAUVEL-ROUIF (1966) "Mouvement ouvriers et dépression économique de 1929 à 1939" in Fauvel-Rouif (ed.) Mouvement Ouvriers et Dépression Economique. Assen: Van Gorcum.
DEPPE, R., R. HERDING, and D. HOSS, (1978) "The relationship between trade union action and political parties" in Crouch and Pizzorno (eds.) The Resurgence of Class Conflict in Western Europe since 1968 (Vol. 2). New York: Holmes and Meier.
DUBOIS, P. (1978) "New forms of industrial conflict," in Crouch and Pizzorno (eds.) The Resurgence of Class Conflict in Western Europe since 1968 (Vol. 2). New York: Holmes and Meier.
DUBOFSKY, M. and W. VAN TINE (1977) John L. Lewis: A Biography. Chicago: Quadrangle Books.
EDWARDS, R. (1979) Contested Terrain. New York: Basic Books.
FAUVEL-ROUIF, D. [ed.] (1966) Mouvement Ouvriers et Dépression Economique. Assen: Van Gorcum.
FINE, S. (1969) Sit-down: The General Motors Strike of 1936-37. Ann Arbor: Univeristy of Michigan Press.
FRIEDLANDER, P. (1975) The Emergence of a UAW Local: 1936-1939. Pittsburgh: University of Pittsburgh Press.
GALENSON, W. (1976) "The labour force and labour problems in Europe 1920-1970," in C. M. Cipolla (ed.) The Fontana Economic History of Europe: The Twentieth Century, Part I. Glasgow: Collins/Fontana.
GESHWENDER, J. (1977) Class, Race and Worker Insurgency: The League of Revolutionary Black Workers. Cambridge: Cambridge University Press.
GREEN, R. (1980) The World of the Worker. New York: Hill and Wang.
KENDALL, W. (1975) The Labour Movement in Europe. London: Allen Lane.
KESSLER-HARRIS, A. (1982) Out to Work: A History of Wage-Earning Women in the United States. Oxford: Oxford University Press.
KINDLEBERGER, C. (1967) Europe's Postwar Growth: The Role of Labor Supply. Cambridge, MA: Harvard University Press.
KORPI, W. (1980) The Working Class in Welfare Capitalism. London: Routledge & Kegan, Paul.
LANDES, D. (1969) The Unbound Prometheus. Cambridge: Cambridge University Press.
LANGE, P. and G. ROSS, (1982) "Conclusions: French and Italian union development in comparative perspective," in Lange et al. (eds.) Unions, Change and Crisis: French

and Italian Union Strategy and the Political Economy, 1945-1980. London: Allen and Unwin.

LICHTENSTEIN, N. (1977) "Ambiguous legacy: the union security problem during World War II." Labor History 18 (Spring).

MILKMAN, R. (1980) "Organizing the sexual division of labor: historical perspectives on 'women's work' and the American labor movement." Socialist Review 49 (January-February).

MILLIS, H.A. and E.C. BROWN (1950) From the Wagner Act to Taft-Hartley: A Study of National Labor Policy and Labor Relations. Chicago: University of Chicago Press.

MITCHELL, B.R. (1976) "Statistical appendix," in C.M. Cipolla (ed.) The Fontana Economic History of Europe: Contemporary Economies, Part II. Glasgow: Collins/ Fontana.

MONTGOMERY, D. (1979) Workers' Control in America. Cambridge: Cambridge University Press.

PHELPS BROWN, E.H. with M.H. BROWNE (1968) A Century of Pay. New York: Macmillan.

PIORE, M. J. (1979) Birds of Passage: Migrant Labor and Industrial Societies. Cambridge: Cambridge University Press.

PIZZORNO, A. (1978) "Political exchange and collective identity in industrial Conflict," in Crouch and Pizzorno (eds.) The Resurgence of Class Conflict in Western Europe since 1968 (Vol. 2). New York: Holmes and Meier.

PORTES, A. and J. WALTON. (1981) Labor, Class and the International System. New York: Academic Press.

SABEL, C. (1982) The Division of Labor: Its Progress Through Politics. Cambridge: Cambridge University Press.

SEIDMAN, J. (1953) American Labor from Defense to Reconversion. Chicago: University of Chicago Press.

SJOBERG, A. (1966) "La vie sociale et les mouvements travaillistes en Suède de 1920 à 1939," in D. Fauvel-Rouif (ed.) Mouvement Ouvriers et Dépression Economique. Assen: Van Gorcum.

SOSKICE, D. (1978) "Strike Waves and Wage Explosions, 1968-1970: An Economic Interpretation" in Crouch and Pizzorno (eds.) The Resurgence of Class Conflict in Western Europe since 1968 (Vol. 2). New York: Holmes and Meier.

U.S. Department of Commerce (1949) Historical Statistics of the United States, 1789-1945. Washington, DC: U.S. Government Printing Office.

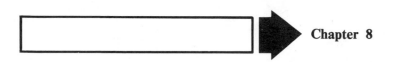

Chapter 8

THE TEXTILE INDUSTRY AND
WORKING CLASS CULTURE

Alice Ingerson
Johns Hopkins University

Most debates over working class culture center on its political and economic implications. Some analysts are interested in the transformation of economically backward peasants into a "modern workforce," while others are interested in the transformation of politically backward peasants into a "revolutionary proletariat." Both kinds of analysis aim to explain why and when working people reject or accept, resist or pursue, a transition from noncapitalist or precapitalist social relations to capitalist ones. Any such explanation depends on comparing societies that became capitalist to societies that did not, or on comparing societies that became capitalist in different ways. Yet the transition to capitalism is not an option presented to each society or working class in turn, but a single global process, without a clear beginning or end. If the world economy has been a single integrated system since the advent of capitalism, if not before, then no national or regional case was truly independent of any other. The capacity of capitalism to take different forms over space and time makes it extremely difficult to declare any given society capitalist or noncapitalist on internal evidence alone, or

AUTHOR'S NOTE: This chapter is a revised version of a paper published by the Instituto de Ciências Sociais, Lisbon, in a special issue of *Análise Social* (1982, 72-74: 1, A Formação de Portugal Contemporâneo). I would also like to acknowledge financial support from the Anthropology Department of the Johns Hopkins University, the Fulbright-Hays Program, and the National Science Foundation (grant BNS 8112850) for fieldwork in Portugal.

even by comparing it with one or two other societies. In a capitalist world system, the crucial question for comparative studies is not the yes-or-no question of *whether* any given society in isolation is capitalist or not, but the historical-process question of *how* each society became involved in the system as a whole.

The world systems approach has thus complicated the question of what counts as capitalism in specific times and places. In contrast with political and economic histories that have at least confronted this complexity, most studies of working class culture still treat each particular culture as an independent unit, classifying it on internal evidence alone as *either* peasant or proletarian, precapitalist or capitalist. Some studies of working class culture expect the cultural unity of precapitalist peasant villages to give way to the cultural diversity of an urban working class, while other studies expect the stubborn individualism of peasants to give way to the class solidarity of urban workers. In claiming to contribute to the study of working class culture in general, many noncomparative case studies imply that all peasants and all proletarians must, or should, share the same cultural characteristics. Only from this point of view can a study of textile workers in Peru test hypotheses derived from studies of Lancashire or New England.

Conciliatory relativists may insist that each working class has its own unique culture, and require any study to treat each working class culture as an insoluble unit. This solution, when it does not rule out comparative study altogether, limits comparison to classification: Any two cases are like or unlike in specific ways, or fall into the same or different general categories.

None of these solutions provides any strategy for studying the history of working class culture in a world system in which a single process—the expansion of capitalism—necessarily produces a variety of cultural results. Working class cultures not only differ from one another, but their very differences are part of capitalism as an ongoing world history. Some peasants were eager and others reluctant to become proletarians. Some populations confronted the world labor market for jobs and wages aggressively, with substantial resources of skills or materials, while others faced the same market at best defensively. Some populations depended on the world market for cloth or clothing because they had lost their capacity to produce these things through the intervention of external forces, while others sought the same commodities in the world market by choice or because they had never been self-sufficient in textiles. From a world systems perspective, the crucial question for comparative analysis is not why different workers in the same system developed different cultures, but why and how the system itself differed over both space and time.

The study of working class culture from this perspective will not prove or disprove any monolithic general theory of working class culture under capitalism, nor will it sort working class cultures into general categories. A general working class culture does not really explain why different groups of workers behaved in similar ways, nor do fragmented preindustrial cultures explain workers' differences from one another. World capitalism did not irrevocably homogenize the world working class, nor did it simply leave workers as it found them; it did some of each. At the same time, the workers themselves did not wait to be made over or preserved, but pursued goals of their own. Determining the relationship between the tendencies of the system as a whole and workers' strategies requires not the testing of ahistorical hypotheses but the explanation of historical events.

The following sections outline a comparative, world systems approach to the history of workers in one basic world industry—textiles. I have used the experiences of textile workers in northwestern Portugal, as the single case with which I am most familiar, to demonstrate that building the experiences of a specific group of workers into the history of world capitalism is more fruitful than treating those workers either as a random sample of the world working class or as culturally unique. This brief discussion cannot integrate every detail of the already voluminous literature on textile workers, but it can at least point out some of the basic issues that need further comparative study.

THE TEXTILE INDUSTRY

Economic historians have been interested in the textile industry because it has often been the first industry, or mills have been the first recognizable factories, in many previously agricultural economies. Social historians have studied the industry because it has often employed larger numbers of workers, and particularly larger numbers of women, than have other industries. Many studies of working class culture have dealt with textile workers as if by accident, simply because their large numbers make them visible or because their early appearance in the sequence of industrialization makes them seem a good test case for general theories about capitalism and working class culture. Most of these studies have made the kinds of implicit assumptions about working class culture in general or about the cultural individuality of each working class, as criticized above. As a result, the large literature on textile workers has not yet begun to build into any world history of textile workers, the textile industry, or capitalism.

The importance of the world market for this industry, however, has very much bound the fate—and the culture—of all textile workers into a single world history. The textile industry has been quintessentially a world industry, probably since the advent of long-distance trade but certainly from the industry's first industrial development. From the late eighteenth century to the late nineteenth century, the British textile industry conquered the world market by both technological innovation and the use of brute military force to transform other textile exporters into textile importers (Farnie, 1979; Manchester Guardian, 1925, 1929; Rostow, 1960).

In the twentieth century, the British textile industry lost markets to new national industries, especially when war interrupted international trade. At the same time, the textile industry in countries such as the United States, Japan, and India left its older centers for new areas where "the wages of textile workers are continually subject to the pressure of unskilled labourers from impoverished rural districts," and where, not coincidentally, unions had little strength (ILO, 1937: 257; Wright, 1981). In 1937, the textiles committee of the International Labour Office called attention to textiles as "perhaps the world trade commodity par excellence," and warned that "the struggle for textile markets has become accentuated to such an extent as to threaten labour standards the world over, and world economic relations in general" (ILO, 1937: 24, 353).

The same struggle continued into the 1970s. In 1980, Froebel, Heinrichs, and Kreye pointed out that the world textile industry as a whole was "relocating" form its older centers in Europe to newer centers in Asia. In the new centers of the industry, workers themselves covered the costs of child raising and caring for the ill and elderly and subsidized their own industrial wages through small-scale agriculture or petty commodity production. National states in many developing countries encouraged these working class "cultural differences," whether as part of rural peasant cultures that had their "roots on the land" or as sets of national or religious values that defended "family unity." Whatever the cultural grounds of these patterns, they saved both states and employers the costs of social welfare programs already established in the older textile centers. These savings helped to keep wage costs down and attracted new industrial employment (Froebel et al., 1980). According to this argument, the world textile industry in the 1970s was actually seeking out and subsidizing what would otherwise appear to be precapitalist working class strategies as a way of cutting labor costs.

This possibility, as well as the long history of textiles as "the world trade commodity par excellence," make a comparative approach to textile workers' history and culture imperative.

THE FAMILY IN WORKING CLASS CULTURE: FROM PATTERNS OF AUTHORITY TO DEMOGRAPHY

The literature on the history of the working class family illustrates the basic problems identified above. Like many studies of working class culture in general, this literature makes diverse and often contradictory assumptions about the cultural transformation of peasants into proletarians. Some studies have expected all proletarians to act economically and politically as either individuals or a class, while all peasants act as members of intermediate units such as families and villages. These assumptions imply that any proletarian attachment to family or locality carried over from a preindustrial culture. Other studies have supposed all proletarians to live in nuclear families and all peasants to live in extended ones. From this point of view, any proletarian extended families must represent cultural continuity from a precapitalist phase. Some studies have taken it for granted that proletarian families are relatively egalitarian and peasant families are patriarchal. This assumption takes any patriarchy or primogeniture among proletarians as evidence of the "incomplete transformation" of peasantry into proletariat. Some studies expected all proletarians to advocate sexual freedom, claiming marriage as a universal right, whereas all peasants had been economically prudish, favoring late marriage and high rates of celibacy along with primogeniture to keep their lands intact and avoid overpopulation. If this were true, then any proletarian tendency toward late marriage must have survived from before capitalism. Other studies took the opposite tack, looking to proletarian families to plan their marriages and childbearing in response to the demand for labor but presupposing that peasants were demographic fatalists, submitting passively to Malthusian checks and balances. If these assumptions were justified, then any tendency toward unbridled procreation amongst the proletariat must have reflected leftover peasant fatalism.

While these assumptions centered on the family, they often had political implications, also often assumed. If capitalism was assumed to favor individualism, then a working class culture that preserved the family was in some sense "resisting capitalism." If capitalism was supposed to favor the nuclear family over the extended family, on the other hand, a working class culture that prescribed the nuclear family was adapting to capitalism rather than resisting it. Studies that see capitalism as creating a labor market that obeyed laws of supply and demand therefore portray a working class culture that manipulates its reproduction in response to the labor market as understanding capitalism better than a culture that does not respond to market forces. Moreover, some scholars interpret a culture that valued sexual freedom and equality or family planning as accepting capitalism, while others see the same culture as preparing to overthrow capitalism.

As general theories not all of these cultural and political assumptions could apply to the development of working class culture, because some of the assumptions contradict others. Very few studies of the working class family have lined these assumptions up against one another clearly enough to examine the contradictions among them or to ask where and when each kind of assumption would make sense even as a hypothesis. A review of the literature on textile workers reveals that this lack of coordination has led new case studies to test hypotheses long after they have been rejected by further studies of the case on which they were first based. From a world systems perspective, many of these studies — particularly those that have "disproven" various assumptions about the transformation of peasants into proletarians — have unwittingly taken on straw people, refuting hypotheses that no other study has defended for the particular case, or the kind of case, at hand. Avoiding this cul-de-sac requires more explicit comparison of the geographical and historical distribution of evidence for and against such hypotheses.

Karl Marx's prediction, for example, that the modern proletariat would abolish all distinctions of sex and age was apparently based on his observations of the early English — and largely textile — proletariat. Neil Smelser "refuted" Marx by arguing that English textile workers strongly defended their own families by working as families in the earliest mills, and later adapted to capitalism by sending both women and children home from the mills. Male weavers organized strikes against the employment of women in the mills, and accused women wage-workers of both wage cutting and immorality, whether for fraternizing with their male coworkers or for neglecting their duties at home (Smelser, 1959: 232, 281-285). Smelser argued that these responses reflected a culture that, like capitalism itself, valued a family headed by a male breadwinner and guided morally by a female homemaker.

While some scholars contested virtually every part of Smelser's interpretation of the English case (Edwards and Lloyd-Jones, 1973), other scholars were confirming Smelser by reporting opposition from male mill workers to women working in mills elsewhere in the world

(Dublin, 1979; Farnie, 1979; Lambiri, 1966; Millis and Montgomery, 1938). Early labor reformers often focused on the working conditions of women and children, arguing that women and children were in special need of government protection (Commons and Andrews, 1936; Millis and Montgomery, 1938; Montgomery, 1923; Phillips, 1922; Smelser, 1959). Recent studies of textile workers have suggested that the gap between women's and men's wages has widened in favor of men, at least in part as a deliberate policy of male-dominated trade unions, thus reinforcing Smelser's argument that working class culture devalued the work of women outside the home (McGoldrick and Tannen, 1980; Millis and Montgomery, 1938: 388). Louise Tilly and Joan Scott attacked both Marx and Smelser by arguing that both men and women saw women's waged work as an extension of their work within the preindustrial domestic economy rather than as a fundamentally new experience. Women in particular used extended kin networks for mutual aid, and shared a cross-class "women's culture" about how to mobilize such networks in times of crisis. While Tilly and Scott in some sense agree with Smelser that the working class family survived and adapted to industrialization, they have a fundamentally different image of that family (Tilly and Scott, 1978: 152).

These accumulating case studies have demonstrated that the family was an important economic and social unit for textile mill workers in many parts of the world and many stages of the industry's development. In none of these cases, however, was the family a straightforward preindustrial survival, or an unambiguous vehicle of either cross-class social integration or class solidarity. There were fundamental differences in the way the family responded to textile industrialization between regions, between propertied and unpropertied peasants, and between Old World peasants and New World farmers. Even a brief survey of studies done within the core of the world system, in Europe and North America, makes it clear that future studies should not focus simply on proving that capitalism destroyed or preserved the family, but must ask how capitalism affected the family and what kinds of families it affected.

Consumption patterns, for example, may not only reflect economic change, but may also contribute to it. Several studies of textile workers have remarked on the tendency of mill wages in Europe and North America to cycle back into finer clothing (Collier, 1964: 40; Eversley, 1967: 212; Women of Lowell, 1974; Lambiri, 1965: 70, 85). In addition to stimulating the demand for labor, at least in textile mills, these expenditures were an integral part of a marriage system based on personal attraction and waged work rather than on land ownership.

This system altered relations between the sexes in fundamental ways, encouraging earlier marriage and thus more children. These changed relations within the family and new way of forming families in some textile areas both stimulated the demand for cloth and, in the long run, helped to provide labor to produce that cloth.

Changes in attitudes toward marriage and children and the resulting changes in demography very much affected the control that workers had over the supply of labor, and thus their control over the conditions of work. David Landes has argued that textile putting-out in Western Europe, beginning in the late Middle Ages, so encouraged population growth that it "destroyed forever the traditional balance between numbers and area" (Landes, 1966: 12). Many studies of textile putting-out have confirmed a tendency among rural textile workers to marry both more universally and earlier, and thus to have more children than did peasant proprietors at the same time or in the same region (Anderson, 1971; Braun, 1966; Krause, 1967; Levine, 1977; Medick, 1981b). Michael Anderson has suggested that decisions about marriage and children for the working class in rural eighteenth- and nineteenth-century Lancashire, both preindustrial and industrial, reflected life crises rather than any deep-rooted cultural continuity or change: these families simply extended themselves in response to economic crises, then "nucleated" again as soon as they could afford to do so. Parents gambled that what their children would eventually contribute to the family income would exceed the amount it had cost to support them until they were old enough to work; but children often abandoned their parents if they had no land to pass on and were too old to work (Anderson, 1971). Rudolf Braun has suggested that textile putting-out and industrialization in eighteenth-century Switzerland extended similar patterns of family relations, and that these had long prevailed among unpropertied peasants, whose children were relatively independent of their parents. Braun argues simply that the extent to which rural textile workers needed land to survive determined the extent to which they accepted both patriarchy and primogeniture (Braun, 1966). In many areas of the world, the income from textile work allowed smaller and smaller parcels of land to support larger and larger families, thus encouraging partible inheritance and further undermining both patriarchy and primogeniture (Chaplin, 1967, Medick, 1981a, 1981b). In contrast to reports that European peasant patriarchs obliged their children (with varying success) to contribute their textile income to the maintenance or expansion of the family holdings, Thomas Dublin reported that nineteenth-century Massachusetts farmers accepted their daughters' mill wages only reluctantly, as "loans" to help pay off farm mortgages (Dublin, 1979: 39). Differences between Switzerland and Massachusetts surely reflected differences between the world textile market over time as much as they did differences between Swiss culture and New England culture. In order to separate capitalist cultural effects from precapitalist ones, future studies must compare the tendencies of capitalism itself across time and space as well as compare (or infer) cultural patterns.

For example, industrial capitalism may have multiplied and fragmented both peasant families and peasant holdings in some parts of the world, but it may have sought out other areas that were already overpopulated for precapitalist reasons. Joan Thirsk has suggested, for example, that a standing preindustrial *imbalance* between numbers and area in some parts of England "compelled [the inhabitants] to seek some other employment in addition to farming" and thus attracted textile putting-out (Thirsk, 1961: 70). Even before capitalist protoindustrialization, farmers in the areas described by Thirsk "recognized not the hamlet or the village, but the family, as the cooperative working unit" (Thirsk, 1961: 86). Similarly, Braun has described the cotton-spinning protoindustry as attracted to the highlands near Zurich because there the typical precapitalist farmer was "an entrepreneur . . . [and] markedly individualistic" (Braun, 1966: 54-55). In the highlands, even minimal physical family unity was a *result* of capitalism:

> [M]any families were enabled for the first time by industrialization to remain in their homeland [whereas] if the father is earning the family's upkeep in Swabia, the daughter is working as a domestic in Zurich, the oldest son is fighting in Dalmatia, and the mother, with the rest of the family, is spinning in Fischenthal, one can hardly speak of an inner and outer family togetherness [Braun, 1966: 64].

According to both Thirsk and Braun, areas with manorial or estate farming in England, and corporate villages in Switzerland, successfully resisted the new industry and thus some aspects of capitalism. The uneven distribution of Thirsk's family-centered and Braun's individualistic peasantries was obviously linked to the uneven distribution of the textile industry, even if the order of cause and effect in that link is not yet clear. Other scholars have found similar links for the textile industry elsewhere (see Medick, 1981b, for example). In contrast to these findings for European textile industrialization, however, the family and the individual in some areas outside the core of the world system seem to have gained in importance relative to larger units even where preindustrial villages had maintained some effective economic unity, as interfamily cooperation became a social option rather than an economic necessity (Chaplin, 1967: 67-70).

The Portuguese case. The history of the textile industry in northern Portugal further illustrates the importance of a world system perspective in sorting out the effects and the causes of capitalist expansion. In the mid-to-late nineteenth century, many rural families in northwestern Portugal were in the same situation that Braun described for eighteenth-century Switzerland, with the individual members earning their keep in different ways and different places. General demographic studies seem to present an image of chronic overpopulation in northern rural Portugal. At the same time, the local population clearly attempted to control both its own growth and land fragmentation through a kind of primogeniture (the *morgadio*), a high average age at marriage, high rates of religious and secular celibacy, and high rates of emigration (Bacci, 1971; Ribeiro, 1961).

Not even preindustrial population density in this region represented a pristine precapitalist peasant culture. High population density in the northwestern province of the Minho in the sixteenth century already reflected major changes in the national and world economies. The cultivation of corn (maize), potatoes, and beans imported from the New World permitted smaller parcels of land to support larger numbers of people, here as elsewhere in Europe (Araujo, 1979; Ribeiro, 1961). Furthermore, the demand for handspun and handwoven linen created an important cottage industry that required and supported an even greater population density. Nor did high population density later reflect any reckless disregard for the economic future among the protoindustrial or industrial working class. The Minho as a whole was famous for its *minifundia*, or smallholdings, but national laws favoring partible inheritance after the mid-nineteenth century tended to fragment these holdings even further. In the twentieth century, textile mills often located in parishes with relatively low population density, after which these parishes soon become among the most densely populated in the region. Oral evidence suggests that the mills eventually competed successfully with agriculture even for the labor of landowners themselves, leading even self-sufficient peasants to subdivide, or even to abandon and sell their land.[1]

Some evidence suggests that, as in Joan Thirsk's putting-out areas, the family rather than the village was the basic economic unit in the Minho. One proverb advised parents to get as much work out of their children as they could (*o trabalho do menino é pouco, mas quem o perde é louco;*[2] Carvalho, 1941: 103). Parents controlled their unmarried children's earnings even in landless families. Whether or not a family-centered peasantry had attracted the textile industry to the area in the first place, by the twentieth century a village in the Minho functioned largely as a social rather than economic unit, much as in textile zones elsewhere (Chaplin, 1967). In addition, even if the textile industry had once fed new income into family budgets administered by patriarchs, by the 1970s sons in particular were resisting this parental authority over their earnings.

Textile industrialization did not reinforce or establish any clear sexual equality in northwestern Portugal. A kind of Portuguese folk sociology claimed that the northwestern province of Minho was originally matriarchal rather than patriarchal (Pimentel, 1905; Carvalho, 1941; Sampaio, 1944; Vaz, 1981), and rural women do seem to have had more of a voice in family decisions here than in southern Portugal, even if only because more of their husbands and fathers were absent through emigration (Caillier-Boisvert, 1968). In some folktales, women cleverly fooled their husbands about the amount of flax the wives had spun for market, suggesting that women could outsmart men but also that they were subject to male authority (Carvalho, 1941). Other sources suggest that in Portugal, as else in rural Europe, female operatives were seen as "loose women" (Pimentel, 1902: 301). In 1888, male weavers in the city of Porto complained, much as had the male weavers studied by Smelser, that the new mechanized mills were "hiring . . . almost exclusively women" so that the "mission of men in society was being transformed, and they were having to perform at home the functions of the [absent] women" (Inquérito, 1889: 18). The first mills, equipped with wooden looms, employed women as *mestras* on a kind of par with men, but mechanization in the twentieth century eventually pushed women out of this "labor aristocracy."

The corporatist dictatorship that governed Portugal from 1928 to 1974 officially discouraged wage work for women outside the home, claiming thereby to express the workers' own basic values. In 1958, the minister for social welfare and labor declared that

> the problem of female work is not, as far as we are concerned, to promote its further development . . . given, as a reality, that some women do work outside the home, we are attempting to make sure that this does not interfere with, much less prevent, the fulfillment of their high calling to motherhood [Veiga de Macedo, 1958: 32-33].

The corporatist state in Portugal claimed to protect the family as a defense against both capitalist individualism and socialist collectivism. Given that labor reforms and textile unions in unabashedly capitalist countries also "defended the family"—particularly the patriarchal family, however—it seems clear that the family thus defended was as much a product of capitalism as a defense against it. The same could be said for partible inheritance or for large family size. This complexity does not mean that Portuguese peasants did not become proletarians in this textile region; it means that they may have done so more than once, without ever abandoning the family or or the land, or migrating to cities. After more thorough comparison than is possible here, the Portuguese case may prove to be typical rather than atypical in its complexity. The literature on textile workers elsewhere suggests that almost no textile workers anywhere abandoned the family or patriarchy completely, or adjusted their rates of reproduction successfully to the labor market, nor did capitalism anywhere necessarily press them relentlessly to do so.

POLITICS IN WORKING CLASS CULTURE: FROM SUBSISTENCE TO STATE PATRONAGE

While assumptions made in studies of working class culture about the political implications of workers' family structures and strategies cover a wide range of possible positions, assumptions made in such studies about the links between economic position and political action cluster at two poles. Some studies expect proletarians who make their living in a complex division of waged labor to be more mobile, both geographically and socially, than are peasants who depend on subsistence agriculture; the free circulation of capital, labor, and information under capitalism should raise the general standard of living so that the industrial working class can advance itself through education and defend itself through electoral politics and collective bargaining. Such studies include in their assumptions the possibility that ingrained peasant conservatism or fear of change might keep some workers dependent on preindustrial patron-client ties and thus prevent them from taking full advantage of the opportunities presented by capitalism. In contrast, another group of studies assumes that the alienation of workers from the means of production will make them resentfully dependent on the world labor market, thus forcing them into an unwanted geographical mobility, if not actually lowering their standard of living. These studies expect that the freedom to be economically insecure under capitalism will force the industrial working class to abandon the patron-client ties that protected the peasantry and organize a militant if not revolutionary class struggle.

Both sets of assumptions often take it for granted that preindustrial peasants and artisans owned their own means of subsistence, and that such ownership made these people politically and economically conservative—either unable to take advantage of capitalist opportunities, or capable of resisting capitalist exploitation. Yet recent studies, especially of textile workers, have increasingly blurred this distinction between peasant proprietors and the propertyless proletariat. Studies of protoindustrialization in Europe have pushed the origins of the unpropertied industrial proletariat back well before the appearance of the first factories (Freudenberger, 1977; Kellenbenz, 1974; Kriedte et al., 1981; Rogers, 1981; Wolff, 1979). David Landes has argued that textile production in medieval Flanders and northern Italy was "organized by typically capitalist entrepreneurs" employing "a true proletariat" (Landes, 1966: 9). On the other hand, medieval cloth merchants developed a rural putting-out system specifically to undercut the power of urban guilds (Freudenberger, 1977; Kellenbenz, 1974; Kisch, 1981; Landes, 1966; Schremner, 1976; Wolff, 1979).

The textile industry continued to seek out low-cost rural labor in the following centuries. In the eighteenth and nineteenth centuries, European handloom weavers were almost universally part-time workers, combining weaving with farming, fishing, or construction (Blythell, 1969). In the nineteenth and twentieth centuries, many textile mill workers were peasant-workers (Chao, 1977; Chaplin, 1967; Dansette, 1954; Dehn, 1913; Freudenberger, 1977; Heywood, 1977; Kellenbenz, 1974; Kisch, 1981; Manchester Guardian, 1925, 1929; Schremner, 1976; Wolff, 1979). In Latin America, "the movement of persons from agriculture to industry and back again appears to have followed the cyclical disturbances in the world economy" (ILO, 1963c; ll). The rise of a precapitalist textile proletariat in Europe and the incomplete transformation of peasants into proletarians in the textile industry throughout the world system challenge both sets of assumptions outlined at the beginning of this section. Some textile workers may have actively resisted expropriation and proletarization by defending their family unity and by part-time farming, but others seem to have preserved the very same patterns only because they had no permanent opportunities to work in factories rather than because they were actively resisting such opportunities. In political and economic strategies as well as in family relations, distinguishing adaptation to capitalism from resistance to capitalism and distinguishing successful from unsuccessful resistance requires the comparative study of capitalism itself as well as the comparative study of workers.

Even when workers themselves explicitly saw family unity or part-time farming as their best defense in the geographically mobile and crisis-prone textile industry, that strategy may also have worked in the interests of their employers. Although many recent studies of working class culture have implied that workers preserved family unity primarily as a defense against capitalist exploitation, some studies have interpreted this working class defense as a subtle kind of capitalist offense. Both Karl Marx and Neil Smelser, for example, argued that family economic unity retarded the development of revolutionary working class politics. Marx believed that capitalism would inevitably undermine such unity, but Smelser argued that capitalism had in fact defended the family, to some extent precisely to head off the political consequences that Marx predicted. Shizeto Tsuru suggested explicitly that "the survival of traditional family relations" was "encouraged for the interest of those who benefitted from cheap labor" in nineteenth- and twentieth-century Japan (Tsuru, 1963: 148). Froebel, Heinrichs, and Kreye similarly argued that family economic unity and part-time farming or other self-employment permitted the Asian industrial working class to reproduce itself for lower wages than European textile workers could afford, and thus simultaneously encouraged the industry to relocate to Asia and discouraged Asian workers from organizing along the lines of European unions or labor parties (Froebel et al., 1980).

The rural dispersion of the textile industry, in particular, has both encouraged textile workers to maintain their links with agriculture and discouraged them from engaging in revolutionary politics. One late eighteenth-century Scottish weaver identified the latter effect of rural industry very clearly—"we being scattered over the whole face of the country, cannot communicate with each other, and we are easily routed by our masters" (Blythell, 1969: 178). Samuel Chapman and Francis Collier both described the early English mills as seeking rural sites with this very effect in mind (Collier, 1964: 60; Chapman, 1967: 160). In England between 1780 and 1840, the government proposed to rent "allotments" of land at low rates to weavers, arguing that "the labourer . . . belonged and had his roots on the land" (Barnett, 1967: 176). Workers with land allotments either did not join, or actively opposed, riots by their landless colleagues in the 1830s (Barnett, 1967: 173). Even in the twentieth century, the ILO explicitly attributed the textile industry's generally low rate of unionization throughout the world to its geographical dispersion (ILO, 1948c: 3, 21, 35), and other studies have drawn the same conclusion (Dansette, 1954; Dehn, 1913; Kellenbenz, 1974).

In general, the political experience of textile workers seems to be one of dispersion and defeat more often than one of either defensive or revolutionary unity. Although E. P. Thompson saw English handloom weavers as the nucleus of a politically militant British working class culture (Thompson, 1963), Duncan Blythell argued that the same handloom weavers had been forced to enter politics and to appeal to the state for economic relief because they had no leverage of their own (Blythell, 1969). David Chaplin offered a very similar account of the "patrón-peon" relationship between Peruvian textile workers on the one hand and both their employers and the state on the other hand, as "due not simply to well-established tradition but also to the workers' objectively weak situation" (Chaplin, 1967: 215). Other scholars have documented similar kinds of paternalism in both German and North American textile towns (Dehn, 1913: 26, 72-73; MacDonald, 1928; Potwin, 1927). A few highly skilled textile workers, like mule spinners and loomfixers in the world-dominant British textile industry, could stage effective strikes on their own behalf (Lazonick, 1981; White, 1978), but textile workers more often relied on the state to improve their working conditions through legislation (Blythell, 1969; Chaplin, 1967; ILO, 1948c).

Often, textile workers could only obtain effective, rather than nominal, state protection when they could already defend their interests through their own organizations; when they could not defend themselves directly, they could not defend themselves through patronage either. Thus many governments only enforced labor legislation in the textile industry when the balance of labor supply and demand shifted in favor of the workers. David Landes has argued that early labor reforms in England, for example, ultimately owed less to working class pressure than to "vested interests opposed to emigration on selfish grounds" (Landes, 1966: 21). However cynical, this kind of naked labor-market argument does seem to apply to textile workers even in twentieth-century Europe. Many countries suddenly passed the ten-hour day and then the eight-hour day during World War I labor shortages and the postwar depression, when textile manufactures in particular wanted to reduce production to maintain profits (Dehn, 1913; ILO, 1916: 1-4; Millis and Montgomery, 1923). The next general wave of wage increases and improved benefits in European textile mills coincided with labor shortages after World War II, when younger workers balked at returning to an industry renowned for low wages and health hazards (ILO, 1948b). Between the two World Wars and after World War II, the world textile industry "stranded" (ILO, 1937: 156) both militant and docile workers with increasing ease, as cheaper labor became accessible elsewhere in the world system. In a kind of Catch-22, textile workers in earlier periods could raise their standard of living both by organizing and by deserting the industry for other kinds of employment, whereas workers in later periods may not have been able to use either strategy.

Given that workers in the older textile centers often found they could not improve conditions by either militance or patronage except during temporary labor shortages, it does not seem peculiar to find workers in the newer textile centers defending their interests through erratic "peasant" work habits rather than through explicitly "proletarian" union drives and strikes. In 1968 the ILO pointed out that strikes were "quite exceptional" in the textile industries of developing countries; that unions were weak, even where they existed; and that workers expressed their discontent through high rates of absenteeism and turnover and overall "low productivity" (ILO, 1968b: 59). Nevertheless, many studies continue to explain the behavior of textile workers in developing countries, particularly in rural areas, as a result of deeply rooted "peasant" conservatism. The 1963 ILO report on textiles, for example, clearly explained that "the movement of persons from agriculture to industry and back again" in Latin America "appears to have followed the cyclical disturbances in the world economy" and thus to have been an adaptive response to capitalism. Nevertheless, the same report cited the "imperfect assimilation of peasant labour to industrial careers" as an obstacle to economic development in the new textile countries (ILO, 1963: 12). From these workers' own point of view, however, assimilating any more perfectly to industrial careers may well have been economically fatal.

Thus the apparently incomplete transformation of any given peasantry into a proletariat may reflect several different histories. In some areas the textile industry deliberately sought out a less-than-self-sufficient peasantry to lower its wage costs. In other cases the proletariat actually predated the peasantry, which was created by renting (or even selling) land to formerly landless workers in return for their economic and political cooperation. In yet other cases both peasantry and proletariat alternated as phases in the lives of the same working class. In all these cases, both assimilation to industrial work and resistance to industrial work require explanation; neither is an economically naive, strictly cultural response to capitalism.

The Portuguese case. As in many areas of the world, a combination of the textile industry and agriculture had a long history in northwestern Portugal. Rural handloom weavers had reduced the wage bills of local linen exporters in the sixteenth century in the very same sort of move undertaken against the urban guilds in other parts of Europe at about the same time. By the end of the nineteenth century, however, the rural linen industry in northern Portugal

> vegetates, in reality it no longer lives . . . the woman who weaves lives precariously in a little hut that serves as both workshop and home. There she passes the years occupied in her craft, taking time from it only for the household chores and to cultivate the tiny plot that surrounds her shack. . . . If it were not for the help that comes to this craftswoman from other small jobs she or her family perform [for money], or from the rent of some small property, or money sent by some relative who emigrated to try to improve their [collective family] condition, she would soon have to abandon her craft in order not to starve to death! [Geraldes, 1913; 17-23]

This linen weaver and her family were in the same position as the Swiss families that Braun described, scattered over the face of the globe and over myriad occupations and, as the English families that Thirsk described, forced to work for wages because they could not live from agriculture. The first statistical evidence, from 1940 and 1954, calculated that from one-half to two-thirds of the agricultural population in northwestern Portugal was less than self-sufficient (Portugal, Recenseamento Geral, 1940; Martins, 1973). By the mid-twentieth century at least, much small-scale agriculture was in effect a subsidiary of the textile industry, depending on factory wages to pay for seeds and fertilizer. In this case, however, the mixture of occupations reflected both a first wave of linen protoindustrialization and a second wave of cotton mill expansion.

In an 1888 inquiry into the textile industry in the city of Porto, the urban weavers complained that textile putting-out in the rural valleys along the new British-built railroads was driving their own wages down (Inquérito, 1889). The rule workers had a reputation for political passivity. The textile unions that responded to the industrial surveys of 1889 and 1910 were concentrated in Porto. In 1910, none of the unions that responded from the smaller northern cities represented textile workers (Cabral, 1977: 263-293). Older workers in the region, however, remember great strikes along the rural textile corridor in 1909. By the 1920s, the same railways that had been built to bring the textile industry out into the rural valleys, within reach of low-cost labor, were also beginning to bring union organizers from the city within reach of that labor force (Vanguarda Operária, 1929, 1930).

In 1933-1934, the corporatist dictatorship made all unions state organizations and outlawed strikes. The corporatist state practiced patron-clientage on a grand scale, presenting Prime Minister António Oliveira Salazer as the "father of the workers." To some extent, textile workers in the northwest seem to have accepted this image as legitimate. In interviews conducted in the early 1980s, textile workers in the northwest blamed Salazar for food shortages during World War II, as had the workers who led hunger marches at the time (Avante!, 1943, 1944). Yet these complaints often accepted the terms of patronage used by the state, blaming Salazar for not fulfilling his "paternal" responsibilities in making sure that his "children" got enough to eat. In interviews many older textile workers who bitterly criticized political repression under Salazar praised the corporatist regime for introducing, and at least in the 1930s for enforcing, minimum wages and the eight-hour day. There were isolated strikes in this region under the dictatorship, but no sustained labor or political uprising.

In Portugal, the corporatist state valued its own prestige above all else. Thus while it forced industrialists to accept some labor reforms, it also forced workers to accept low wages. Both textile firms and the corporatist state explicitly hoped that the rural location of the textile industry in the northwest would encourage workers to retain some subsistence base in agriculture, and thus to be satisfied with low industrial wages. One Portuguese textbook about the textile industry, published in 1965, pointed out

> the appreciable advantages, from the social point of view, of the rural population finding industrial work without ever leaving home. Under these conditions, the peasant transforms himself into a factory worker during the 8 hours of industrial work, and uses the rest of his time in cultivating the smallholding that, normally, he rents. In this way he can live off a relatively low industrial salary. . . . It seems that this system is the most appropriate to the circumstances of modern life in the most populous areas, as is demonstrated . . . [by experiences in] other countries such as Japan, India, China, and Italy [Ribeiro, 1965: 257-258].

At the same time, of course, the corporatist regime was prepared to use political force against any workers who for some reason did not accept this economic logic.

In the Portuguese textile industry, as in other textile industries throughout the world, wages and working conditions improved most dramatically not through state patronage alone but when labor shortages allowed the workers themselves to confront both their employers and the state from a position of strength. In the late 1960s, massive emigration to northern Europe created labor shortages in the textile mills, which in turn gave workers the confidence to stage an increasing number of illegal strikes. These conditions forced the state to enforce its own labor litigation more consistently, and often forced millowners to exceed official minimum wages. Shortly after the 1974 revolution made strikes legal, however, the demand for both Portuguese labor and Portuguese textiles abroad began to retract. The resulting increase in unemployment restored in some mills the combination of paternalism and repression, and the appearance of "peasant" conservatism among the workers, that had prevailed under the dictatorship. In the 1980s, many older workers argued that they had no reason to support strikes, because even low mill wages were a big improvement on what they had earned as day laborers or tenant farmers before the mills were built. These workers knew from personal experience that the mills had not always been there, and often argued that too many strikes might drive the mills away. Many slightly younger workers, with no memory of the preindustrial period, would not support strikes for a different reason. Even if the state would protect them against being fired for striking, it could not guarantee that their children would not be denied jobs in retaliation against the parents. In the Portuguese case, and in may other cases of textile industrialization throughout the world, family unity and a class historical memory may have defended workers against the vagaries of a highly mobile industry precisely by forcing them into political passivity.

CONCLUSION

Betty Messenger has argued that most industrial workers have their own culture, including the kind of "industrial folklore" that she collected from linen workers in Northern Ireland (Messenger, 1978). Along with Messenger and many studies of working class culture, the preceding discussion has simply assumed that the industrial working class *has* a culture—that is, that class is an important, if not the most important, cultural unit for workers. This possibility is certainly worth considering for each case, but so are other cultural units such as geographical community, sex, and age group. Immanuel Wallerstein has suggested, for example, that "in a world-economy the political structure tends to link culture with spatial location" (Wallerstein, 1974: 231). In several of the studies discussed above, state support for the geographical "cultural differences" that made rural or peripheral labor relatively docile and cheap seem to support this hypothesis. A number of other studies of textile workers have examined cultural units other than class. Anthony Wallace argued that a nineteenth-century Pennsylvania mill hamlet maintained a community culture across class lines (Wallace, 1978). Louise Tilly and Joan Scott argued that a specifically working women's culture survived and adapted to industrialization in Western Europe (Tilly and Scott, 1978), while Thomas Dublin argued that such a culture was born and died within two generations in Lowell, Massachusetts (Dublin, 1979). Tamara Hareven has recently argued that generations, along with and across family and class, were fundamental cultural units in Manchester, New Hampshire (Hareven, 1982). If world capitalism tends through national states to support geographical cultures (such as the one that Wallace described) then class-, sex-, or age-based cultures could in themselves be forms of "resistance to capitalism" under such circumstances, whether or not that resistance was overtly political.

General theories of working class culture would compare all of these studies with one another with the aim of discovering which cultural unit was in the end *the* most important to *the* textile proletariat. General cultural categories would compare case studies in order to classify them, without necessarily explaining their similarities and differences. From a world systems perspective, however, the crucial questions are how and why each group experienced capitalism differently. Early twentieth-century linen workers, relatively protected within the then-dominant British textile industry, may have had the urban concentration and above all economic security to develop their own folklore. Mill workers on their way to becoming frontier farmers in early nineteenth-century Pennsylvania may have had neither the security nor the incentive to develop such lore. Specifically women's cultures may have thrived in some places and not in others, or legislative protection focused on women may have changed their culture by allowing or forcing them to spend more time at home. Finally, as the world textile industry became increasingly mobile in the twentieth century, the very real threat of losing their jobs may have forced all workers in the newer textile centers to behave like first-generation workers. A capitalist world system that is heterogeneous over both space and time may thus create as much cultural variation as it discovers.

In addition to place, time, sex, and age, capitalism may vary and provoke cultural variation by industry. The textile industry, for example, although one of the first and largest employers under capitalism, may not be very representative of that system. Many studies of the textile industry have made ungrounded assumptions about the "normal" dedication of capitalist culture to economic growth, technological innovation, class distinctions, and laissez-faire politics. Many textile industrialists in particular have fallen short of these norms, hanging onto outdated technologies or investing their industrial profits in landed estates (Barnett, 1967; Chaplin, 1967; Chapman, 1973; Coleman, 1973; Heywood, 1977; Hoffman, 1963; Jones, 1967; Kisch, 1981; Landes, 1966; Schremner, 1976; Wolff, 1979). Some textile entrepreneurs, although certainly not a majority, rose from the ranks of the proletariat, thus blurring the class distinction between themselves and their coworkers or employees (Chapman, 1967; Dansette, 1954; Dehn, 1913; Farnie, 1979; Freudenberger, 1977; Strew, 1977). Many textile entrepreneurs relied on their national governments, rather than on their own ingenuity, to finance their industrial expansion (Freudenberger, 1977; Heywood, 1977; Manchester Guardian, 1925, 1929; Strew, 1977; Wolff, 1979). In virtually every case, state intervention, often in the form of war, was critical in controlling markets (Dehn, 1913; Farnie, 1979; Freudenberger, 1977; Heywood, 1977; ILO, 1937, 1948; Rostow, 1963; Strew, 1977).

Thus the textile industry, even in the core of the world system, may not have been "really" capitalist, and textile workers may not therefore have been representative of working class culture under capitalism. From a world systems perspective, however, the textile industry's quirks do not suggest that studies of working class culture should concentrate on some more representative industry. Instead these atypical characteristics suggest that such studies should concentrate on specific analytical questions, such as when and why particular workers adopted patriarchal families or revolutionary politics. Both case studies and comparative studies must consider world economic conditions and state intervention as possible causes of specific cultural changes, rather than describing or classifying each working class culture as a fixed or indissoluble whole. The textile industry was very much "really" capitalist, and textile workers were very much a real industrial working class—not because they followed a fixed set of capitalist rules, but because they played an important role in real historical capitalism. The importance of world systems theory for the study of working class culture lies in its capacity to organize both economic and cultural variation not into rules and exceptions or a proliferating series of categories, but into a single complex world history.

NOTES

1. Some of the conclusions in this chapter are based on unpublished sources, including a series of oral history interviews and items from the archives of the corporatist state textile unions and regional labor ministry delegations in the northwestern Portuguese districts of Braga and Porto. I have also consulted the official newspaper of the Portuguese Communist Party, *Avante!*, published clandestinely from 1933 to 1974 (and hence without place of publication), available at the PCP headquarters in Lisbon. In particular, these materials were my sources for conclusions about the labor practices of the corporatist dictatorship and textile workers' responses. Readers interested in the actual evidence for these conclusions should consult "Corporatism and Class Consciousness in Northwestern Portugal" (Ingerson, 1984).

2. "The child's work is little, but anyone who wastes it is crazy."

REFERENCES

ANDERSON, M. (1971) Family Structure in Nineteenth-Century Lancashire. Cambridge: Cambridge University Press.

ARAUJO, I. A. (1979) "A revolução do milho vista duma aldeia do Minho serrano." Histórias e Ideias 3-4. Avante! (1943, 1944)

BACCI, M. L. (1971) A Century of Portuguese Fertility. Princeton, NJ: Princeton University Press.

BLYTHELL, D. (1969) The Handloom Weavers: A Study in the English Cotton Industry During the Industrial Revolution. Cambridge: Cambridge University Press.

BRAUN, R. (1966) "The impact of cottage industry on an agricultural population," in The Rise of Capitalism. See Landes 1966.

CABRAL, M. V. (1977) O operariado nas vésperas da República, 1909-1910. Lisboa: Editorial Presença.

CAILLIER-BOISVERT, C. (1968) "Soajo, une communauté feminine rurale de l'Alto Minho." Bulletin des Etudes Portugaises 27: 237-278.

CARVALHO, A. L. de (1941) Os mesteres de Guimarães, vol. 2: estudo histórico e etnográfico do linho. Guimarães.

CHAMBERS, J. D. (1972) Population, Economy and Society in Pre-Industrial England. London: Oxford University Press.

CHAO, K. (1977) The Development of Cotton Textile Production in China. Cambridge, MA: Harvard University Press.

CHAPLIN, D. (1967) The Peruvian Industrial Labor Force. Princeton, NJ: Princeton University Press.

CHAPMAN, S. D. (1967) The Early Factory Masters: The Transition to the Factory System in the Midlands Textile Industry. Newton Abbott, England: David & Charles.

———(1972) The Cotton Industry in the Industrial Revolution. New York: Macmillan.

COLEMAN, D. C. (1973) "Textile growth," in N. B. Harte and K. G. Ponting (eds.) Textile History and Economic History. Manchester: Manchester University Press.

COLLIER, F. (1964) The Family Economy of the Working Classes in the Cotton Industry, 1784-1833. Manchester: Manchester University Press.

COMMONS, J. R., and J. B. Andrews (1936) Principles of Labor Legislation. New York: Harper & Row.

DANSETTE, J. L. (1954) Origines at évolution d'une bourgeoisie: quelques familles du patronat textile de Lille-Armentières, 1789-1914. Lille: Emile Raoust et Cie.

DEHN, R. M. R. (1913) The German Cotton Industry: A Report. Manchester: Manchester University Press.

DUBLIN, T. (1979) Women at Work: The Transformation of Work and Community in Lowell, Massachusetts, 1826-1860. New York: Columbia University Press.

EDWARDS, M. M. and R. Lloyd-Jones (1973) "N. J. Smelser and the cotton factory family—a reassessment," in N. B. Harte and K. G. Ponting (eds.) Textile History and Economic History. Manchester: Manchester University Press.

EVERSLEY, D. E. C. (1967) "The home market and economic growth in England, 1750-1780," in E. L. Jones and G. E. Mingay (eds.) Land, Labour and Population in the Industrial Revolution. New York: Barnes and Noble.

FARNIE, D. A. (1979) The English Cotton Industry and the World Market. Oxford: Clarendon Press.

FISHER, F. J., ed. (1961) Essays in the Economic and Social History of Tudor and Stuart England. Cambridge: Cambridge University Press.

FREUDENBERGER, H. (1977) The Industrialization of a Central European City: Brno and the Fine Woollen Industry in the Eighteenth Century. Edington, England: Pasold Research Fund, Ltd.

FROEBEL, F., J. Heinrichs and O. Kreye (1980) The New International Division of Labor. Cambridge: Cambridge University Press.

GERALDES, M. de M. N. (1913) Monografia sobre a indústria do linho no distrito de Braga: relatório de inquérito oficial. Coimbra: Imprensa da Universidade.

HAREVEN, T. K. (1982) Family Time and Industrial Time: The Relationship Between the Family and Work in a New England Industrial Community. Cambridge: Cambridge University Press.

HARTE, N. B., and K. G. Ponting (1973) Textile History and Economic History. Manchester: Manchester University Press.

HEYWOOD, C. (1977) The Cotton Industry in France, 1750-1780: An Interpretive Essay. Loughborough University Department of Economics.

HOFFMAN, W. G. (1963) "The take-off in Germany," in W. W. Roston (ed.) The Economics of Take-Off. Cambridge: Cambridge University Press.

INGERSON, A. (1984) "Corporatism and class consciousness in Northwestern Portugal." Ph. D. dissertation, The Johns Hopkins University, Baltimore, MD.

Inquérito sobre o estado da indústria de tecelagem na cidade do Porto e a situação dos respectivos operários (1889) Lisboa: Imprensa Nacional.

International Labour Office (1921) Tendencies of European Labour Legislation Since the War. Geneva.

International Labour Office, Textiles Committee

(1968a) General Report: Recent Events and Developments in the Textile Industry. Geneva.

———(1968b) Labor Problems in the Textile Industry in Developing Countries. Geneva.

———(1968c) The Effects of Structural and Technological Changes on Labour Problems in the Textile Industry. Geneva.

———(1963) Conditions of Employment and Related Problems in the Textile Industry in Countries in the Course of Industrialization. Geneva.

——(1950) General Report. Lyons.

——(1948a) General Report. Geneva.

——(1948b) Employment Problems, with Special Reference to Recruitment and Training. Geneva.

——(1948c) Industrial Relations. Geneva.

——(1937) The World Textile Industry: Economic and Social Problems. Geneva.

JONES, E. L. and G. E. MINGAY [eds.] (1967) Land, Labour and Population in the Industrial Revolution. New York: Barnes and Noble.

KELLENBENZ, H. (1974) "Rural Industries in the West from the End of the Middle Ages to the Eighteenth Century," in P. Earle (ed.) Essays in European Economic History, 1500-1700. Oxford: Clarendon Press.

KISCH, H. (1981) "Proto-industrialization between industrialization and deindustrialization," in P. Kriedte et al. (eds.) Industrialization before Industrialization. New York: Cambridge University Press.

KRIEDTE, P. H. Medick, and J. Schlumbohm [eds.] (1981) Industrialization before Industrialization: Rural Industry in the Genesis of Capitalism. New York: Cambridge University Press.

LAMBIRI, I. (1965) Social Change in a Greek Country Town. Research Monograph Series 13. Athens: Center of Planning and Economic Research.

LANDES, D. S. (1966) The Rise of Capitalism. New York: Macmillan.

LAZONICK, W. H. (1981) "Production relations, labor productivity, and choice of technique: British and U.S. cotton spinning." Journal of Economic History 41: 491-516.

LEVINE, D. (1977) Family Formation in an Age of Nascent Capitalism. New York: Academic Press.

MACDONALD, L. (1928) Southern Mill Hills: A Study of Social and Economic Forces in Certain Textile Mill Villages. New York: Alex L. Hillman.

MACEDO, H. V. de (1958) Alguns princípios da política social e corporativa portuguesa. Lisboa: Ministério das Corporações e Previdência Social.

McGOULDRICK, P. and M. Tannen (1980) "The increasing pay gap for women in the textile and clothing industries, 1910 to 1970." Journal of Economic History 40: 799-814. (See also further discussion in Journal of Economic History 42.)

Manchester Guardian (1929) Special supplement on "World Textiles." July 11.

——(1925) Special supplement on "European Textiles."

MARTINS, J. S. (1973) Estruturas agrárias em Portugal continental, Vol. 1. Lisboa: Prelo Editora.

MEDICK, H. (1981a) "The proto-industrial family economy," in P. Kriedte et al. (eds.) Industrialization before Industrialization. New York: Cambridge University Press.

——(1981b) "The structures and function of population-development under the proto-industrial system," in P. Kriedte et al. (eds.) Industrialization before Industrialization. New York: Cambridge University Press.

MESSENGER, B. (1978) Picking Up the Linen Threads: A Study in Industrial Folklore. Austin: University of Texas Press.

MILLIS, H. A. and R. E. Montgomery (1938) Labor's Progress and Some Basic Labor Problems. New York: McGraw-Hill.

MONTGOMERY, B. G. de (1923) British and Continental Labour Policy. London: Oxford University Press.

OLIVEIRA, E. V. de, F. Galhano, and B. Pereira (1978) Tecnologia tradicional portuguesa: o linho. Lisboa: Instituto Nacional de Investigação Científica.

PHILLIPS, M. (1922) Women and Children in the Textile Industry: An International Survey of Hours of Work and Age of Entry. Amsterdam: International Federation of Trade Unions.

PIMENTEL, A. (1905) As alegres canções do norte. Lisboa: Livraria Viuva Tavares Cardosa.

———(1902) Santo Thyrso de Riba d'Ave. Club Thyrsense.

Portugal, Instituto Nacional de Estatística (1940) Recenseamento geral da população. Lisboa: Imprensa Nacional.

POTWIN, M. A. (1927) Cotton Mill People of the Piedmont. New York: Columbia University Press.

RIBEIRO, E. K. de Q. (1965) O algodão: novos processos de produção, comércio, e indústria. Porto.

RIBEIRO, O. (1961) "Agricultura," in J. Serrão (ed.) Vol. 1, Diccionário de história de Portugal. Lisboa: Editora Iniciativas Editorias.

ROSTOW, W. W. [ed.](1963) The Economics of Take-Off into Sustained Growth. New York: St. Martin's.

———(1960) The Stages of Economic Growth: A Non-Communist Manifesto. Cambridge: Cambridge University Press.

SAMPAIO, G. (1944) Cancioneiro minhoto. Porto: Livraria Educação Nacional.

SCHREMNER, E. (1976) "The textile industry in southern Germany, 1750-1850: some causes for the technological backwardness during the industrial revolution." Textile History 7: 60-89.

SMELSER, N. J. (1959) Social Change in the Industrial Revolution: An Application of Theory to the British Cotton Industry. Chicago: University of Chicago Press.

STREW, R. J. (1977) "The birth of the textile industry in western Columbia." Textile History 8: 131-149.

THIRSK, J. (1961) "Industries in the countryside," in F. J. Fisher (ed.) Essays in the Economic and Social History of Tudor and Stuart England. Cambridge: Cambridge University Press.

———(1978) Economic Policy and Projects: The Development of a Consumer Society in Early Modern England. Oxford: Clarendon Press.

THOMPSON, E. P. (1966) The Making of the English Working Class. New York: Vintage.

TILLY, L., and J. SCOTT (1978) Women, Work and Family. New York: Holt, Rinehart, & Winston.

Vanguarda Operária (1929, 1930) Porto.

VAN HOUTE, F. (1949) L'évolution de l'industrie textile en Belgique et dans le monde de 1800 à 1939. Institut de Recherches Economiques et Sociales.

VAZ, A. L. (1981) O culto da mulher em portugal. Separata de Revista Presença e Dialogo 3 (Setembro).

WALLACE, A. F. C. (1978) Rockdale: The Growth of an American Village in the Early Industrial Revolution. New York: Knopf.

WALLERSTEIN, I. (1974) The Modern World System, Vol. 1. New York: Academic Press.

WHITE, J. L. (1978) The Limits of Trade Union Militancy: The Lancashire Textile Workers, 1910-1914. Westport, CT: Greenwood Press.

WOLFF, K. H. (1979) "Guildmaster into millhand: the industrialization of linen and cotton in Germany to 1850." Textile History 10: 7-74.

Women of Lowell (1974) New York: Arno Press.

WRIGHT, G. (1981) "Cheap labor and southern textiles, 1880-1930." Quarterly Journal of Economics 96: 605-630.

Chapter 9

THE IMPACT OF
WORLDWIDE INDUSTRIAL RESTRUCTURING
ON A NEW ENGLAND COMMUNITY

June Nash
City College of the City University of New York

In the day-to-day relations in an industrial plant, the opposed interests of labor and management are tempered in the rules that order production. Strikes reveal the stresses as well as supports for a given structure of production (Warner and Low, 1947: 1). If the strength of each side could be measured without a conflict, then agreement might be reached without a strike (Coser, 1956: 133). As this cannot be anticipated because of the alliances that may develop among parties to the conflict and other interest groups in the community, strikes must be enacted as "the symbolic displays of political energy" (Shorter and Tilly, 1974: 243).

By examining a series of strikes over time and in industries that are integrated differently in the world capitalist system, we can assess the changes in structure and how these relate to a particular cultural context. In this analysis of strikes in western Massachusetts from 1916 to 1975 I shall try to show how workers in the electrical machinery and electronics industry developed a cultural form of mass action that

AUTHOR'S NOTE: Research was done in part with funds received from the National Science Foundation and the National Endowment for the Humanities in the summer and fall of 1982. I am indebted to them for the assistance enabling me to do the research, and to the invaluable comments and criticisms of Carl Chiaretto, John S. Foley, Theresa Kielman, and Al Litano, and to Max Kirsch who later joined the research project.

effectively allied local business and political forces. This alliance reached the peak of its potential in the post-World War II period when nationally integrated corporations confronted nationally integrated unions. Following the strike wave of 1946, corporations fought organized labor directly by promoting legislation that curbed the right to strike, and indirectly by fomenting the ideological schism of "communism" versus "patriotism." These strategies wore thin in the 1960s as organized labor pulled its ranks together for the strike wave at the end of the decade. But they encountered an even more formidable obstacle in the global integration of production promoted by the tariff and tax laws of that decade. The move overseas in the 1960s and 1970s was part of a long-term trend negating the mutual dependency of industry and community (Arensberg, 1942) when factories were tied to investments in a particular plant and work force. In the nineteenth century the community provided an infrastructure of shops, schools, municipal maintenance, and consumer services while depending on income generated by primary manufacturing establishments. The development of corporations with several plants located in different regions within the United States gave management greater flexibility to operate throughout the nation prior to World War I and during the interwar period. The growing power of the corporations was checked by nationally integrated industrial unions organized in the 1930s. The current movement overseas and the deindustrialization of the United States threaten the base for corporate hegemony.

The strikes that occurred in the Pittsfield plant of General Electric show how this hegemony was constructed in the mutual interaction of organized labor and corporate control. The strikes occurring in the Sprague Electric Company in North Adams and in the owner-operated firm of Wesco in Greenfield reveal the impasse in labor's attempt to come to terms with firms that operate in the sector directly in competition with off-shore producers.

INDUSTRIAL CONFLICT IN PITTSFIELD

Capital accumulation in local textile industries in the nineteenth century provided the infrastructure and the capital for what was to become the dominant industry in Pittsfield in the twentieth century. William Stanley, the inventor of the first polyphase alternating current generator, established an electrical machinery factory in Pittsfield in 1887. He was forced to sell most of the shares of the company that grew tenfold within a decade because of a patent suit threatened by Westinghouse, and in 1903 the company was bought by General Electric (Boltwood, 1916: 269; Passer, 1953: 306; Willison, 1957). The new corporation threatened to close the shop in the very beginning (Berkshire Eagle, February 10, 1903). However, as the efficiency of the alternating current generator became appreciated, the plant was given several new contracts and capital investments of $7,000,000.

The 1916 Strike

World War I stimulated local industries as Europe bought guns, ammunition, and food produced in the United States. Workers, who had remained relatively quiescent as successive waves of immigrants arriving in the nineteenth century outstripped the demand for labor, began to protest the rising cost of living and the decreasing value of their wages. Labor conflicts were frequent in Pittsfield as in other industrial cities. Spinners, organized by 14 craft unions, had a two-month strike by 1,156 workers in the woolen mills in July and August, 1916. A strike in General Electric (GE) followed on September 2, 1916. Of the 6,000 workers, 4,800—including 600 women—walked out. Inspired by the textile workers' gains of a 5 percent wage increase and reduction of the 55-hour workweek to a 50-hour week, GE workers called for similar gains. I first heard about the strike from retired workers at a meeting in the IUE union hall. One recalled the police repression:

> I remember I was standing on Kellogg and Parker Street and Maggie Malloy, she worked in the plant, sassed these big six-by-six cops that was pounding everyone, and they beat her. She was standing right there on her own property and they beat her. My brother went out and beat up the cops. And GE blacklisted him for the rest of his life. . . . The GE would beat people right in public, right over on our lawn. They used to bring in these metropolitan cops from Boston. They wore these helmets, hats, like bobbies.

Piqued by the story, I checked the archives of the local newspaper. The pending strike was reported in the *Berkshire Eagle* on August 26, 1916, the same day that a national railroad strike was said to be "paralyzing the country's transportation system" and "crippling the allied war effort." Labor officials from seven unions including machinists, pattern makers, metalworkers, and electrical workers that dealt with the firm arrived in town. Although 3,600 of the 6,000 workers in the plant were union members, the company did not recognize any bargaining representatives.

The union representatives failed to get an audience with Cummings C. Chesney, the local manager, who was accused of trying to "parcel out" work to the Lynn plant with the intent of a lockout in Pittsfield if a strike were called (Berkshire Eagle, August 29, 1916). The reasons for the strike, set for Labor Day, September 2, were the failure of GE to consult with workers and firing those who joined unions. The cooperating unions requested wage increases of 10 percent to make up for shortening hours from 55 to 52½ per week. The Schenectady GE plant, where 20,000 people were employed, had just accepted a reduction of hours to 52½ with a 5 percent increase in wages. Settlement with this plant early in the game reduced the chances of concerted action by workers of the same corporation.

On September 2, 80 percent of the 6,000 workers quit work and 2,176 of them took part in a parade leading up to a protest meeting on the commons. No disorders were reported and neither city nor special policemen had anything to do as crowds up to "hundreds" reportedly cheered the marchers (Berkshire Eagle, September 2, 1916). The strike included not only the unskilled but also machinists getting $15 to $24 a week. Systematic picketing was reported in the following week, with only 300 workers, including tool and die makers, engineers, and firemen, reporting to work. Although not yet organized, these technicians were reported to be in sympathy with the strike (Berkshire Eagle, September 5, 1916).

The power play involved two major strategies: The union tried to gain the support of other GE plants in a sympathy strike, which was countered by issuing a statement that each plant of the GE Corporation "is handled as an independent unit" (Berkshire Eagle, Sept. 8, 1916). Each side tried to mobilize wider support in the community and the state. While the corporation organized the Berkshire Manufacturers' Association with the stated aim of "defending the American principle of the open shop" (Willison, 1957: 95), the unions secured the endorsement of the Massachusetts State Federation of Labor.

The corporation backed their strategy by bringing in a special force of Boston police, first reported at the plant along with private detectives on September 8. They were joined by 52 Boston Metropolitan Park police requested by Police Chief Sullivan. This provoked the anger of local citizens, who were footing the bill of $400 a day for the police. They drew up a petition with 500 signatures asking that the city council hold a public hearing on the matter of "police harassment of property-owners." In these New England communities, "taxpayers" and "property-owners" are categories that supercede "class" and "occupation" because city officials and services are supported by property taxes.

As the strike wore on in the month of September, a division between machinists and unskilled workers from assembly lines appeared to be emerging, as the International Association of Machinists' president commented that their workers were in high demand and could get jobs elsewhere (Berkshire Eagle, September 22, 1916). Although some other jobs such as those of winders were very skilled, workers could not transfer their skills from electrical machinery to any other industry and so were limited in their bargaining power. The only hope for settlement was a sympathy strike at the Schenectady plant; and when this failed, the strike dissolved. On October 2, the union agreed to the original GE offer. The only concession by the company was an agreement to hear grievances presented by a committee made up of one representative for 200 workers chosen by the workers themselves, but not a union representative.

Both sides claimed a victory, the union asserting that it had accomplished what it had set out to do in demonstrating the ability to coordinate a walkout of nearly 5,000 workers with the concrete gain of shop representation.[1] The company claimed that it had won because it had not moved from the original wage offer and had not accepted union representation.

The outstanding feature of this strike was the moderation of the union demands—always referred to as requests—and the apparently unchecked power of the corporation. Management could ignore the Massachusetts State Conciliation Board and use public funds and police to protect the strikebreakers brought in at the taxpayers' expense. The greater integration of the company, which had several different plants to which it could shift production, enabled management to hold out against labor, which could not gain the support even of the neighboring plant.

Union Organization and the Post-World War II Strike

The National Recovery Act and the National Labor Relations Board that implemented the new laws governing labor relations during Franklin Roosevelt's first term as president, brought about a fundamental change in industry. The struggles for the right to unionize now guaranteed in law did not take place at the General Electric plant in Pittsfield but at small local companies. The first CIO union was brought in by workers at the Lichtman Tanning Corporation in 1937 and other locals were organized in the textile and button mills (Willison, 1957: 177-185).

General Electric did not recognize an independent union as bargaining agent for the workers until 1940 in the Pittsfield plant. This may have been due to the fact that the company-sponsored union had negotiated a pension and wage that was slightly higher than the average for industrial workers in the state. It was only after the Wagner Act had been tested and proven to guarantee the right to organize that organizers from the Schenectady plant, where the United Electric

Radio and Machine Workers (UE) union had won an election in 1938, were able to get workers signed up in the Pittsfield plant in 1940. The union succeeded in overcoming some of the ties based on personality and favoritism to foremen and supervisors who had exercised arbitrary power and in regularizing work schedules. When war was declared on December 7, 1941, a no-strike pledge was signed and wages were frozen for the duration of the war.

Following V.J. Day on August 14, 1945, the long-suppressed drive by labor to catch up with inflation went into effect. On December 14, 1945, UE locals throughout the country voted on whether to go out on strike. The strike vote was 86,229 for and 17,225 against (or 5 to 1 nationally), and in Pittsfield it was 4.6 to 1 in favor. In January 1946, an industrywide strike was declared and 200,000 UE members set up picket lines across the nation in GE, Westinghouse, and GM plants. A week later, 800,000 steel workers shut down steel plants, revealing the unprecedented scope of the organization of workers (Matles and Higgins, 1974: 40).

Strikers encountered support from local police, farmers, congress-men, and the mayors of over a dozen cities in which General Electric was the biggest employer. A special public statement was made by 55 U.S. senators and congressmen declaring, "UE strikers deserve full moral and financial support in their grim struggle for a substantial wage increase and for a decent American standard of living." In nearby Lynn, Massachusetts, merchants contributed $3,000 the first day of the strike and the town community fund gave help to needy cases. All the trade unions in the city of Pittsfield came to the support of the strikers and contributed funds.

In Pittsfield, picketing began on January 15 with 600 participating in the line. Massachusetts state law prevented women from picketing after 6 P.M. and before 7 A.M., a carry-over of protective legislation operating in the plant. This did not hinder their full participation on the daytime picket line; on the tenth day of the strike, over 100 working women and wives of workers with their children marched in the severe cold (Berkshire Eagle, January 24, 1946). Patriotism was at a high tide, and the workers, not the "war-profiteering corporations," were clearly the heroes. The men wore their uniforms on picket duty. Invoking the spirit of the American Revolution, one picket sign read, "America Don't Tread on Me!" (Berkshire Eagle, January 18, 1946). Police Chief Sullivan—the same person who had been in charge of the 1916 strike— no longer responded to company demands such as calling in the Boston police as he had done 30 years before. His commands were limited to forbidding pickets from setting fires in the gutters to keep warm and restricting the size of the signs.

A new management strategy segmenting the work force as ineligible for union membership surfaced in this strike. Engineers, commercial workers, cost and accounting workers, production supervisors, and personal secretaries were declared ineligible because of the sensitivity of their work and were required to work in the plant during the strike. The union's business agent tried to turn away four supervisors, stating that "they will have the stigma of scab until the day they die," but management's prerogative in defining this category was supported by an injunction issued by the superior court against union interference with any persons "lawfully entitled to do so" from entering the plant. The local newspaper editorialized that "the decision [to admit ineligibles] must have been made by the company nationally. We do not believe the local company would ever, of its own volition, ask 1,800 residents of Pittsfield, friends and neighbors of strikers, to endanger the cordial and democratic relations between them by asking them to cross their picket lines."

Local community support for the union was strong. The city council, now including five GE workers, voted 10 to 1 for a resolution urging GE management "to enter immediately into negotiations with the union . . . and alter its present policy in favor of a just and equitable attitude toward the wage needs of Pittsfield's GE employees." A Cadillac dealer who headed the Citizen's Aid Committee said that he "unqualifiedly supported the union because their cause was just." At a meeting in the commons he addressed the workers as follows:

> You are the largest consumers, you buy the goods you yourselves and people like you produce. You are the life of the community and there is no doubt about it. Businessmen realize your importance to this community.

The manager of the plant expressed his belief in unions and his "sincere conviction that the complexities of industrial life today require them." He was a respected man, and the union took the tactic of separating him from the corporation he represented, stating in the newsletter that "there is little doubt in our mind that if it were possible for him to personally negotiate the issues at stake, an early settlement might be forthcoming." They went on to note, however, that "he must conform with the policy set down in New York."

The strike ended by the middle of March. Workers gained a 10 percent pay increase (slightly higher for those getting less than $1.00 per hour). For the first time in history, all GE plants were out, along with all competitors in the electrical machinery industry. Two months later, GE laid off 500 employees (Willison, 1957: 215).

Anticommunism and the Cold War Strikes

The power of the union demonstrated in the early postwar period provoked a profound change in managerial tactics. A drive to curb unions resulted in the passage of the Taft-Hartley Act in 1947. This required a 60-day cooling-off period enabling management to plan its counterattack at the same time that it deprived unions of their most effective weapon, that of surprise. The newfound unity of unions was broken with the requirement that union leaders must sign noncommunist affidavits. When the CIO endorsed the anticommunist campaign, the UE withdrew in 1949 and the International Union of Electrical, Radio, and Machine Workers (IUE) was formed the following day, led by former UE president James Carey. In the elections to determine which union would represent them in the shops organized by the UE, IUE took over half the existing contracts and two-thirds of its members between 1953 and 1956 (Matles and Higgins, 1974: 180).[2]

The anticommunist attack on local union leaders resulted in the defeat of the UE in Pittsfield. General Electric management supported the McCarthy committee by firing workers who refused to testify under oath whether or not they were members of the Communist Party, a tactic that the local newspaper editor called "GE's own Fifth Amendment firing policy."

A new personnel policy spearheaded by Lemuel Boulware, a vice president of the General Electric Corporation, sidestepped the collective bargaining process. Just before the end of a contract period, the management met separately with local union heads to try to ascertain what were the minimal, irreducible demands of workers; and once they decided what their offer would be, they did not budge. The company then proceeded to publicize what it called its "firm, fair offer" in all of its plants and in the communities where they were located (Matles and Higgins, 1974: 251).

It was in this climate of labor relations that James Carey, the man who led the purged ranks of the IUE, called a strike against GE in 1960. GE employed 240,000 workers in 166 plants, and the IUE had a total membership of 58,000. As a result of this divided work force, and with many Canadian and domestic plants not affected by the strike, the company had "great flexibility in productive capacity to meet customers' needs" according to Northrup, an industrial relations consultant who was involved in GE's expansion and decentralization in the 1950s (Northrup, 1964). Backman (1962: 295) quoted Northrup as saying that in the expansion at home and abroad "GE has built second or satellite plants in many cases where operations of a group of plants might be jeopardized by a strike in a sole supplying plant." While labor disunity was spreading throughout the 1950s, GE was strengthening its position to confront the union.

Following the Boulware tactic, the company advertised its "firm, fair offer" in the plants where contracts were due to terminate in September 1960. A full-page ad in the Berkshire Eagle (September 1, p. 20) announced that, "over the past two years, employees have made it clear that their main concern is security. What does this mean?" The answer management gave was (1) keeping a good job free from worry as to skills becoming obsolete; (2) financial protection in case of layoffs; and (3) opportunities for better pay and medical benefits. "Therefore GE has made a proposal for improvements in present contracts providing greater employment opportunities, income protection in case of layoffs, general wage increases, increased security on retirement, and greater insurance protection."

The *Berkshire Eagle* (September 4, 1960) maintaining as always a remarkable degree of independence in spite of the income earned from GE ads, pointed out in an editorial that "the cost of living increase is not (as the company says) inflationary, but rather a result of inflation." The editor did, however, agree with the company position that private companies should not pay unemployment security and proposed that this should be paid by the state.

Advertisements placed by the company in the local press questioned what the effects of a strike would do to job security, pinpointed as the chief concern of workers. Their answer was cast in terms affecting each of the three divisions of the Pittsfield plant: The Polaris Missile contract being negotiated by the Ordnance Division with the U.S. Navy might go to Hughes with a loss of 300 union jobs; plastics would lose contracts to competitors causing a loss of 100 jobs; and the Transformer Department might lose up to 78 jobs. In addition to advertising in the local press, the company sent 277 different written communications to their employees (Kuhn, 1980: 231). In their ads the company urged its employees to vote, adding, "If you vote for a strike, you will jeopardize your pay, family welfare and job."

Pittsfield's Local 255 voted against the strike with a 2-to-1 margin in a meeting attended by 2,600 of the 4,200 production and maintenance workers, but the strike was approved by 45 of 51 IUE locals nationwide. Aware of the split within the ranks, Carey tried to avert the strike by presenting the dispute to a fact-finding board, but his plea was rejected by the president of GE, Ralph J. Cordiner (Berkshire Eagle September 27, 1960). Other attempts by the clergy and governors of the states with large GE plants failed and the strike began on October 2. Despite the discontent in the ranks, only one percent of the workers showed up in the Pittsfield plant on the first day; but by the fourth day the union mobilization began to falter as one after another of the locals began to back out.

Despite the unpopularity of the strike, there was a marked change in the city officials' handling of it compared to earlier strikes. They refused to give the policy authority to open the picket lines and let the trucks into the plant (Berkshire Eagle, October 20, 1960). A GE petition for restraint against mass picketing was denied by three superior court justices on the grounds that if the company had taken advantage of the assistance of a panel of mediators on September 30, the strike could have been averted.

On October 24, the union capitulated and the workers returned to work with little gained except a retraining program for employees whose jobs were being eliminated by technological change, and the loss of a cost-of-living increase contained in the previous contract. Management analysts gave a technical explanation for the failure of the strike: Northrup (1964) based the lack of unity on the variety of jobs related to the great diversity of products in electrical machinery companies. But union leaders blamed it on the ideological schism. Albert Litano, business agent for the IUE in the 1960s, said, "When we started choosing up sides, Boulware said a plague on both sides. We should have cleaned up our own house."

The union brought a suit against General Electric for unfair labor practices in the 1960 strike. Although they won the case four years later, there was no chance of regaining the losses.[3] When a strike was called in 1966, President Johnson urged postponement because of the Vietnam war; and Boulware's offer of a four percent wage increase in the first year of the new contract with three percent increases in the subsequent two years was accepted.

Union leaders spent the time mending the breach. Al Litano, business agent in Pittsfield's IUE local, said that "when we saw what we lost, I, along with Matles and Fitzgerald of the national UE and Foley, Chief Shop Steward of Local 255 IUE, started meeting. It was the birth of coordinated bargaining." This development was an important advance that helped the locals gear up for the big strike in 1969.

The 1969 Strike

In the summer of 1969 as the contract deadline neared, the unity in leadership was matched by unity at home. In the 1946 and 1960 strikes, management had appealed directly to the wives of workers to go against the strike. This taught union leaders to extend their lines of communication. Al Litano told me,

We cautioned the people, "Go home and talk to your wives." In the '46 and '60 strike, pressure from the wives was terrific. [Why did this change?] They saw what they had lost in contracts, especially from 1955 to 1960 in the five-year agreement. They'd see it in take-home pay. Also, the assignment of jobs was by the company, and they wouldn't like the shifts their husbands had to work.

Although a growing awareness of women's effect on a working man's decisions is apparent, the perspective is still that of the male worker although 40 percent of the work force in the Pittsfield plant was female. In the late sixties, women were becoming more active in the union, and 25 of the 265 stewards were women.

October 1, the date for renewal of contracts set by Lemuel Boulware in 1950, gave the company an added advantage because of the cold weather in store for pickets. The climate of opinion, however, was against the company and against the Vietnam war, which was becoming increasingly unpopular. A series of slowdowns, caused by lack of parts (a possible side effect of the war itself since U.S. plants depended on subassembly work in Asian plants) had cut down the pay of contract workers throughout the year.

The union demands were for a 30-month contract with an increase of 35 cents an hour in the first year, 30 cents the second, and 25 cents in the last six months, with 50-cent increases for skilled workers. GE countered with an offer of a three-year contract and increases only in the first year, refusing an escalator clause based on cost-of-living increases (Berkshire Eagle, October 27, 1969). Behind these economic demands was the accumulated resentment against Boulwarism, the labor policy of Vice President Lemuel Boulware that culminated in the year that he published his book outlining the strategy (Boulware, 1969). By circumventing the ritual of collective bargaining in his tactic of presenting a firm, fair offer based on research on what the rank and file wanted, he removed the cultural trappings that had masked the sterile negotiations with a weakened and divided union. Labor was determined to seize back the initiative. UE and IUE were united in supporting the strike and the AFL-CIO backed it as a "struggle against a company. . . determined to destroy not only the union but the whole process of collective bargaining," in George Meany's words (Baer, 1975: 5-6). On the negative side, there were many more unorganized shops in the electrical machinery industry than there had been the decade before, and Northeastern industrial workers were competing with lower-wage workers in the South and overseas. Furthermore, there were many more technicians in proportion to assembly operators, and they often did not join labor unions (Matles and Higgins, 1974: 273).

On October 27, 140,000 of the 310,000 workers in GE plants throughout the nation walked out. In Pittsfield, 1,000 pickets were on duty in the morning when the 7:00 shift came in. The temperature was just above freezing. Most of the incidents that occurred on this morning and in the months that followed occurred at the Ordnance Department where, according to Al Litano, GE tried to break the strike. Community support from local businessmen and professionals as well as other working people was strong. Banks did not foreclose on unpaid mortgages, and local businesses (especially those with long histories in town) gave money and gifts at Christmas, but chain stores gave no help at all.

By November, the area economy was hurting from the strike. The loss of patronage by 5,500 strikers—20 percent of the county's 20,000 industrial workers—meant the loss of one million dollars for businesses in the first month of the strike. Luncheonettes closed, barbershops reported few customers, sales of cars were down 20 percent, and there was a 5 percent drop in supermarket sales.

General Electric lost orders to Detroit Edison and to foreign companies. Sales dropped by almost 2 billion dollars over the same period in the preceding year, and profits were down 100 million dollars. GE stock hit a 5-year low, at 79⅛ per share. GE management countered the union's elation over their ability to close down production with the statement in an advertisement published in the local press that "lost customers mean lost business and lost business means lost jobs" (Berkshire Eagle, November 17, 1969). The company stepped up its attempts to get strikers back to work for the Thanksgiving holiday, reiterating their same offer. But on Thanksgiving Day, the pickets set up a charcoal grill with a plucked bird suspended over it, bearing a sign reading, "No More Pigeon; Let's Talk Turkey."

Christmas season posed another goal for ending the strike because workers always needed extra cash for holiday spending. The union charged GE with hiring strikebreakers and giving bonuses to supervisors and nonunion workers for recruiting "Cinderellas"—18-to-21-year-old women who couldn't work on the third shift and were ordinarily last to be hired. The business agent sent out a call for reinforcements on the picket lines and dozens more showed up on a freezing December 10 morning when the strikebreakers were expected. The company issued a new offer on December 12, but the union turned it down. Pickets adorned a dormant thornapple tree with Christmas lights and one of the pickets arrived on the line dressed as Santa Claus carrying "GE's big bag of nothing."

With the failure of any new developments at Christmas, political pressure was mounted for a settlement. Senator Javits, Republican of

New York, called for a fact-finding board, which was accepted by the union and rejected by GE. Wage losses in Massachusetts were reported as being 3 million dollars a week, and an estimated 3,000 employees were on public assistance. Congressmen met in Beverly to bring about a settlement. Leaders of the AFL-CIO brought pressures for a strikers' benefit bill. In response, GE Vice President Clement E. S. Sutton, Jr., said, "If the strike benefit bill passes, we'd have no alternative but to set in motion programs for a more serious scaling down of our operations here and further expansion to other states."

On January 30, 1970, the IUE and the UE accepted a new offer by the company, subject to ratification following 101 days of strike. Fitzgerald and Matles called it the first contract negotiated by collective bargaining in 20 years. "It took 14 weeks on the picket lines for the organized GE workers to convince GE to respect the union at the bargaining table," they announced.

The final agreement was only slightly better than that offered in December, and both Lynn and Syracuse locals rejected the contract. The union felt pressured by the press buildup of a "fantastic offer" that GE was making. Even more to the point, the union treasury was down to a few thousand dollars—no more than a week's strike benefits for the needy. According to Al Litano, this was one of the best-kept secrets during the last month of the strike. On the other hand, management was forced to yield because of the refusal by longshoremen to unload ships with components from GE plants abroad to fill in for products made in the strike-bound plants.

Despite the claims of victory on both sides, the impact of the strike was negative for the work force and the community. In May of 1970, GE announced plans for a 5 million dollar expansion of its transformer department in their plant in Hickory, North Carolina. Opened in 1956 as a satellite for the GE Pittsfield division, the plant provided the flexibility the corporation liked to have in case of labor disputes.

INDUSTRIAL STRIKES IN NEIGHBORING CITIES

Strikes in Greenfield's Wesco Company in 1979 and North Adams' Sprague Electric Company in 1970 reveal recent trends affecting the industry and the regional economy. Both companies manufacture capacitors, which are components in all electronic products that were formerly manufactured in Pittsfield GE but are now made in their offshore plants or purchased from suppliers such as Sprague and Wesco. Most of the workers are women who earned slightly more than the minium wage before the strike. As suppliers of the kinds of products produced cheaply in foreign plants, both companies maintain that they can only remain in operation if they keep wages down. Both communities have experienced high unemployment rates, ranging from 8 to 13 percent since 1975.

The Sprague Electric Company Strike

Sprague Electric Company was started by Robert C. Sprague in his Quincy, Massachusetts, kitchen in 1926. His sales of $54,000 in 1927 jumped to $234,000 the following year; and in 1930 he purchased the vacated textile mill in North Adams where the headquarters of what is now a minimultinational with plants in Vermont, New Hampshire, other states in the West and South and overseas in Puerto Rico, Mexico, and the Philippiness. Incorporated with General Cable Corporation, the firm maintains a separate identity with Sprague's son serving as vice president.

I first heard of the strike while interviewing the manager in charge of personnel. When he said that the North Adams plant had reduced the work force from 4,500 in the 1960s to 1,800 in the early 1970s I asked what the reason was and he replied,

> With much of our manufacturing, we build a branch plant somewhere and the pilot plant is built here, but the major part of the production goes elsewhere. So it has diminished employment, no question about it, but it's been over a period of years. Well, we had a strike here in 1970. It was a sort of a catharsis. It built up over many, many years, and it blew. When the strike was over, we lost a lot of business, which often happens, not just here, but with other companies.

Until 1970, Sprague's work force was represented by the Independent Condenser Workers and by other unions representing distinct components of the work force: the national Association of Machinists, Technical and Office Workers, and the American Federation of Technical Engineers. Shortly before a vote scheduled to consider the IUE as representative for the production workers, the engineers went out on strike on March 2, the first strike in 21 years. The IAM and those workers signed up with the IUE respected the strike and stayed home.

By mid-March, negotiations had reached an impasse, which Chief Steward Joseph Lord decried as Boulwarism. Sprague followed the Boulware practice of running ads in the local paper, in an attempt to sway the vote on whether IUE or the ICW would be the bargaining agent.

The company carried out practices that had not been used by GE since the 1916 strike. They hired Pinkerton detectives to protect property, and company trucks were accused of driving into picket lines, injuring pickets. During the course of the strike, the company moved an entire floor of machinery to a Nashua, New Hampshire, plant that was not on strike.

Action on the picket lines was not entirely without humor, however. On April 1, pickets took up a collection—40 pennies—and gave them to Robert S. Sprague "to help make up the pay cut Mr. Sprague took last year." Pickets had signs reading, "We Got Ten Percent!" followed by a sign reading "April Fool!" on April 1. When Robert S. Sprague, Jr., attempted to enter the line, the picket nearest him bowed as he ushered him through while other pickets looked on smiling (North Adams, transcript, April 1, 1970).

On May 25, Sprague reached an agreement with the three bargaining units. The victory was short-lived. The three-year contract provided for a six percent raise—one-and-a-half percent less than the union called for and one-and-a-half percent more than the company offered in earlier negotiations. But in early July, the company discontinued most of production at their Union Street plant and was studying operations at the Beaver Street shop with an eye to cutting them. The work force has continued to experience attrition in the 1980s.

Wesco Electric Company Strike

Wesco Electrical Company started producing capacitors in Greenfield in 1949. The company now employs about 125 workers—all female except for 3 male production workers and 6 supervisors. In 1976 the UE started to organize the shop. The union lost the first election by two votes, but when the organizers discovered that "group leaders" who had been talking with management had also voted, they took the case to the NLRB. After winning the court case, the union held another election, which they won on December 9, 1976. The UE was certified as bargaining representative for the employees of Wesco on September 28, 1977, but the company refused to enter into collective bargaining. Finally in February 1979 the UE began contract negotiations calling for a 40-cent across-the-board pay increase and a 15-cent merit raise. When the company refused to consider paying any increase over $3.40 an hour, the women went out on strike on September 26, 1979.

Like many workers in less-skilled jobs in shops belonging to the competitive sector of the economy, the 85 women employed on piecework at Wesco were long-term employees with 10 to 20 years of service. The range of pay was $2.90 to $4.20 an hour with an average of $3.40—only 50 cents above the minimum wage. Benefits were nearly nonexistent; there were no paid sick days, no guaranteed pay raises, and overtime was mandatory. The company threatened to close down if the strike was called, and to fire or give less desirable shifts or jobs to those who went out on strike.

One of the workers commented to me shortly after the strike was over, "They never thought a bunch of women would do like we did do, walking out and everything. That was amazing. I don't think they thought we could get the support we did from the community either." Their support came from workers at GTD, Bendix, and Mayhew, as well as students from the University of Massachusetts. "Restaurants donated soups for our lunches," my informant said, "because we had soup kitchens here. One of the stores was giving us coffee and the trailer park let us use a trailer for four months." Donations came in from organized shops throughout the area. The strike committee held a dinner every week or two, and at Thanksgiving and Christmas there were gate collections of money and food. "This was important in keeping up morale," Ruth said. "We had a big Christmas party for the kids. We had a collection and went shopping to an auction. I felt my kids had a better Christmas than they had had for a while, even with the pull we had to go through."

During the strike, women's perceptions of themselves changed. Two of the leaders left their husbands, who objected with their union involvement. One of the workers said that the owner-manager "would like to think that the union was the cause of a lot of personal problems," but that for her it was gaining the self-respect that came with working for the union that made the difference.

The company was able to maintain some production with 6 supervisors, 15 foremen, and 35 "managerial" employees along with 25 to 30 scabs. Except for winding, which takes close to three months to learn, most of the jobs were unskilled and could be learned in a couple of days. Close work on small parts means intense eye strain, especially in the glare of neon lights with tinfoil reflectors. "The climax came," I was told, "when the owner put an ad in the newspaper calling for strikebreakers to replace workers. That had never happened in Greenfield before, and that is what really rallied help from other shops." When 500 union members from other companies arrived, management agreed to close down the plant. The company's request for an injunction was denied, as was their appeal for state police. Instead the governor sent in the State Commissioner of Labor and Industries to initiate full-time mediation on contract negotiations. The motivation to arrive at a settlement was stimulated by a citizen's petition calling on the company to negotiate in good faith. According to an interview with UE News reporter, this movement, initiated by a local druggist, was motivated by a reaction to the owner's "1920's style union-busting" (UE News, February 25, 1980).

The strike was settled on February 6. The contract substituted the "merit" system (which workers called a policy of favoritism pitting worker against worker) with a standardized set of procedures for wage raises, sickness and accident benefits, and vacation schedules, along with the wage increases of 90 cents per hour. However, the contract included extensive statements of management's rights

> to manage its business, to determine the size and composition of the work force, to decide the number and location of plants, the quantity and type of equipment, the speed of operation for equipment, the manning requirements of equipment, the products to be manufactured, the method and place of manufacturing, work-break schedules, processes of manufacturing and assembling, control of raw materials, determination of the quality and quantity of work done, decisions as to contract out work or to discontinue work, scheduling the starting and quitting time, overtime, the number of hours and all other rights and prerogatives subject only to such regulations and restrictions governing the exercise of these rights as expressly stated in the agreement.

The contract language clearly leaves management in control of the house.

As a result of the strike, union organizers felt that the company was directing production to New York, where a handicapped persons sheltered shop was in operation. Assembly-line workers had noticed a slowing down in production and inferior materials put into use. Although they had no direct proof that the company owned a subsidiary to which they were sending material, they had seen another shop linked with theirs in the United Fund appeal.

STRUCTURAL CHANGES IN INDUSTRIAL RELATIONS

What do these strikes in Pittsfield, North Adams, and Greenfield tell us about structural changes in industrial relations? How are these changes related to cultural patterns and beliefs?

In the day-to-day routines of work and living, the class conflict inherent in the capitalist system of production is obscured in American culture. Charles Walker, who wrote *American City, a Rank and File History* (1971/1937), brought out this contradiction between American culture and structure. "Working class [people] approximate the style of living of the classes above them in America in contrast to the distinct life style of England," he wrote. "Only in strikes do they develop a sense of class solidarity and distinct modes of thinking and acting." In strikes there is a break from the boredom, monotony, and subservience of everyday life. The threat of violence provokes some fear, but excitement and even gaiety and a festival atmosphere prevail on the picket line; and there is a spontaneous creativity in the tactics, songs, and organization. Egalitarianism among strikers breaks the hierarchy that divides them on the job and links them in a solidary group that is denied in the enterprise. At the same time, it clarifies the break between those who work for a living and those who manage the work of others.

In everyday life one perceives a mosaic of class alliances in which the generational mobility related to the great growth of American enterprises tied an aging production work force to their children, many of whom became technicians, sales representatives, and professionals in the expanding service and bureaucratic sectors. A trickle-down of wealth accumulated at home and abroad enabled a blue-collar worker to buy a home, furnish it with a refrigerator, washing machine, and even an air conditioner and stereo. Everyone has an automobile, and some have motor boats and skidoos. Union officials maintain the same life-style as other skilled workers. This is almost indistinguishable from that of the middle class.

The frustrations of American workers do not evoke the heroic forms of militant action I had seen in Bolivia and other Third World countries. The frustrations are those of having an 18-foot motor launch and two skidoos parked in your two-car garage and not having the time to use them because you have to work overtime six days a week. It is being retired and living in a house with eight rooms and having to keep the thermostat at 50 degrees Fahrenheit because the $350-a-month pension you negotiated when you were working can barely cover your food and medical expenses. It is having a right to organize and not trusting the representatives at the negotiating table, or of seeing some of the most militant trade union activists put into supervision and thus become ineligible as members. Hard work and ability don't seem to bring rewards, as mobility within the enterprise depends more than ever on education and contacts. "There's no way you can get up by yourself," an old-timer from Maine told his son when he started to work in the GE, "you're going to have to have someone pull you up by the bootstraps."

These day-to-day frustrations are forgotten on the picket line. The belly-to-back formation at the gates turned back trucks and cars in the 1969 strike. The soup kitchens and parties for the children of workers at Christmas in Greenfield demonstrated the feelings of community that overcame the alienation in the workplace. The picket line carries the symbolic freight of this solidarity. This is especially evident when union sympathizers are forced to violate the taboo against entry into the workplace, which, in effect, is declared polluted by the pickets. In one case, a supervisor, whose brother was business agent for the union, was forced to report to work as one of the ineligibles. The pickets were so aware of his distress that they picked him up bodily and lifted him over the line. Or in another case, a man who had organized the union in the 1930s when it was illegal and who was working out his last month in order to be able to collect his retirement hesitated to cross the line when it vanished before his eyes, and the pickets did not regroup until he was out of sight.

These cultural features in which the power of class solidarity becomes manifested do not necessarily make for structural change. That can only be realized in a new hegemony resulting from a change in the balance of power. The trends in which this is coming about can be retraced in the strikes recounted.

(1) Changes in class alliances. At the time of the 1916 strike, city service employees and shopkeepers were separate ethnically and economically from production workers. The police were clearly on the side of the corporation. There was no support for the strikers from the banks and shopkeepers; only the small grocers extended credit to strikers, since these were their only customers. The work force itself was divided, "foreigners" reportedly taking over the jobs of the striking workers were Italian and Polish workers often employed in textile factories or in odd jobs for GE outside the factory. The "segmented labor market"[4] did not separate workers at that time since skilled winders and machinists allied themselves with assembly-line workers in the strike action. GE was strong enough to resist the pressures of the State Federation of Labor as well as attempts by the State Board of Conciliation to bring about negotiations, and there was no higher authority that could prevent their use of strike breakers or special police force.

The alignments were different in the 1946 strike. The city council was clearly in favor of the strikers; many of them were workers in GE or children of GE workers. But the most remarkable change was in the business community that formed a coalition supporting strikers with money and credit.

In 1969 the union's outreach to the business community was more organized than ever before. However, there were few remaining local stores, and the chains rarely express support to strikers. The buying power of GE workers won at the negotiating tables in the post-World War II period was the strategic factor in the alliance of workers and small businessmen.

American workers, especially since 1946, share a common culture as consumers with professional and commercial people at the local level. The emic categories for class in American culture do not contrast "proletariat" and "bourgeoisie" but rather "little" and "big" business. This was even beginning to surface in the 1916 strike. The workers who were being accosted by the alien Boston police force brought in by GE were standing on their own lawns. Many owned their houses and they were paying the wages of the local police force with their taxes. Although GE could then ignore state machinery in labor disputes, this was no longer possible in the post-World War II period.

(2) The codification of rules in industrial relations. Workers' organizations and strikes were legally established with the passage of the National Recovery Act in 1933 and the Wagner Act in 1935, and codified by rulings of the National Labor Relations Board. Subsequent regulations—particularly the Taft-Hartley Act—have reduced labor initiative in setting the time for the strike. Since no strike can be called during the contract period, management can plan its production schedules to weather a strike more effectively than can the workers. The cooling-off period required by the Taft-Hartley Act reduces the effectiveness of collective action. Place as well as time is also under the control of management, as the pickets must not trespass on "company property." The sit-down strikes of the 1930s were a more revolutionary statement in that the workers were asserting, if only temporarily, control over place as well as time.

The strikes in Pittsfield illustrate the trend Brecher (1972: 139) notes, "that, by the twentieth century, workers by and large have accepted the wage system and their position within it as an accomplished fact." In 1916 management would not even enter into a dialogue with the union, but by 1970, leadership in the union was often a step into a managerial position.

(3) National integration of unions and international integration of industry. In the period from 1916 to 1946, trade unions moved from a situation in which they were unable to coordinate joint action even among neighboring plants of the same corporation to one in which unions coordinated strikes at a national level in 1946. The nationwide industrial unionism of the CIO paid off in the joint strike action of the post-World War II era. However, the cold war and anticommunist attacks broke that unity until the mid-1960s when IUE and UE locals joined to fight Boulwarism. But by that time, the integration of firms at an international level posed a greater threat to trade union action. This was more evident in the case of Sprague Electric in North Adams, where workers were in competition with the unorganized shops owned

by the company in the United States as well as overseas. Because of its national prominence, GE could not be as direct in such moves; but long after the 1969 strike, workers who had been out on strike were not called back. Wesco in Greenfield had the least flexibility because it had no subsidiaries, but striking employees suspected that it was operating in conjunction with a sheltered shop plant with state-subsidized handicapped workers in New York. The difference in the way the three companies used the threat of job loss is related to their flexibility in deploying work among different plants. Wesco was the only firm to advertise for strikebreakers, an act that mobilized union workers throughout the region and ended the strike. Sprague simply shipped production to their New Hampshire plant, reducing the assembly-line work force by one-half. These workers have never been replaced even though the company expanded nonunion shops in the United States and in Mexico and the Philippines. GE could not risk an open threat of employment cuts. Instead they carried full-page ads in the local press detailing the contract losses as a result of the strike and warning workers of future retrenchment that would take place in the Pittsfield plant if this occurred. Employment levels have never gone back to pre-1960 levels, and expansion of middle-sized transformers that are the most profitable have been in Southern plants since the strike. The corporation now seems to be phasing out the entire operation of large power transformers in Pittsfield.

The immediate result of the growing unemployment is to make workers conform to the demands of management. However, as their position in the productive system continues to weaken, it is quite possible that production workers will become more politicized. In Greenfield, Wesco workers, who typify the secondary work force in that they are predominantly female, low paid, and have no job security, showed the greatest militance in their 1979 strike. None of these women enjoyed seniority benefits that tie workers to a particular firm, and their wages were so little above welfare that they did not have a great deal to lose. Political action may indeed be on the agenda as workers lose the economic rewards they have gained as members of a primary work force and find themselves falling into the secondary work force or unemployed.

Workers accept the daily constraints on the job not out of "false consciousness" but out of true perception of their dependency on the job and the sale of the products they make in a world market. Despite this compliance at a surface level, strikers have begun to sense the power that they can mobilize. As Brecher (1972: 244) states, this "is in large part because they undermine the rhythm of daily life, the pattern of adaptation to which people have become accustomed and to which they had to cling even when it is impoverished."

That pattern of adaptation is now being undermined by management as they seek the lowest labor costs and minimize corporate responsibility to the work force, community, and nation. In this context, the old forms of scheduled, contract-defined strikes may become obsolete. New strategies are evolving as workers are attempting to slow down production without yielding the site to management. Random walkouts based on prearranged selection of payroll numbers are another means of expressing discontent without risking a strike showdown. If an all-out strike is considered necessary in the future, labor might well consider the advantages of the sit-down strikes; the company might simply walk off with the machinery, as Sprague did in 1970.

Structural analysis tells us about the limitations on human action. It cannot define the motivations and commitments that promote collective behavior and gain alliances in the wider society. This requires a cultural synthesis that puts the concrete historical responses into the perspective of patterns of behavior integrated at local, regional, national, and international levels. Wildcat strikes prior to the development of institutional controls were a moment when workers stood outside the hegemony that regulated their behavior in everyday life and became actors in history. Corporations are now subverting the institutional controls that ensured their hegemony as they escape the controls of unions and state regulation by going abroad. As yet, unions have not countered this move by extending their organizational links internationally.

NOTES

1. The difficulty with the committees set up to represent workers was in retaining some autonomy. In the years following the strike, the independent unions—never recognized as a bargaining agent until the NLRB ruling—constantly put pressure on the company to respond to these committees. They fought to use company billboards to announce meetings and to hold the meeting outside the shop so foremen would not influence the vote. Strikes were threatened to gain these apparently insignificant victories (Berkshire Eagle, September 12, 1916; September 21, 1918; September 23, 1918).

2. Kuhn (1980: 224) claims that the disunity was brought about by the UE union leaders who emerged in the 1930s and brought with them "the seeds of disunity that later, in sprouting and rank growth, were to split and weaken the electrical workers in their bargaining." Considering that they were the ones who organized the unions, it would appear that anticommunism fostered in the postwar McCarthy era engendered disunity.

3. Kuhn (1980: 232) argues that the board and court based their judgment of GE's illegality on a "narrow and conservative definition of collective bargaining." The theatrics of collective bargaining at the negotiation table that Kuhn deplores affirm the position of

the union as representative of the membership. Like all ritual, it stabilizes a hegemonic relationship and is not, therefore, trivial.

4. Segmented work refers to the structural divisions in the labor markets through which workers secure their livelihood (Gordon, Edwards, and Reich, 1982). These authors consider segmentation to be the latest strategy in managerial control of the work process. In fact, a preferred core of workers were found in nineteenth-century textile mills and persisted throughout the twentieth century (Smith, 1876). Like managerial analyst Northrup (1964), Gordon, Edwards, and Reich argue that fissions in the labor movement are derived from the segmented work process. They differ in that the latter assert that the division of jobs is programmed by management to divide the work force into ethnically and gender specific jobs while the former sees it as an inadvertent consequence of technology. Labor leaders, on the contrary, assert the importance of ideological divisiveness in the cold war period and emphasize how the persistent differences in the work force are overcome in the periods of labor crisis. In today's marginal work shops operating in the competitive sector, ethnicity is probably less significant than are gender, age, and physical condition. As the Wesco case shows, the suspected shift of production to "sheltered shops" for handicapped workers subsidized by the government is a new facet of segmentation. The division of labor by gender in the electrical manufacturing industry is less exclusively segregated than in other major industries, as Ruth Milkman (1982) convincingly demonstrates. The shift from a preferred male labor force was often threatened, and not only in war time. As a consequence, the United Electric fought for equity in wage scales more consistently than any other union.

REFERENCES

ARENSBERG, C. (1942) "Industry and communities." American Journal of Sociology 7 (July): 1-12.

BACKMAN, J. (1962) Electronic Imports: The U.S. Consumer and Employment. New York: Sydney S. Baron and Co.

BAER, W. E. (1975) Strikes. New York: American Management Association.

Berkshire Eagle (1903-1969) selected issues.

BOLTWOOD, E. (1916) The History of Pittsfield Massachusetts from the Year 1876 to the Year 1916. Pittsfield: Eagle Printing Co.

BOULWARE, L. (1969) The Truth about Boulwarism. Washington, DC: Bureau of National Affairs.

BRECHER, J. (1972) Strike! San Francisco: Straight Arrow Books.

COSER, L. (1956) The Functions of Social Conflict. New York: The Free Press.

GORDON, D. M., R. EDWARDS, and M. REICH (1982) Segmented Work, Divided Workers; The Historical Transformation of Labor in the United States. Cambridge: Cambridge University Press.

KUHN, J. (1980) "Electrical products," pp. 209-262 in G. C. Somers (ed.) Collective Bargaining, Contemporary American Experience. Madison, WI: Industrial Relations Research Association Series, University of Wisconsin.

MATLES, J. J. and J. HIGGINS (1974) Them and Us: Struggles of a Rank and File Union. Englewood Cliffs, NJ: Prentice-Hall.

MILKMAN, R. (1982) "Female factory labor and industrial structure: control and conflict over 'woman's place' in auto and electrical manufacturing." Presented at the Colloquium for Social History, City University of New York Graduate Center.

NORTHRUP, H. R. (1964) Boulwarism. Ann Arbor: University of Michigan, Bureau of Industrial Relations, Graduate School of Business Administration.

PASSER, H. C. (1953) The Electrical Manufacturers 1875-1900; A Study in Competition, Entrepreneurship, Technical Change and Economic Growth. Cambridge, MA: Harvard University Press.

SHORTER, E. and C. TILLY (1974) Strikes in France 1830-1968. Cambridge, MA: Harvard University Press.

SMITH, E.A. (1876) The History of Pittsfield, Berkshire County, Massachusetts, from the Year 1800 to the Year 1876. Springfield, MA.: C.W. Bryan and Co.

WALKER, C. (1971) American City: A Rank and File History. New York: Arno Press. (originally published in 1937)

WARNER, W. L. and J. O. LOW (1947) The Social System of the Modern Factory. New Haven, CT: Yale University Press.

WILLISON, G. F. (1957) The History of Pittsfield, Massachusetts, 1916-1955. Pittsfield: The Sun Printing Co.

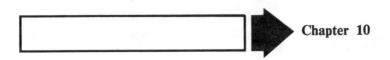
EXPORT MANUFACTURING
AND LABOR: THE ASIAN CASE

Frederic Deyo
State University of New York
at Brockport

Labor movements in the more industrially advanced countries of Latin America have long played a powerful role in national politics. During the 1940s and 1950s, organized labor comprised an important political support base for development-oriented ruling elites. In Mexico, the oil boom and rapid economic development have permitted the government to support escalating wage and welfare demands, and thus to maintain labor peace.

In other cases, particularly in Argentina and Brazil, early corporatist labor support gave way to unmanageable popular protest as economic stagnation undercut the ability of economic and political elites to meet escalating labor demands. It is this conjuncture of economic stagnation and growing labor militancy that largely explains the imposition of highly repressive, military regimes in the most developed Southern-cone countries during the last two decades (Kaufman, 1979). But it is important to recognize that even under repressive regimes, organized labor has retained its capacity to challenge economic and political elites through effective, organized protest. Even in hitherto industrially peaceful Mexico, increasing labor protest appears to be threatening the

AUTHOR'S NOTE: I am grateful for helpful comments by Richard Abrams, Richard Barrett, Charles Bergquist, Charles Hirschman, and Hagen Koo. Support for this research was provided by the SUNY University Awards Program and by the National Science Foundation.

old corporatist labor alliance as economic crisis demands politically unpopular "austerity" policies.

While the power of organized labor in Latin America originated in mining and, to a lesser degree, foreign-controlled plantation agriculture, its consolidation in the newer industrial sectors of Argentina, Brazil, Chile, and Uruguay was dramatic. By contrast, labor movements in the newly industrializing countries of Asia have found but weak footing in the rapidly growing export industries that have been the pacesetters for economic change in that region. Contrary to the Latin American pattern, the social transformations of industrialization have there been associated with a progressive diminution, rather than growth, in the power of organized labor. Such an observation applies with special force to Korea, Hong Kong, Singapore, and Taiwan, the countries with which this chapter deals. Industrialization in these countries, collectively known as the "gang of four," has been associated with rapid generation of an industrial proletariat. Table 10.4 suggests that by the late 1970s, manufacturing alone generally absorbed a larger proportion of total employment in these countries than in the more industrialized Latin American countries, with their larger agricultural sectors. But despite this profound and rapid transformation in employment structure, with its associated increase in the numbers of potentially "organizable" workers, labor unionization, protest, and power have generally stagnated or declined. Table 10.1 shows unionization trends for the gang of four since 1960. While such trends in themselves, without additional indication of their political independence and responsiveness to worker demands, give little indication of the strength of labor movements, they do at least measure the extent of labor's potential organizational base for collective action. It is clear that until the state corporatist efforts of the early to mid-1970s, unionization levels among the gang of four countries generally stagnated. It will be noted later that this decline was not so much the result of falling levels of organization in established industries as of a lack of organization among workers newly mobilized into the rapidly expanding light consumer-goods industries that led industrial change during the 1960s.

Data on work stoppages (Table 10.2) show similarly low or declining levels of industrial conflict (particularly for Hong Kong and Singapore) during the 1960s and 1970s period of rapid industrialization. Such statistics may be contrasted with the rising levels of protest during recent years among the Latin American NICs.

While data on unionization and industrial conflict generally suggest stagnation over the course of Asian industrialization during the 1960s and 1970s, such findings do not effectively demonstrate a weakening of

TABLE 10.1 Union Members as Percentage of the Labor Force

Year	Hong Kong	Taiwan	South Korea	Singapore
1960		9	4	29
1961	18	9	NIL	32
1962		9	NIL	36
1963		9		26
1964		9	3	28
1965		9	3	27
1966	12	10	4	
1967		9		
1968		9		
1969		9	5	
1970		11		15
1971	13	11		17
1972		12		22
1973		13		23
1974		13	4	24
1975		15	6	24
1976	20	15	6	24
1977		16		
1978	20	16		
1979	18	16	7	
1980		17		

SOURCES:
Hong Kong: Registrar of Trade Unions, Annual Departmental Report; England and Rear (1975: 86); Turner (1980: 23).
Taiwan: ROC, Report of Taiwan Labor Statistics; ROC, Yearbook of Labor Statistics.
South Korea: Han (1974: 189); Federation of Korean Trade Unions, reported in Korea Annual.
Singapore: Ministry of Labour.

labor movements among the gang of four countries. First, unionization declines have not been great, while conflict levels fell most sharply at the outset of industrialization in the early 1960s and showed only moderate decline thereafter. Second, neither unionization nor conflict statistics are valid indicators of the vitality of labor movements. High levels of unionization may often be associated with government preemptive organizational efforts, especially under corporatist regimes, in which case high levels of unionization may reflect tight government controls over labor rather than strong, independent union organization. Similarly, manifest conflict levels, even where accurately reported, are very poor indicators of the power of labor. In the context of supportive political elites or economic expansion, for example, workers may rarely find it necessary to engage in costly work stoppages.

TABLE 10.2 Workdays Lost To Stoppages per Thousand Labor Force

Year	Hong Kong	Taiwan	South Korea	Singapore
1961	34	1	(very high)*	804
1962		2	NIL	314
1963		1		717
1964		1	NIL	65
1965		3	2	80
1966	17	1	4	
1967		3	1	
1968		1	6	
1969		2	17	
1970		5	1	4
1971	16	1	1	
1972		1	NIL	
1973			NIL	
1974			1	6
1975			1	6
1976	3		1	3
1977			1	
1978			1	NIL
1979			1	NIL
1980	9		4	NIL

SOURCES:
Hong Kong: Turner (1980: 88); ILO Yearbook; Hong Kong Monthly Digest of Statistics.
Taiwan: Report of Taiwan Labor Statistics; ROC: Yearbook of Labor Statistics.
South Korea: ILO Yearbook.
Singapore: Minister of Labor, Annual Report.
*A period of social protest preceding the Park coup of 1961.

Given these problems in interpreting unionization and conflict indicators of labor movement strength, a third, less easily quantifiable measure suggests itself. This measure refers not to conflict per se, but rather to its characteristics and outcomes (Shorter and Tilly, 1974). Here, attention is directed to the ability of workers to organize protest effectively so as to exert maximum pressure on employers, as well as to the frequency with which such protest gains elite concessions or at least is not summarily defeated (Ragin, Coverman, and Hayward, 1982). This measure may profitably be used under conditions of either high or low levels of industrial conflict, and asks not how frequently protest occurs but rather how effective or consequential it is when it does occur.

One indicator of the organizational effectiveness of labor protest is the extent to which large numbers of workers within and across firms and industries can quickly be mobilized for work stoppages or other

TABLE 10.3 Workdays Lost per Work Stoppage: Five-Year
Averages*

Period	Hong Kong	Taiwan per stoppage	per dispute	South Korea	Singapore
1961-65	3984(5)	176(5)	—	1105(2)	3269(5)
1966-70	1127(5)	857(5)	—	5018(5)	3303(5)
1971-75	865(5)	75(2)	(59)	350(3)	1029(5)
1976-81	519(5)	n.a.(13)	(13)	207(5)	800(5)

*Averages based on any years for which data is available. Number of years for
which data are available in each time period is indicated in parentheses.

types of collective action (see Britt and Galle, 1977; Shorter and Tilly,
1974). Table 10.3 presents trend data on the size of work stoppages, as
measured by number of workdays lost per stoppage, in Korea, Hong
Kong, Singapore, and Taiwan. It will be noted that EOI expansion
(beginning in the 1950s in Hong Kong, and the mid-1960s in the other
three countries) has been associated with a clear trend toward ever
smaller work stoppages. This shift, in turn, has been accompanied by a
progressive increase in the proportion of stoppages that are poorly
organized, largely defensive, and quite easily dealt with by employers.
In many cases, stoppages are confined to small groups of workers in
particular parts of individual plants who are protesting retrenchment or
declining real wages during times of recession (Salaff, 1981: 21; Turner,
1980; Ogle, 1979; Deyo, 1981). In summing up the postwar strike
experience in Hong Kong, Turner (1980: 89, 102) argues as follows:

> The most obvious points about the summarised record are, first, that
> the number of strikes and lockouts has never been great, and their
> incidence has certainly been declining over the period as a
> whole . . . the number of workers involved in any year has—with
> the possible exception of 1967—always been low, despite the great
> increase in employment over the period . . . [and] stoppages have
> generally been rather small . . . [I]t is quite notable, again, that the
> yearly average of "days lost per workers involved" in stoppages is
> rather high in most years of the immediate post-war period and the
> 1960's; but after 1967, strikes have almost always been not merely
> small, but short . . . [in the context of a more general] inability to
> deal with continuing problems of pay structure and employment as
> more than transitory occasions for protest.

The major portion of this chapter offers an explanation of Asian
labor's very weak response to industrialization in the gang of four by

reference to the economic structural and political changes that have accompanied economic growth. But before moving on to this substantive issue, it is first necessary to introduce the analytical framework within which the discussion is organized.

WORLD ECONOMIC LINKAGES
AND THIRD WORLD LABOR MOVEMENTS

An understanding of the consequences of external economic linkages for domestic labor movements requires an integration of two largely independent bodies of literature. The first of these deals with the immediate determinants of labor organization, militancy, and power. Here, attention focuses on the consequences of variation or change in the structure and level of employment, community organization, direct elite controls over workers (hereafter referred to as "labor regime"), and political structure for labor (see Figure 10.1). In particular, it has been argued that the strength of labor movements is typically enhanced in the context of full employment (Sturmthal, 1973); simple, undifferentiated industrial structures (Form, 1974); cohesive work groups (Seashore, 1954; Sturmthal, 1973); employment concentration in large factories and urban places (Lincoln, 1978; Shorter and Tilly, 1974; Britt and Galle, 1974); class-homogeneous worker communities (Langton and Rapoport, 1975); freedom to organize and to engage in collective action; and elite disunity (Warner, 1973).

The second body of literature, comprised substantially although not exclusively of writers in the "dependency" and "world system" tradition, deals with the implications of particular types of economic and political linkages connecting national political-economies with those of other countries. This literature suggests that Third World economic change is powerfully conditioned by the nature of economic (Chase-Dunn, 1975) and political (Snyder and Kick, 1979) linkages with industrial or "core" countries. It should be noted that economic and political linkages are themselves interdependent. The nature of external political linkages with core states, for example, may encourage particular types of economic linkage, just as the latter may reciprocally deepen or alter political linkages. Such external linkages in turn have profound consequences for employment, community organization, and political structures, and thus for labor movements as well.

This analytic framework suggests three general observations. First, one often-cited weakness in much of the earlier dependency and world system literature on Third World economic change was its relative lack

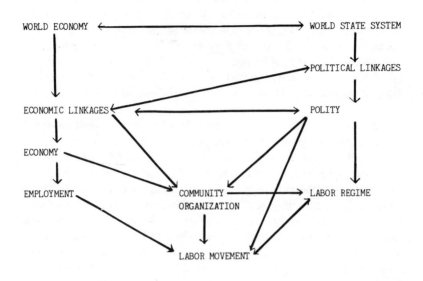

**Figure 10.1 World and Third World Labor Movements: An Analytical
Framework**

of systematic treatment of factors within countries that may influence or mediate the social or economic consequences of external linkages in particular countries (Portes, 1976; Delacroix and Ragin, 1978; Bornschier, Chase-Dunn, and Rubinson, 1978; Snyder and Kick, 1979). The conceptual framework utilized here explicitly takes such factors into account in examining the implications of external economic linkages for Third World labor movements. Indeed, state development strategy, an endogenous political factor, is seen as a significant *determinant* of such linkages.

Second, the literature on Third World labor movements has demonstrated the profound role of political factors in general, and of the state in particular, in shaping such movements (Kerr et al., 1960; Friedland, 1963; Amin, 1974; Kreye, 1980). Such a political emphasis appropriately reflects the paramount importance of authoritarian controls frequently imposed by elites both to encourage economic investment and to contain the social tensions resulting from delayed, unequal development (Apter, 1976). While fuller treatment of Asian labor regimes is presented separately (Deyo, forthcoming) this chapter deals primarily with economic structural changes associated with EOI that have impinged on domestic labor movements in these countries. But it should be noted in Figure 10.1 that such economic influences on labor movements are in part *indirect*, through their impact on communities and the polity. Figure 10.1, then, suggests that economic and political factors interact at various levels in mediating the consequences of external linkages for domestic labor movements.

Finally, the framework implicitly underscores the causal importance of variation in "world system time," and phases or changes in external economic linkages (see Bornschier, Chase-Dunn, and Rubinson, 1978). This chapter emphasizes cross-national variation in type of economic linkage. But it is clear that linkage type depends very much on the state of the world system at the time such linkages are forged. That Latin American industrialization was initiated in response to world economic depression while that in Asia began during a period of world trade expansion influenced the types of world economic linkage established in these two regions, with important implications for economic change and labor movements.

ECONOMIC GROWTH IN THE GANG OF FOUR

Table 10.4 presents comparative economic data on middle-income, Third World countries that produced over US$1 billion in manufactur-

ing value-added in 1978, and in which at least 20 percent of the
workforce was employed in manufacturing (World Bank, 1982). It is
clear that while the major manufacturing countries are in Latin
America, the gang of four, despite very small size and minimal resource
endowment, comprise the most important Third World export manufacturers. It may also be noted that the contrasting ratios of manufactured exports to manufacturing value-added between Latin America
and Asia reflect quite different industrialization strategies (import-
substituting and export-oriented, respectively), which shall be discussed
below. Also clear is the exceptionally high percentage of the Asian
workforce in manufacturing, a difference that makes the relative
weakness of Asian labor movements all the more surprising.

Between 1960 and 1979, the gang of four countries maintained
average annual growth rates per capita of over 7 percent, higher than
those of any other developing countries. During this period, Hong
Kong's gross domestic product (GDP) increased from US$950 million
to $17,390 million. That in South Korea rose from $3,810 million to

TABLE 10.4 Middle-Income, Third World Countries with over
US$1 Billion Value Added in Manufacturing and
more than 20 Percent of the Labor Force in Manufacturing[a]

Country	1978 Millions of Dollars in Manufacturing Value Added	1978 Dollars in Manufacturing Value Added per Capita[b]	1978 Percentage of Labor Force in Manufacturing	1978 Millions of Dollars in Manufacturing Exports
Asia				
Hong Kong	2,629	520	57	10,693
Taiwan	—	—	38 (1978)	14,565[c]
Singapore	1,815	900	38	4,679
South Korea	9,064	236	30	11,220
Latin America				
Uruguay	1,008	330	32	290
Argentina	10,641	380	28	1,674
Mexico	24,856	370	26	1,620
Brazil	37,685	320	22	4,335
Colombia	3,078	110	21	430
Chile	2,561	240	20	118
Peru	3,685	210	20	205
Africa				
Egypt	3,178	80	29	504
South Africa	—	—	29	2,576
Algeria	2,220	120	24	35
Morocco	1,802	90	21	345

a. World Bank, *World Development Report,* 1981.
b. Population base from World Bank, 1980.
c. *Taiwan Statistical Data Book,* 1979.

$60,660 million, while Singapore's GDP rose from $700 million to $9,010 million (World Bank, 1981). Taiwan's GDP, expressed in million NT dollars, rose from $62,566 in 1960 to $1,164,073.

This remarkable economic growth was led by expansion in labor-intensive manufacturing for world markets (Chen, 1979: chap. 6) beginning in the 1950s in Hong Kong and in the 1960s in the other three countries. The associated economic structural shift is reflected in changes in the percentage of GDP accounted for by manufacturing. During the 1960-1979 period, South Korean manufacturing increased from 14 percent to 27 percent of the GDP, that of Singapore from 12 percent to 28 percent (World Bank, 1981) and that of Taiwan from 15 percent to 43 percent (Republic of China, Monthly Bulletin of Statistics, 1978-1980: 18) respectively. Corresponding increases in manufactured exports were equally significant during this period. Between 1962 and 1978, such exports increased from $642 million to $10,693 in Hong Kong, from $10 million to $11,220 million in South Korea, and from $328 million to $4,679 million in Singapore. For Taiwan, Galenson (1979) reports an index rise from 36 in 1963 to 157 in 1973.

This Asian pattern of export-oriented industrialization (EOI) comprises a special type of economic linkage with the world economy, involving as it does the mobilization of cheap, disciplined domestic labor to manufacture light consumer goods for world markets. Asian EOI contrasts sharply with the earlier Latin American experience. Unlike the gang of four, early industrialization in Argentina, Brazil, Uruguay, and Mexico was developed in response to declining primary export prices during the years of the world depression. In this context, domestic industrialization was sought as a necessary part of a more general economic restructuring that might reduce vulnerability to international market fluctuations. The larger countries, with their more adequate domestic markets, embarked on an import-substituting industrialization (ISI) strategy. Such a strategy emphasized development of a diversified, internally integrated industrial and economic structure, unlike the more specialized, externally articulated industrial structures of the gang of four. The following discussion explores the implications of these differences in development strategy for domestic labor movements in Asia and Latin America.

THE POLITICS OF LABOR DEMOBILIZATION IN ASIA

The literature on dependent industrialization would suggest that an obvious possible explanation for the declining power of Asian labor movements is to be found in state-imposed political controls over unions and collective action. While Asian labor regimes are discussed elsewhere (Deyo, forthcoming), it is necessary briefly to deal with the impact of such political controls before moving on to economic structural factors, which are the major concern of this chapter.

The Latin American experience suggests that during most of the period of postdepression industrialization, political factors powerfully shaped emergent labor movements: first by channelling them into corporatist union structures, and later in many cases by controlling them under repressive regimes. Similarly, Otto Kreye (1980) and others have argued that EOI development has generally been associated with highly repressive labor regimes, and that such regimes account in large measure for the unhappy fate of Asian labor movements. In fact it is true that in the cases of South Korea and Singapore, the EOI initiative was accompanied by imposition of drastic controls over labor, in both cases including deregistration of unions, jailing of labor militants, and enactment of major legislative restrictions on collective action. Reflecting these new restrictions, levels of unionization and conflict dropped sharply in both countries during the 1960s. On the other hand, new repressive controls did not accompany EOI initiative in Hong Kong, while tough Taiwanese labor legislation was never effectively implemented at the local level (see U.S. Bureau of Labor Statistics, 1962).

During the two decades of EOI development, there was some shift toward increasingly authoritarian controls in Korea (Kim, 1978), while Singapore's labor regime moved in the direction of remobilization of workers into government controlled unions but without the imposition of further controls. In Taiwan, there has been some effort to invigorate a dormant trade union movement already controlled by employers and state, and there is indication of a gradual easing of restrictive controls (New York Times, 1983: May 22). In the case of Hong Kong, Turner (1980) similarly reports that there was some liberalization of already permissive labor legislation during the 1970s. In both Taiwan and Hong Kong, state-level controls have been far less significant that in Korea or Singapore, while enterprise-level authority has remained more important.

How useful, then, is an explanation for a continuing decline in the size and efficacy of labor protest that centers on changes in political restrictions over labor? It is clear that at the point of EOI initiative both in Singapore and South Korea, government repression was an overwhelmingly important factor underlying the decline in labor movement strength, while Korea's increasingly authoritarian regime during the 1970s may constitute a further explanation for subsequent declines there. But this explanation, by itself, leaves much to be accounted for. First, it fails to explain why, despite minimal labor repression and even some relaxation of controls during the period of EOI industrialization in Hong Kong and Taiwan, labor movements there followed the course of movements in the other two countries, becoming and remaining ineffective in representing workers' interests. Insofar as a *continuing* decline in protest efficacy would suggest an explanation based on continuing political changes, only Korea presents a case of progressively more authoritarian controls during the 1970s. But even here, it should be noted that in fact such controls were directed less at industrial workers than at students, intellectuals, church groups, and oppositional political parties.

Second, and more important, an explanation centering on repressive controls fails to account for important cross-regional and interindustry differences. Southern-cone Latin American labor movements have, especially since the mid-1960s, been confronted by highly repressive, military-backed, state labor controls whose only Asian parallel has been in Korea. Yet, despite more repressive labor regimes, Latin American labor movements have displayed far greater vigor than their Asian counterparts. Similarly, interindustry differences in labor militancy *within* the Asian countries, where organized labor is weaker in the new export industries than in traditional and heavy industry, suggest that industry-differentiating economic structural factors may be as important as more general political ones for an understanding of the impact of EOI development on Asian labor movements.

An alternate political explanation, which articulates more directly with economic structural factors, relates less to the formal contours of political controls than to their economic underpinnings. If labor regimes among the gang of four have not generally become more comprehensive or repressive, it is still possible that they have become more *effective* over time and, in some cases, despite a gradual *relaxation* of controls. Such enhanced effectiveness, in turn, may be explained in part by the nature of EOI development itself (see Figure 10.1).

It is clear that the dramatic increase in EOI investment during the 1960s was encouraged by close political/military linkages with the West that provided a security umbrella for investors. But EOI development has, in turn, led to a substantial increase in core economic stakes in Asia, thus further consolidating core support for domestic elites. It may be assumed, therefore, that ruling groups are less vulnerable than before to domestic political pressures, and in a stronger position effectively to implement existing regime controls. Second, export-oriented industrialization has generated economic structural changes that have increased elite unity. Such unity was initially guaranteed by colonial rule or by quick transition from colonial to single or dominant party rule, with but brief interludes of political conflict in Korea and Singapore. But subsequent EOI development has tended to undercut any existing independent economic resource base for opposition movements by bypassing or reducing the political independence of the domestic bourgeoisie. In the case of Singapore, massive direct foreign investment by core multinational corporations has bypassed the local bourgeoisie altogether (Deyo, 1981). Korean reliance on loan capital channeled to local manufacturers through government-controlled banks has reduced the bourgeoisie to a politically dependent class, while subcontract manufacturing in Taiwan and Hong Kong similarly ensures dependency and lack of opposition on the part of business groups to an EOI development strategy or to the political elites upon whose external clientage the success of such a strategy rests. Finally, rapid labor-intensive industrialization in these small Asian countries has bolstered the political legitimacy of ruling elites by substantially reducing earlier high levels of unemployment, while at the same time permitting a relatively equitable income distribution by encouraging entry into employment on the part of young women from low income families.

These three consequences of EOI (mobilization of external, core support for ruling elites; undercutting of an independent domestic bourgeoisie; and enhancement of elite political legitimacy) have likely increased the effectiveness of existing labor regimes in Asia and thus indirectly enhanced labor peace. It may be noted that such consequences clearly differentiate the Asian pattern from Latin American ISI, which was associated with a far less intimate political linkage with core elites, development of a more independent and dynamic domestic bourgeoisie, increased inequality and unemployment, and growing economic stagnation. It was precisely these quite different socioeconomic consequences of Latin American ISI development that contributed to later political instability.

But if Asian EOI has indirectly assured labor peace through its political consequences, it has more directly influenced labor movements through its implications for industrial and occupational structure. In the following section, it is argued that EOI has been associated with rapid expansion in occupations within which effective organization and protest is difficult; and in this sense EOI differs from Latin American

ISI, which has generated greater growth in occupational sectors wherein labor movements are afforded more secure social anchorage.

EOI AND THE STRUCTURAL DEMOBILIZATION OF LABOR: LIGHT INDUSTRY

Latin American ISI has encouraged development of a relatively diversified industrial structure, including intermediate, heavy and chemical industries. Asian EOI, on the other hand, has overwhelmingly emphasized light, low-skill, female-intensive, consumer goods industries. The employment consequences of this difference are reflected in available data on the industrial distribution of the workforce for various countries and years. Official employment data (Table 10.5) suggest that the percentage of the manufacturing workforce in such heavy industries as transport equipment, chemicals, machinery, and basic metals in Argentina and Mexico stood roughly at 49 percent and 35 percent, respectively, by the late 1970s (ILO, 1982). Similarly, by the late 1960s, a substantial portion of Brazilian intermediate and capital goods was being produced locally. Brazil's iron and steel and chemical industries are the largest in Latin America, while automobile production comprises the largest private enterprise sector in manufacturing. Conversely, Asian EOI has centered on rapid expansion in a few light consumer goods industries. By the late 1970s, heavy and chemical industrial employment accounted for a far smaller proportion of total manufacturing employment in the gang of four than in the Latin American NIC, while employment in the major light consumer goods industries (textile products, footwear, and electronics) was more substantial.

The general stagnation in Asian unionization and protest noted earlier are in large part a consequence of the relative weakness of

TABLE 10.5 Manufacturing Employment in Selected Industries (in percentages)[a]

Heavy		Light
49	Argentina (1979)	3
32	Brazil (1976)[b]	23
35	Mexico (1980)	20
23	Singapore (1980)	43
17	South Korea (1978)	42
5	Hong Kong (1980)	62
19	Taiwan (1980)	38

a. ILO, 1982
b. The Economist Intelligence Unit (1981).

organized labor in the new export-industries. The general union decline of the 1960s was not so much a result of declining levels of organization in established industries as of lack of organization among workers newly mobilized into the rapidly expanding light consumer goods industries that led industrial change during the 1960s. Turner (1980: 25-26) reports, for example, that much of the apparent increase in unionization strength in Hong Kong during the 1970s was confined to utilities and public services, while unionization levels in such light export industries as electronics, plastics, and garment manufacturing were quite low.

The heavier industries that have played so important a role in Latin American ISI development are associated with relatively high-wage, high-skill, and male-intensive employment, whereas the light consumer goods industries that have been industrial pacesetters in Asia tend to generate low-wage, low-skill, female-intensive employment. Especially striking has been the dramatic mobilization of young, unmarried women into those labor-intensive, export-oriented industries that grew most rapidly during this period. By 1980, over 50 percent of Hong Kong's manufacturing workers were female (Hong Kong Monthly Digest of Statistics September 1981), while data for Taiwan show an increase in the female share of manufacturing employment from around 12 percent at the outset of EOI in the early 1960s to 43 percent in 1978 (ILO Yearbook). The corresponding increase for Korea was from 26 percent in 1960 to nearly 40 percent in 1980 (ILO Yearbook), and from 23 percent in 1966 to 46 percent in 1980 in Singapore (Republic of Singapore, Ministry of Labour). In all cases, females constitute a far larger proportion of the manufacturing labor force than in Mexico (28 percent in 1979), Brazil (22 percent in 1975), or Argentina (21 percent in 1970). And in all cases, too, female production workers are disproportionately employed in a few light export industries. In 1973, for example, nearly 70 percent of Singapore's female production workers were in the textile, electronics, apparel, and footwear industries (Deyo, 1976; for Korea see Ogle, 1977).

The rapid expansion in employment of young, unmarried females in EOI manufacturing was based on a number of considerations. First, because their employment often provides a secondary rather than primary family income and because they do not support dependents, they may be hired at relatively low wages (Diamond, 1979). Second, their competence and discipline are assured by childhood socialization that emphasizes both job-relevant skills (e.g., fine needle work) and acquiescence to male authority. Finally, and of equal importance, they tend to view work as a temporary interlude between childhood on the one hand, and marriage and motherhood on the other. Their resulting status as a "part-time proletariat" (Gates, 1979) has the further consequences of increasing workforce flexibility in these market-vulnerable industries and of reducing seniority-based wage increments.

The creation of an increasingly dominant light industries sector tends to impede independent organizational efforts by unions and to ensure that unions may easily be controlled by agencies of the government. High rates of employment turnover and low levels of skill among production workers are associated with difficulties in local unionization efforts in the context of minimal and short-term commitment to job, employer, and industrial employment in general. By and large, except where the government has actively encouraged unionization, organizational levels in these industries are very low. Salaff (1981: 21) notes, for example, that only 8 percent of Hong Kong's female workers in textiles, apparel, and leather goods, and 4 percent of those in electronic assembly were union members in 1974. Similarly, only 18 percent of Korean textile and clothing workers were unionized in 1974, as against 50 percent in mining and 37 percent in a large group of industries including chemical, petroleum, rubber, cement, and glass manufacturing (based on data from Park, 1974: 56-57).

In addition, unionization efforts become increasingly dependent on leadership from outside the ranks of workers themselves. Thus, lack of dynamic, independent, union federation leadership, as in Hong Kong and Taiwan, becomes a significant depressant on labor action. Conversely, in cases of extensive government control over more active national union federations, as in Korea and Singapore, weak local organization ensures preemptive government control over unionization efforts themselves, thus similarly undercutting the independent organizational base for effective protest. Thus may be explained the observed pattern of ever-smaller and more easily contained stoppages in all four countries, as well as the relative success with which the governments of Korea and Singapore—where restrictive regulation has been more significant—have been able to contain militance through controls at federation and national levels with relatively little intervention at plant and local levels.

Corresponding to low levels of unionization, industrial conflict in EOI sectors tends to be both less well organized and less successful than in other economic sectors. Hong Kong's moderate increase in militancy and unionization during the late 1970s in large part reflects gains by organized labor in public services and utilities (Turner, 1980). This is not to deny the existence of continuing industrial conflict in the new EOI sectors, although such conflict tends more often to manifest itself in individual behavior such as high rates of turnover and absenteeism, gossip, personal complaints, and work apathy. Where protest does take collective forms, however, it occurs among small isolated groups, with minimal organization and little chance of success. Instructive in this regard is the contrast between major industrial disputes among Korean dockworkers on the one hand, and textile workers on the other. In 1974, there was a major strike at the Hyundai Shipyard in the port city of Ulsan. The strike involved 3,000 workers, and was only put down after 1,000 riot police conducted massive arrests during which 80 persons were injured. By contrast, a number of stoppages and disputes among young workers in the export-processing zones occurred in the late 1970s and early 1980s. While involving large numbers of workers, most of these stoppages were short and spontaneous, and few required substantial police intervention.

LABOR AND EMERGENT ECONOMIC TRENDS

Rapid, successful, export-oriented industrialization has transformed earlier labor abundance into labor shortages. By the early 1970s, upward wage pressure began to alarm employers, and governments became concerned about an apparent shift of investment to cheaper labor countries in the region. The implications of this change are many. It is clear that the economic bargaining power of labor has been increased somewhat by growing labor scarcity. But given the lack of effective, independent unions, such power has primarily been reflected in growing rates of job turnover as workers turn to job mobility as an alternative to bargaining. More important, governments in the gang of four countries have sought to meet the problem of labor shortages through efforts to induce greater investment in higher-technology, high-skill manufacturing in such fields as advanced electronics and engineering in order to maintain internationally competitive labor costs. This effort to alter the position of domestic economies in world markets has thus necessitated heightened efforts to increase worker skills and achieve greater workforce stability.

The new strategy has two important implications. First, it is likely that such an economic restructuring, if successful, would encourage stronger, more independent labor movements by stimulating more rapid growth in occupational sectors characterized by higher skills and greater job stability as well as by reducing demand for young, low-skilled female workers seeking short-term work prior to marriage. But given the new and still tentative nature of this policy shift, it is too early to ascertain the longer-run structural consequences of restructuring. Table 10.5, for example, suggests a continuing vitality in light, female-intensive export-industries, although such data, especially for electronics, may conceal technological upgrading. Second, even if economic restructuring is not yet reflected in occupational changes, it has in some cases been associated with labor regime changes deriving from a need for greater workforce stability and commitment. During the early and mid-1970s, Singapore's ruling People's Action Party energized and used a previously stagnant trade union federation, the National Trades Union Congress (NTUC), as the basis for both disciplining and encouraging greater productivity among workers (see Deyo, 1981). More recently, the NTUC structure has been decentralized in favor of greater efforts to enhance worker attachment to local firms. Similarly, during the mid-1970s, the government-controlled national union federations in both South Korea and Taiwan have been given greater encouragement as means for a fuller economic mobilization of the workforce, although in the Taiwanese case, the enterprise remains the major focus of such efforts. All such attempts to incorporate workers more fully into enterprise and union control structures stand in marked contrast to the primarily repressive approaches taken during the 1960s and have generally been associated with a reversal of earlier periods of union stagnation (see Table 10.1).

If Mexico's labor regime has drawn strength from the early revolutionary origins of the ruling party and from a buoyant economy, another possible explanation for its apparent success until the late 1970s is that it consolidated preemptive corporatist structures well before the rapid industrialization of the 1940s and 1950s. To the extent that late Asian EOI has now moved into a development stage conducive to more vigorous labor movements, the new corporatist labor regimes may play a similarly preemptive role, despite their quite different origins in largely economic rather than political considerations. For this reason it is unlikely that Asian corporatism will eventuate in the sort of populist explosion that ultimately evoked repressive military actions in many Latin American countries.

CONCLUSION

Insofar as the literature on Third World economic dependency speaks to the issue of emergent labor movements, emphasis has generally been placed on the political ramifications of linkage to core economies. While political factors are clearly important, inadequate attention has been given to economic structural consequences of such linkages for labor. This chapter has presented a tentative framework for the study of the ways in which Third World economic linkages to core countries may shape domestic economies in ways that impinge on labor both indirectly, through their political and community consequences, and directly, through their impact on employment and occupational structures.

Both the speed with which Asian industrialization has occurred, and the power of political elites to control labor's response to this economic change derive from the peculiar political and economic linkages of these countries to the world system. EOI has been most successful in those countries whose deep economic links to the West and Japan have been sustained by strong political bonds. Hong Kong's colonial status, and the political-military client status of Singapore, South Korea, and Taiwan vis-à-vis the West have provided not only the political security necessary for capital and technology flows from core countries, but support as well for ruling political groups against domestic opposition.

More importantly, however, EOI development has itself further undercut the independent power of labor through both its political buttressing of ruling elites and through its association with a disproportionate expansion in light-industrial employment drawing mainly on a temporary proletariat of young unmarried women whose docility is ultimately guaranteed by subordination to patriarchal family authority (Salaff, 1981).

Finally, EOI has generated pressures at later stages of development for a government-sponsored reinvigoration of labor unions, at national and enterprise levels, through creation of corporatist structures that simultaneously address the needs for control and economic mobilization. Such structures, it is argued, may play an important preemptive role in ensuring continued elite domination over labor movements even as such movements are energized by structural changes associated with late EOI.

REFERENCES

AMIN, S. (1974) "Accumulation and development: a theoretical model." Review of African Political Economy 1, 1.

APTER, D. (1976) "Charters, cartels, and multinations—some colonial and imperial questions," in D. Apter and L. Goodman (eds.) The multinational corporation and social change. New York: Praeger.

BARRETT, R. and M. WHYTE (1982) "Dependency theory and Taiwan: a deviant case analysis." American Journal of Sociology 87, 5: 1064-1089.

BOLLEN, K. (1979) "Political democracy and the timing of development." American Sociological Review 44, 4: 572-587.

BORNSCHIER, V., C. CHASE-DUNN, and R. RUBINSON (1978) "Cross-national evidence of the effects of foreign investment and aid on economic growth and inequality: a survey of findings and a reanalysis" American Journal of Sociology 84, 3.

BRAVERMAN, H. (1974) Labor and Monopoly Capital. New York: Monthly Review.

BRITT, D. and O. GALLE (1974) "Structural antecedents of the shape of strikes: a comparative analysis." American Sociological Review 39,5: 642-651.

CARDOSO, F. (1979) "On the characterization of authoritarian regimes in Latin America," pp. 33-57 in D. Collier (ed.) The New Authoritarianism in Latin America. Princeton, NJ: Princeton University Press.

CHASE-DUNN, C. (1975) "The effects of international economic dependence on development and inequality: a cross-national study." American Sociological Review 40, 6: 720-738.

CHEN, E. (1979) Hyper-Growth in Asian Economies: A Comparative Study of Hong Kong, Japan, Korea, Singapore, and Taiwan. New York: Holmes and Meier Publishers.

DELACROIX, J. and C. RAGIN (1978) "Modernizing institutions, mobilization, and Third World development: a cross-national study." American Journal of Sociology 84, 1.

DEYO, F. (forthcoming) "Labor regimes and the new Asian industrialism," in F. Deyo (ed.) The Political Economy of The New Asian Industrialism.

———(1981) Dependent Development and Industrial Order: An Asian Case Study. New York: Praeger.

———and P. CHEN (1976) Female Labour Force Participation and Earnings in Singapore. Bangkok: Clearing House for Social Development in Asia.

DIAMOND, N. (1979) "Women and industry in Taiwan." Modern China 5, 3.

DICKENSON, J. (1978) Brazil. Boulder, CO: Westview.

DJAO, A.W. (1981) "Traditional Chinese culture in the small factory of Hong Kong." Journal of Contemporary Asia 11, 4.

The Economist Intelligence Unit (1981) Quarterly Economic Review of Brazil: Annual Supplement, 1981. London: Author.

EDWARDS, R. (1979) Contested terrain: the transformation of the workplace in the twentieth century. New York: Basic Books.

ELDRIDGE, J.E.T. (1973) "Industrial conflict: some problems of theory and method," in J. Child (ed.) Man and Organization. London: George Allen and Unwin.

Federation of Korean Trade Unions. FKTU News. Seoul.

FORM, W. (1973) "The internal stratification of the working class: system involvement of auto workers in four countries." American Sociological Review 38, 6: 697-711.

FRIEDLAND, W. (1963) Unions and Industrial Relations in Underdeveloped Countries. Ithaca: New York School of Industrial and Labor Relations.

GALENSON, W. (1979) "The labor force, wages, and living standards," in W. Galenson (ed.) Economic Growth and Structural Change in Taiwan: The Postwar Experience of the Republic of China. Ithaca, NY: Cornell University Press.

GATES, H. (1979) "Dependency and the part-time proletariat in Taiwan." Modern China 5: 381-408.

HAN, S. (1974) The Failure of Democracy in South Korea. Berkeley: University of California Press.

HO, S. (1979) "Decentralized industrialization and rural development: evidence from Taiwan." Economic Development and Cultural Change 28: 77-96.

Hong Kong, Registrar of Trade Unions. Annual Departmental Report

———Monthly Digest of Statistics.

INGHAM, G. (1974) Strikes and Industrial Conflict. New York: Macmillan.

International Labour Office (annual) Yearbook of Labor Statistics. Geneva: Author.

KANAPPAN, S. (1968) "Bargaining theory and developing countries," in B. C. Roberts (ed.) Industrial Relations: Contemporary Issues. New York: St. Martin's.

KAUFMAN, R. (1979) "Industrial change and authoritarian rule in Latin America: a concrete review of the bureaucratic-authoritarian model," in D. Collier (ed.) The New Authoritarianism in Latin America. Princeton, NJ: Princeton University Press.

KERR, C. J. DUNLOP, F. HARBISON, and C. MEYER (1960) Industrialism and Industrial Man. Cambridge, MA: Harvard University Press.

KERR, C. and A. SIEGEL (1954) "The interindustry propensity to strike: an international comparison," in A. Kornhauser et al. (eds.) Industrial Conflict. New York: McGraw-Hill.

KIM, C.I.E. (1978) "Emergency, development and human rights: South Korea." Asian Survey 18, 4: 363-378.

KOO, H. (1981) "Center-periphery relations and marginalization: empirical analysis of the dependency model of inequality in peripheral nations." Development and Change 12: 55-76.

KREYE, O. (1980) "World market-oriented industrialization and labor," in F. Froebel et al. (eds.) The New International Division of Labor. London: Cambridge University Press.

LANGTON, K. and R. RAPOPORT (1975) "Social structure, social context, and partisan mobilization." Comparative Political Studies 8, 3.

LINCOLN, J. (1978) "Community structure and industrial conflict." American Sociological Review 43, 2: 199-200.

LITTLE, I. (1979) "An economic reconnaissance," in W. Galenson (ed.) Economic Growth and Structural Change in Taiwan. Ithaca, NY: Cornell University Press.

LLOYD, P. (1982) A Third World Proletariat? London: George Allen and Unwin.

MALLOY, J. (1977) "Authoritarianism and corporatism in Latin America: the modal pattern," in J. Malloy (ed.) Authoritarianism and Corporatism in Latin America. Pittsburgh: University of Pittsburgh Press.

MORRIS, M. (1969) "Labor relations: developing countries," in W. Faunce and W. Form (eds.) Comparative Perspectives on Industrial Society. Boston: Little, Brown.

New York Times, selected issues.

OGLE, G. (1979) "South Korea," in A. Blum (ed.) International Handbook of Industrial Relations. Westport, CT: Greenwood Press.

PARK, Y.K. (1974) Labor and Industrial Relations in Korea: System and Practice. Seoul, Korea: Institute for Labor and Management, Sogang University.

PORTES, A. (1976) "The sociology of national development." American Journal of Sociology 82, 1.

RAGIN, C., and S. COVERMAN (1982) "Major labor disputes in Britain: 1902-1938." American Sociological Review 47, 2.

Republic of China, Monthly Bulletin of Statistics. Department of Budget, Accounting, and Statistics.

——Report of Taiwan Labor Statistics.

——Yearbook of Labor Statistics.

Republic of Singapore, Ministry of Labour. Annual Report.

SALAFF, J. (1981) Working Daughters of Hong Kong: Filial Piety or Power in the Family? Cambridge: Cambridge University Press.

SEASHORE, S. (1954) Group Cohesiveness in the Industrial Work Group. Ann Arbor: Survey Research Center, University of Michigan.

SHAW, T. (1979) "The semiperiphery in Africa and Latin America." Review of Black Political Economy 9.

SHORTER, E. and C. Tilly (1974) Strikes in France: 1830-1968. London: Cambridge University Press.

SMELSER, N. (1976) The Sociology of Economic Life. Englewood Cliffs, NJ: Prentice-Hall.

SNYDER, D. and E. Kick. (1979) "Structural position in the world system and economic growth, 1955-1970." American Journal of Sociology 84, 5: 1096-1126.

SONG, B.N. (1977) "Production structure of the Korean economy: international and historical comparisons." Econometrica 45.

STITES, R. (1982) "Small-scale industry in Yingge, Taiwan." Modern China 8, 2.

STURMTHAL, A. (1973) "Industrial relations strategies," in A. Sturmthal and J. Scoville (eds.) The International Labor Movement in Transition. Urbana: University of Illinois Press.

Republic of China (1979) Taiwan Statistical Data Book.

TURNER, H.A. et al. (1980) The Last Colony: But Whose? A Study of the Labour Movement, Labour Market and Labour Relations in Hong Kong. Cambridge; Cambridge University Press.

United States Bureau of Labor Statistics (1962) Labor Law and Practice in The Republic of China (Taiwan). Report 404. Washington, DC: U.S. Government Printing Office.

VANNEMAN, R. (1980) "U.S. and British perceptions of class." American Journal of Sociology 85, 4.

WARNER, M. (1973) "Industrial conflict revisited," in M. Warner (ed.) The Sociology of the Workplace. London: Allen and Unwin.

World Bank (1980) World Development Report. Washington, DC: U.S. Government Printing Office.

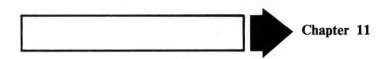

Chapter 11

THE ROLE OF WORKERS IN BOYCOTT MOVEMENTS, 1905-1931: A COMPARISON OF INDIA AND CHINA

Nesar Ahmad
Lawrence Weiss
Friends World College

The use of boycott movements by nations to achieve political and economic goals is common. In the colonized regions of the modern world system, nationalists frequently used boycott tactics to pursue a united front strategy. In India and China boycott movements played a crucial role in mobilizing an overwhelming portion of the population in support of nationalist objectives. In this chapter our central purpose is to assess the role played by the urban workers in the boycott movements that took place in India and China in 1905, 1920, and 1930.

In looking at the role of the urban workers in these boycotts, we must examine the proletariat's actions within the context of the roles played by other classes. When political movements occur, classes act in relation to each other; they coalesce or oppose each other. Major political movements usually do not result from the actions of a single class. True nationalist struggles, in particular, must involve all classes. We are focusing on boycott movements to elucidate the role of diverse classes in the nationalist struggle in two very large colonized regions.

The first part of the chapter discusses the role of the workers in the boycott movements that took place in India; the second part discusses their role in China. We have found that Indian and Chinese workers played very different roles in the boycott movements in their respective countries.

Specifically, we are faced with the fact that in India the workers remained aloof from the boycott movements. The intelligentsia, in alliance with the native capitalist class, initiated and led these movements. In China, however, the workers joined the other classes — the professional and the commercial bourgeoisie — in organizing boycotts.

This chapter explains the dominance of the national bourgeoisie in Indian movements that eclipsed the workers, as well as the circumstances that necessitated the national bourgeoisie in China to seek support and cooperation from the workers.

THE FIRST BOYCOTTS (PRE-1905 AND 1905)

In the following narrative of Indian boycotts, we have emphasized the role of the national bourgeoisie as opposed to that of the workers. The national bourgeoisie succeeded in bypassing the workers and in assuming supremacy over the nationalist movement in general and the boycott movement in particular, while the workers exhibited a lukewarm attitude toward these movements.

As indicated below, the explanation of this phenomenon lies in the key factor of the colonial state. The colonial state encouraged the bourgeoisie, preferring this class over the proletariat; besides encouraging the bourgeoisie, it pursued a policy of suppression of the workers movement, rendering the latter weak. In addition, the workers, as the pace of industrialization increased through the decade, came in conflict with the native mill owners over the economic issues. As these owners exercised an influence over the nationalist movement, the workers were alienated from it. This explains their indifference toward boycott movements. While the workers remained indifferent, the emerging native capitalist classes took the lead in organizing boycott movements.

M. G. Ranade, a politician representing the interests of the commercial and the emerging industrial classes, spoke of boycotting foreign goods as early as the 1890s. The first organized boycott movement in India occurred, however, in 1905. The proletariat as a class had hardly emerged by then. The intelligentsia of the eastern province of Bengal organized this movement.

Bengal was the province where, after 1757, the British had been building the colonial state apparatus. The British recruited local functionaries for the bureaucracy, mostly Hindus of upper caste. In time, the number of educated Bengalis grew. The Great Depression of the 1870s hit this group hard. By the turn of the century, the number of educated Hindus exceeded the number of available jobs. During this period, the educated classes in India analyzed the problems of the nation and concluded that imperial policies were stunting indigenous industrial growth, Indian agricultural resources were being exploited in the interest of British industries, and "free trade" disfavored local entrepreneurship. Remesh Dutt, the Bengali economist, developed these views at the turn of the century in his classic work on the Indian economy; his work prefigured contemporary dependence theory. (Dutt, 1963). Intellectuals such as Dutt gained support from the emerging native commercial and industrial classes by developing such analyses of economic issues.

The British administration, partly to stem the tide of the emerging antiestablishment movement among the intelligentsia and partly for administrative convenience, decided in 1905 to partition Bengal (Broomfield, 1960: 29-41). Whether intentionally or not, this action was bound to weaken the Bengali Hindu elite. Many members of this elite were the offspring of landlords. They held land in East Bengal, but lived in metropolitan Calcutta, jostling each other in and around the seats of power—the bureaucratic centers, the municipal government, and the university. Many earned a living through representing rural litigants in urban courts. The formation of a new provincial urban center at Dacca in East Bengal therefore severely limited opportunities for the Calcutta-based elite.

The educated Bengali Hindus thus opposed the partition. The antipartition movement assumed the character of a *Swadeshi* (national) movement. This involved not only the boycott of foreign goods, but also the building of national institutions (e.g., "national" schools and colleges). There seem to be two reasons why political grievances resulted in an economic boycott. First, the intelligentsia needed the support of the emerging native commercial and industrial classes. It could ensure this support by raising economic issues that interested that class. Second, the intelligentsia, confronting the harsh economic problems of the time, had come to the realization that economic autonomy was indispensable for the improvement of its condition. Boycott movements, it reasoned, would help promote Indian products, thus benefitting the local population.

Incipient native capitalists quickly approved the move to shun foreign goods. The necessity for preferential treatment of indigenous articles was vigorously pressed in a Provincial Conference in Bengal at Burdwan as early as 1894. In 1902 a formal resolution was submitted to the Subjects Committee of the Indian National Congress, but it failed to pass (Mazumdar, 1915: 174). In 1901, the Indian National Congress had begun to hold industrial exhibitions during its sessions. The Indian Industrial Conference was instituted in 1905 in association with the Congress. During the boycott movement that started in 1905, joint stock companies were launched. The native capitalists, however, had limited goals. Their purpose was to use the boycott as a substitute for a protective tariff. They became the moderates of the movement— refusing to engage in the terrorist activities that the intellectuals, hoping to arouse nationalist feelings among the masses—had spread far beyond Bengal.

By 1911, the state succumbed and annulled the partition, bringing an end to the first Swadeshi movement. Conflict in aims led to a split in Congress between "moderates" and "extremists." The colonial state repressed the "extremists" (who were also thrown out of the Congress Party) and conceded to the moderates limited power through the Morley-Minto Reforms of 1909.

The boycott movement resulted in the decline in the importation of cotton goods. By the turn of the century, India was well into the "textile revolution." She was beginning to move toward self-sufficiency in the production of cotton textiles, and eventually emerged as a major exporter of cotton piece goods, a process completed by World War II. The role of the national bourgeoisie (the native capitalists) in political movements was to increase in the decades to come.

Along with the bourgeoisie, the ranks of the proletariat also began to swell. Slowly, it emerged both as the bourgeoisie's ally and adversary. It participated in the nationalist movement alongside other classes. But it came in conflict with the native bourgeoisie and its supporter, the intelligentsia, as it pressed its demands for the amelioration of its own economic condition. What is significant, from the point of view of this chapter, is the fact that the proletariat, despite its increasing numbers, could never assume a dominant role in the nationalist movement.

NONCOOPERATION MOVEMENT OF 1920

As in 1905 the main thrust of the noncooperation movement of 1920 came from the educated elite. This time, however, its stronghold was in the inland provinces (Gujrat, United Provinces, Bihar, etc.), which had hitherto not shared any power within the colonial administration. More important, for the first time in the history of the Indian freedom movement, Muslims and Hindus united to wage a common battle against the British.

This movement received much more mass support than the boycott that began in 1905 because general economic crisis had gripped the colonial state. The decline of the British hegemony that began in the 1870s continued into the twentieth century. Attempts at recovery by Britain had a telling effect on India. "The brightest jewel in the British crown," India was useful for Britain in three respects: (1) in providing the Army to defend the Eastern Empire; (2) in serving as a market for British manufacturers; and (3) in helping the British balance of payment by paying "home charges" (i.e., payments for the cost of running the civil and military colonial administration both in India and in Britain). The rise of other imperial powers led to the intensification of interimperialist rivalry, and caused Britain to expand the Indian army, particularly during and after World War I.

As the cost of running the colonial administration rose, India repeatedly faced severe balance of payment crises. The rise in import prices worsened the situation. The crisis affected all classes of people. In 1920, the rupee value plummeted. The disastrous effect of this drop upon Indian import houses with their long-term contracts in sterling brought the commercial classes into noncooperation and led to organized repudiation of the contracts for the importation of British goods. At this time the growing Indian capitalist class found it opportune to revive its demand for "fiscal autonomy." It wanted a radically different tariff policy. Because India was a colony rather than a core country, the state used its control over customs, railway rates, and shipping regulations to promote free trade or, as the Indians claimed, to discourage home industry (Bagchi, 1972). The most blatant of these measures was the "countervailing" cotton excise duty, a 3.5 percent tax imposed on all cotton piece goods manufactured in India. The measure was designed to offset the revenue customs duties that penalized Lancashire goods.

Meanwhile, as a consequence of the deterioration of agricultural prices, the peasantry was hard hit and soon began to organize. Some peasants joined the boycott movement, but pressed their own demand for the abolition of rent. The Executive Committee of Congress had to take action to halt the no-rent campaign in various parts of the country, which threatened to throw the zamindars (land owners) into the arms of the government (Philip, 1932: 223; Chakrabarty and Bhatta-Charyya, 1935: 43).

Urban workers, by now a significant social force, also joined the boycott movement to project their growing grievances. However, they seemed more interested in their own struggle against the industrial class and were not attracted to the intelligentsia-led boycott movement in very large numbers.

The movement of 1920 also marked the emergence of Gandhi as a national leader. Gandhi rose to leadership by uniting the new forces, seeking recognition at the all-India level (Brown, 1972). The intelligentsia from the inland provinces and the emerging commercial and industrial classes found in Gandhi a national spokesman. With the assumption of leadership by Gandhi, therefore, the power of the Presidency elite (Bengal, Bombay, and Madras) declined. Many of these people were driven to radical politics, both right and left. As a result, some of them turned to organizing workers.

This reconsolidation of the Indian bourgeoisie under Gandhi's leadership had profound significance. With the removal of the exclusive control over Congress by the Presidency elite, the party was able to draw in a much larger following from many parts of India and to mobilize the peasantry and some workers under its cautious guidance and control.

The first major example of Gandhi's restrained leadership was the manner in which he brought an abrupt end to the noncooperation movement. That movement had consisted of civil disobedience, nonpayment of taxes, and boycotts of educational institutions and foreign clothes. Gandhi called off the movement when it was at its zenith because a violent incident had broken out in a small village in the United Provinces. Some writers claim that the movement was interrupted more by the internal splits than by the outbreak of violence. Evidence of such splits can be found in the resolution passed in the Bardoli Congress in 1922, which chastised the peasantry for defying the property rights of the landowning class (Orr, 1939: 167). Congress did not want the peasant movement to assume an independent dynamic.

There was much trade union activity among the workers in the wake of the noncooperation movement. A number of trade unions were formed in 1920. Some Congressites took the lead and formed an All India Trade Union Congress (AITUC) to coordinate labor activities. Ironically, they proceeded to organize workers in mills owned by Congressites. Meanwhile, the Communists proved enormously successful in union organizing, particularly among the cotton textile workers and railwaymen (Haithcox, 1971: 79). Eventually, they were to capture the AITUC. Their influence on the trade union movement slackened only after the wrath of the colonial state fell on the radical organizers in the late 1920s.

While the colonial state sought to suppress the radical organizers—especially in response to the boycott movement—it began to move toward accepting the demands of the native capitalists. It formed a fiscal commission in 1922 and accepted the principle of discriminative protection in 1923. It appointed for the first time a Tariff Board in 1923, and abolished the cotton excise duty in 1926 (Orr, 1939: 299). Finally, for those (mainly the intellectuals) seeking a share in the running of the state apparatus, the colonial state announced in March 1921 the goal of a Dominion Status. The British state was actually responding to the changes in trade relationships between England and India, which were already taking place and which were further accelerated by the boycott movement of 1920. These changes included a decline in the importation of cotton piece goods and woolen and silk goods, and a decline in the British share of imports of consumer goods generally. It should be pointed out, however, that during this period there was a rise in import of machinery from England, which reflected the rise in local textile production.

CIVIL DISOBEDIENCE MOVEMENT, 1930

Gandhi had brought the noncooperation movement to an abrupt end. His action gave rise to dissension and controversy among the ranks of the Congress. One such controversy concerned the question of participation in elections and in the Reformed Councils. The Congress had at first taken an unusually clear and decisive stand against parliamentary collaboration with their alien rulers. Then came the discouragement that followed the failure of Gandhi's militant noncooperation. This played into the hands of the moderates who controlled the Maharashtra Congress organization. What was more important, the militant Bengal Congress, led by C. R. Das, abandoned the boycott of the Councils and espoused a limited form of parliamentarianism thus allowing the Nationalists to seek office in order to "wreck the Councils from within." Local Congress organizations were allowed to experiment along this path, although it was considered a treacherous one by Gandhi, who preferred to continue taking an uncompromising stand.

A most unprecedented result was achieved. C. R. Das's Swaraj Party won by a clear majority both in 1923 and in 1927 elections, and actually carried out its announced policy of sabotaging the Councils without succumbing to the wiles of Parliament and without abandoning its opposition to foreign rule. In spite of this unexpected success in discrediting the Reformed Councils, the path that the Swaraj Party followed led nowhere. It was only a question of time until the spirit of militant nationalism would rise once again against the British rulers.

It was an act of the British government rather than exhortations from the nationalist leaders that served to provoke the new wave of national sentiment in India. This was not the first time that a British blunder played into the hands of Indian nationalism. Back in 1921, the faltering ranks of Congress, and indeed the whole Indian population, had been aroused by the visit of the Prince of Wales. So again in 1927 the government unwittingly came to the aid of the Indian nationalists— this time by naming a committee composed exclusively of British members to study Indian conditions as the basis for the regular decenial constitutional revision.

No single administrative act could have exasperated India more; even the most moderate Indian was outraged by the fact that no Indian was considered worthy of a responsible part in drafting India's constitution. The nationalist cry that instantly went up against the Simon Commission was louder and more united than it had ever been, and, for a time, the will to boycott the commission was practically unanimous, uniting all spheres of political opinion.

The wild demonstrations as well as the silent *hartals*, which followed the Simon Commission everywhere in India, were simply rehearsals for a gigantic nonviolent struggle against the Empire that was already in the making—the Civil Disobedience campaign was to grip India in the early 1930s. During this struggle the demand was raised for complete independence for the first time.

Two prominent new classes had emerged by now—the industrialists and the urban working class. The years between the world wars saw the collapse of the pattern of world trade, investment, and multilateral settlement that had become established in the second half of the nineteenth century. Along with other countries, India's participation in international trade changed significantly (Tomlinson, 1979: 30ff). Rivalry was intense among the important powers, and world trade was disrupted by war conditions. These factors contributed further to India's balance of payment crisis, making it more difficult to import goods. India was forced to transform its relationship with the world economy through a process of import substitution in consumer goods. Indian industries as a whole, although stagnant for much of the 1920s, suffered relatively little during the Depression and made striking advances after 1934. By 1945, India was the tenth-largest industrialized country in the world (Tomlinson, 1979: 31).

The monetary policies of the Colonial State severely threatened this process of industrial expansion. In 1926 and 1927 the state set the Rupee exchange rate at 18 pence rather than the traditional 16 pence, a policy that severely penalized Indian manufacturers in competition with

British manufacturers. This measure was counteracted in part by suspension in 1926 of the 3.5 percent countervailing duty on the production of cotton goods in India. That move was an attempt by the British at once to counter Japanese competition and to court the Indian capitalists. But the long years of discrimination against Indian industrial development had left a deep conviction concerning the role of alien *raj* that could not be suddenly altered by belated concessions. Indian producers saw in boycott both an opportunity to air their grievances and an occasion to unload their *swadeshi* stocks at an immediate profit.

Behind Gandhi and the independence struggle, therefore, was the Indian Chamber of Commerce. Support from the business classes was strongest in Bombay where it included the stockbrokers and the wealthy Parsi merchants and wholesalers. These latter had long remained unfriendly to political agitation; but when they finally espoused it, they were particularly well situated to aid in effective boycotting. Funded by the native capitalists, the Indian National Congress was able to mobilize the largest number of people during the Civil Disobedience movement of 1930. Almost the entire nation rose in defiance of foreign rule and in support of complete *swaraj*, or self-rule.

As a result of the movement, India came closer to achieving political independence, although the immediate impact was confined to certain economic gains attained by the industrial class. The Indian textile industry continued to grow as imports declined and protection increased both against the British and the Japanese. During the Great Depression, Indian mills continued production and ran double shifts. Lancashire felt the impact; its production declined drastically.

SUMMARY

With each new campaign, the boycott movement extended its geographical base and drew in broader strata of the Indian population. Each time with more participation, the campaigns increased in economic effectiveness. What Remer said of the Chinese boycotts applies to India as well:

> Over the whole period of about thirty years Chinese boycotts have become more numerous, more extensive in the territory covered, and more general in their appeal to the various classes in the Chinese community. These developments have made them more effective, and economic effectiveness is the first condition of success in boycotting [Remer, 1933: 232].

From one campaign to the next the boycotts maintained a continuity of aims. In each case, they represented opposition toward the authority of the British government and support of increased political and economic autonomy for India. The protest against the dismemberment of Bengal that motivated the first campaign was symbolic of the rising resentment against British rule. Late in the campaign, a minority voiced the hidden motive in terms of *swaraj*, but the only independence they envisaged was the gradual attainment of Dominion Status. In the postwar noncooperation campaign, swaraj became one of the three announced goals, and the one that united Muslims and Hindus. In 1930 the majority of the nation rallied to the cry of purna swaraj (total independence), but it was eventually found that the mill owners and commercial classes could be appeased with much less. Over the period of three decades Indian nationalism had moved persistently toward the goal of complete independence, and the boycotts had been pursued to achieve that goal. The principal achievements of Indian boycott campaigns include legislative reforms, the annulment of the partition of Bengal, the introduction of a protective tariff policy, and the Federal Constitution of 1935.

INTRODUCTION TO CHINESE BOYCOTTS

Perhaps the most striking example of worker participation in revolutionary struggle anywhere in the world during the 1920s involved the groups of armed proletarian pickets that enforced compliance with the great Chinese boycotts of British and Japanese goods in 1925-1926. These boycotts, known in Chinese historiography as the "May 30 Movement," provided the occasion for a significant revival of the Chinese labor movement after several years of decline. Labor militance culminated in impressive shows of proletarian force, directed primarily against foreign-owned enterprises in Shanghai—China's industrial and commercial center—in 1927.

Chiang Kai-shek, who in 1925 succeeded the deceased Sun Yat-sen as the leader of China's Nationalist Party, the Kuomintang, decapitated the Chinese proletariat in a dramatic purge of Communists and union leaders in Shanghai in mid-April 1927. The annihilation of Communist cadres in China's largest city and the growing power of expansionist Japanese imperialism set the stage for the reorientation of Chinese Communist revolutionary strategy under the leadership of Mao Tse-tung. Ultimately successful, Mao's strategy emphasized the mobilization of China's massive peasantry by a militarized party under the banners of land redistribution and patriot resistance to Japanese imperialism and gave only lip-service to the leading revolutionary role of the proletariat.

The Chinese boycott movement from 1905-1931 established a pattern of mass participation in anti-imperalist activities that the Chinese Communists were able to build upon in succeeding decades. The boycotts also provided an important link between the political culture of traditional Confucian China and the twentieth-century political environment that featured the participation of the newly emergent bourgeoisie and intelligentsia as well as the proletariat.

As C. F. Remer notes in his definitive work, *A Study of Chinese Boycotts With Special Reference to their Economic Effectiveness*, a tradition of passive resistance to authority was well established, particularly at the local level, in Imperial China (Remer, 1933: 10-12). Indeed, the power of local elite groups vis-à-vis the District Magistrates who represented the central government was often sufficient to allow for major, coordinated resistance to central government authority. Such resistance frequently took the form of withholding services or tax payments. Although such movements were usually led by the gentry elite, the mass peasantry provided the manpower. Secret societies possessed the ability to enforce mass participation through an interlocking loyalty system that reached well into the villages, across class lines.

During periods of dynastic decline, passive resistance and violent rebellions became especially pervasive in Imperial China. Considering that the anti foreign movements of the 1890s (of which the Boxer Rebellion is best known) coincided with the final decline in 1911 of the Qing Dynasty, it is not entirely surprising that passive resistance evolved into a successful, anti-imperialist tactic. Not only did anti imperialist boycotts excite the newer urban middle and working classes, they struck resonant chords in the consciousness of traditional peasant and gentry groups that were familiar with the logic of passive resistance movements on a large scale.

THE EARLY BOYCOTTS (1905-1924)

The process of imperialist encroachment on Chinese sovereignty that began with the Opium Wars of 1842 reached a climax with the "scramble for concessions" of the 1890s. Despite the fact that Britain, France, Germany, and Japan were the major actors in "slicing the Chinese melon," it was the United States that served as the first target for a modern Chinese boycott in 1905. The infamous Chinese Exclusion

Acts infuriated Chinese on both sides of the Pacific. Consequently, merchant guild and secret society organizations of Chinese in America as well as within China provided financial support for a nationwide boycott of American goods, centered in Shanghai and Canton. Remer attributes certain subsequent American modifications of the Exclusion Acts to the political aftermath of the boycotts and considers them to have been fairly effective economically within south China with particular reference to such commodities as cotton piece goods, kerosene oil, and wheat flour (1933: 33-39).

In a larger sense, the most illustrative feature of the 1905 boycott concerns the role played by commercial bourgeois elements. Acting through traditional guild organizations, many of the merchants were new actors on the Chinese political and economic stage. This is perhaps most true of the overseas Chinese merchants of San Francisco who were just one or two generations removed from the indentured Cantonese peasants who had been brought to the United States to construct the transcontinental railroads.

The central role of the bourgeoisie in the boycott movements became all the more evident in the major 1915 and 1919 anti-Japanese boycotts. World War I played an important role as well in shaping these protests.

The war's effects on China were generally positive. Preoccupied by the fighting on their own continent, the European imperialists could not maintain their prewar presence in China. As the war progressively drained the European economies and weakened the trade controls that the imperialist treaty system had imposed on China, native bourgeois elements moved to take advantage of the economic power vacuum. Their efforts were all the more encouraged by the ever-increasing commodity and industrial needs of the European war economies, some of which expanding Chinese factories and trading companies were able to satisfy.

The Japanese also moved to avail themselves of economic opportunities in China made possible by European preoccupation with the war in France. Chinese bourgeois, intellectual, and to a small extent proletarian interests collided with those of the Japanese when Japan (an ally of Britain and France, as was China) attempted to assert control over former German concession areas in Shandong. The Japanese initiative, known to history as "The 21 Demands," elicited a strong patriotic response across China that manifested itself as a powerful boycott of Japanese goods, as Remer (1933: 53-54) explains in the following:

> The boycott of 1915 was the first which revealed the power of this weapon in the hands of the Chinese. The decline in Japanese trade was

great for the brief period of the severest boycotting. This decline was
not confined to a single part of China as had been the case during
earlier boycotts. . . . The stimulus to domestic industry from boycotting had added a new feature but otherwise this boycott was not
different, except in extent, from those of an earlier day.

Although the Japanese failed to achieve all of their immediate
territorial goals with respect to Shandong in 1915, their efforts to
improve their political and economic position in China progressed
dramatically during World War I. The failure of the 1911 Revolution
against the Qing Dynasty to produce an effective central government
greatly encouraged such efforts.

By the end of World War I, the "Republican Government" with its
capital in Beijing consisted of little more than a congeries of warlord
factions. Sun Yat-sen, leader of the 1911 Revolution, had long since
abandoned Beijing for Canton, where he too was surrounded by rival
warlords. The foreign concessions remained small islands of foreign
sovereignty within China's largest ports.

Coincident with China's political dissolution, however, new centers
of economic and political power arose during World War I consisting
largely of national bourgeoisie and intelligentsia elements, with a small
but significant industrial proletariat following the anti-imperialist lead
provided by such groups.

The first major test of strength for the new bourgeois groups came
on May 4, 1919. Japanese designs on Shandong once again provided the
issue. The result became one of the key events in the development of the
modern Chinese Revolution.

In the early days of May 1919 news arrived from Paris that the
Council of Prime Ministers at the Versailles Peace Conference had
decided to turn German rights in Shandong over to the Japanese. Many
leaders of the subsequent protest movement immediately inferred that
pro-Japanese members of the Beijing Government had cooperated with
the Japanese in achieving this result.

An outpouring of spontaneous protest erupted in Beijing initially
involving students and rapidly growing to include merchants and
workers. The protestors called for boycotts of Japanese goods in all
major cities and quickly set up headquarters to implement their
decision. Students organized propaganda teams that deliberately set out
to organize mass support for the anti-Japanese movement (see Chow,
1960).

Over the next three years, boycott activity exacted a heavy price on
Japanese trade in China. As Remer notes, some of the decrease in

Japanese trade in China can be explained by the return of European goods to the China market after the hiatus of World War I, and a further portion of the decrease was due to the effects on Japan of the global postwar depression (Remer, 1933: 65-69). Nevertheless, the May 4 Movement's massive boycotts and strikes clearly played a central role in bringing about the Japanese decision to abandon their claim to German rights in Shandong in 1921 after the Washington Conference.

A wave of strikes hit China during the 1919-1921 period, most of which were directed against foreign-owned industrial and commercial establishments. As Jean Chesneaux indicates, however, the leadership of such strikes came from other classes—the intellectual and national bourgeois elements that were carrying out the larger May 4 Movement (Chesneaux, 1968: 153).

The alliance between left-wing intellectuals and workers forged during the May 4 Movement provided a foundation upon which the Chinese Communist Party and other progressive political groups were built in the early 1920s. The Russian Revolution's success had a great impact on China, and the willingness of the Bolshevik authorities to assist Sun Yat-sen's efforts to unify China by force encouraged Sun to incorporate Communist, intellectual, and national bourgeois elements into a rejuvenated Kuomintang movement.

Many factors contributed to the success of the May 4 Movement. China lacked an effective central government able to suppress dissident activity. The old agrarian and bureaucratic elites divided along geographic lines and were basically controlled by the regional "warlords" who came to power after the collapse of the Republic, which occurred soon after its founding in 1911. With the end of World War I, interimperialist rivalry resumed in China with Japan, Russia, and the United States emerging as more powerful actors and England attempting to recapture its traditional position of leadership. The divided and competitive nature of political power within China created opportunities for revolutionary activity. Many warlord and civilian contenders for national power regarded support for anti-imperialist activity as in their interest, while antiregime and antiwarlord protest was often coordinated within the more tolerant borders of the foreign concessions. Interimperialist competition, which often inspired attempts to develop supporters among the divided warlords, contributed to the anarchic environment in which protest could develop quickly.

THE GREAT ANTI-BRITISH AND ANTI-JAPANESE BOYCOTTS OF 1925-1926

The revival of the Nationalist Party under Sun Yat-sen's leadership, supported by the Soviet Union and allied with the growing Chinese Communist movement, accelerated the pace of both anti-imperialist activity and worker organization. While some members of China's traditional landlord and merchant elite groups remained powerful figures in Kuomintang, they were eclipsed (only temporarily as events later proved) by the more progressive national bourgeoisie and intelligentsia elements.

The postwar depression that beset most of the world in the early 1920s served to encourage interimperialist competition in China at precisely the time that anti-imperialist consciousness and activity were on the rise. The depressed world economy and the return of European competitors to the China market also affected the Chinese national bourgeoisie, threatening to wipe out many of the gains that had been made in industry and commerce during the war. Important bourgeois elements responded with increased support for nationalist and anti-imperialist initiatives.

Thus, for the Chinese industrialist and merchant facing increased foreign competition, for the man in the street seeing more and more foreign troops in Shanghai and the other treaty ports, and for the warlord aching to flex his newly procured muscle of modern armaments, the antiforeign impulse stimulated increasingly active responses. Moreover, as the 1911 Revolution faded further into history with each passing year, the frustration felt by virtually all segments of the Chinese population as a result of the Revolution's failure to fulfill its great expectations led to rising nationalist fervor and a hunger for a comprehensive solution to China's manifold political problems.

The death of Sun Yat-sen in March 1925 and continuing preparations for the "Northern Expedition" against the Beijing warlords by the modern Kuomintang army added tension to an already explosive situation. Several specific events involving violent confrontations between Chinese and foreigners provided the igniting spark in the spring of 1925: the killing of a striking millhand at a Japanese-owned textile mill in Shanghai on May 15; the killing of 14 Chinese protestors in front of the Louza Police Station by foreign members of the Shanghai Municipal Police on May 30; the shooting of several Chinese in Hankow by British troops protecting an armory on June 12; and finally, the killing of over 40 Chinese in an armed confrontation with British troops in the Shameen District of Canton on June 23. Chinese historiography records the widespread response to the events in Shanghai and Wuhan as the "May 30 Movement." The Movement consisted of a series of strikes, boycotts, and demonstrations against British and Japanese commerce and industry in China unlike any mass movement previously seen in the Middle Kingdom (Borg, 1967: 20-46). As Remer (1933: 97) notes, "an interesting feature of the boycotting during 1925 was the alignment of students with laborers in leading the Shanghai agitation." Indeed, the 1925-1926 boycotts and strikes, including the gigantic Hong Kong seamen's strike and related boycott, represented the high water mark of direct action by the Chinese urban proletariat and intelligentsia. Such action stopped short of protracted armed struggle, however, as the spontaneously organized units of armed pickets can scarcely be reckoned as a revolutionary military force. In fact, the well-trained Kuomintang military units, in which Communist officers and men were fully incorporated at the time, normally stayed quite clear of strike and boycott activity.

The Third Conference of the All China General Union Conference, convened in Shanghai on May Day of 1926 represented the single most significant symbolic event of the May 30 Movement period as far as the proletariat was concerned. Attended by 502 delegates, representing 690 labor organizations, the Conference claimed to speak on behalf of 1.2 million workers. Jean Chesneaux estimates that more than half of all Chinese industrial workers were represented at the Conference (Chesneaux, 1968: 302).

There is no question that in the major ports of south and central China, such as Hong Kong, Canton, Wuhan, and Shanghai, the alliance of militant workers, students, Communist and left-wing Kuomintang political activists, and some national bourgeois merchants and industrialists became a political force to be reckoned with by foreign imperialists and domestic reactionaries.

For the British, the boycott caused very serious repercussions. According to Remer, Britain's share of the China trade in 1925 reached a level lower than in any previous peacetime year. Entrepôt trade through Hong Kong also suffered dramatically (Remer, 1933: 112).

For the Kuomintang, poised to march north under Chiang Kai-shek, the success of the May 30 Movement represented an unquestioned anti-imperialist success and a warning of the independent power that left-wing elements were developing within the party. Never a highly unified group under the best of circumstances, the Kuomintang contained many volatile and mutually antagonistic factions after Sun Yat-sen's death. Representatives of the landed gentry, conservative merchants, labor racketeers, and regional militarists occupied positions very close to the center of power in the KMT. Such groups worried a great deal about the rising power of the Communists and the workers. With the Party's military strength developing dramatically as a result of help from the USSR and growing popular support for the Northern Expedition, control of the army represented the major point of contention between the KMT's factions.

Chiang Kai-shek, relying on his position as Director of the KMT's modern military academy as a power base (ironically Chiang's chief assistant for political affairs at the Whampoa Military Academy during the period of KMT-Communist collaboration was Chou En-lai), managed to gain supreme control of the Nationalist army without revealing very many of his own political predilections. Chiang had spent some time in the Soviet Union undergoing military training but also had close links to Shanghai's reactionary "Green Gang." As Chiang's armies swept north to the Yangtze River and Shanghai in 1926, military rather than political concerns appeared to predominate. Crucial differences in policies became evident in early 1927, however, as the Nationalist armies divided to take over the central Yangtze valley to the west and Shanghai to the east.

Left-wing elements in both army and political leadership predominated in the forces active in the central Yangtze. When in January 1927 the Nationalists officially moved their capital from Canton to Hankow (one of the Wuhan cities on the central Yangtze), Communist and left-wing elements controlled many key positions in the political and military hierarchies, much to the alarm of more conservative domestic and foreign constituencies. The reactionaries can scarcely have been comforted by the increased muscle flexing of the Shanghai labor movement as it awaited liberation from warlord control by the approaching KMT armies.

On February 28, 1927, a sustained labor mobilization began with the calling of a one-hour general strike to protest the presence of British and Japanese troops in Shanghai. Two million workers participated in the action. Throughout the month of March, proletarian and popular activity in Shanghai was highly developed and diversified. When KMT soldiers conquered Shanghai in late March, they found a city seething with anti-imperialist, nationalistic, and politically progressive sentiments, much to the consternation of the foreign community clustered around the city's International Settlement and the domestic right-wing that historically had controlled China's largest port (Chesneaux, 1968: 347-367).

Upon entering Shanghai, Chiang Kai-shek faced a momentous decision. The Hankow Government certainly expected that its military commander would support the established policies of KMT-Communist collaboration and militant anti-imperialism. On the other hand, Chiang was far from Hankow and owed no particular allegiance to its political leadership. As the supreme military commander, he had the capacity to mobilize right-wing and foreign support behind his leadership by crushing the left in one surprise stroke.

Chiang, of course, decided to decapitate the Chinese workers movement in a series of brutal execution and suppression missions throughout Shanghai on April 12-13, 1927. Known Communists were the first targets of the attacks, and many were killed. The Shanghai counter-revolutionary purge, together with the killing of Communist leader Li Ta-chao in warlord-controlled Beijing on April 6, delivered a fatal blow to the urban workers movement. Chiang nearly succeeded in exterminating the Chinese Communist leadership, but many Communists remained in Nationalist-held areas beyond his immediate control or were able to seek protection in the foreign concessions of Shanghai (see Malraux, 1934; 1968).

RECAPITULATION

Although use of boycotting techniques continued in China after 1927, and particularly in 1931 in response to the Japanese invasion of Manchuria, the workers movement never again played an important independent role in such movements. Indeed, after 1927 it is not really possible to regard the proletariat as an important force in Chinese politics. The center of gravity in the revolutionary conflict in China shifted to the countryside as the Communists, under the leadership of Mao Tse-tung, Chou En-lai, and Chu Teh, developed an independent military capability and a power base in the vast reaches of rural China.

Following initial defeats at the hand of Chiang's superior army in the early 1930s that forced the Communists to undertake their famous Long March, the Chinese Communist Party (CCP) successfully established a major base area in north-central China that became a center of effective anti-Japanese activity after 1937. By the end of the War of Resistance Against Japan in 1945, the Communists controlled most of North China outside the major cities. Unquestionably, in building their anti-Japanese united front, the Communists used many of the techniques that they had first learned during the boycotts. During the war, the Communists proved especially successful in constructing a patriotic coalition of intellectuals, national bourgeois elements, and peasants.

In the 1945-1949 Civil War, as the Communists liberated the cities first of Manchuria, then North China, and finally in 1949 of Shanghai and the south, the workers movement became active once again but under far tighter Communist control than had been the case in the 1920s. The Chinese proletariat never regained the leading and independent role that for a brief decade it enjoyed at the head of anti-imperialist boycotts and strikes. In China, ultimate political power developed from the guns of the 3-million-man People's Liberation Army rather than from the staves wielded by several thousand armed, proletarian pickets.

CONCLUSION

Our assessment of the role of the workers in the boycott movements has required an analysis of the roles of other participant groups and classes belonging to diverse economic and social status. It should be remembered that participation of workers and peasants in a mass movement does not necessarily make that movement one in which the working people have leadership. In both India and China, the boycott movement was primarily led by the industrial, commercial, and intellectual classes. The urban workers assumed a more active and enthusiastic role in the boycott movement in China, even though the movement was initiated by the national bourgeoisie. In India, the urban workers hardly participated. This was so despite the fact that by 1920, and certainly by the 1930s, the industrial working class had grown to a formidable size in India—more numerous than in China.

To understand the different role of Indian and Chinese workers in the boycott movement, we have examined the nature of the leadership of the movements. In India the bourgeoisie that initiated boycotts was cohesive; it began to gain strength steadily since the turn of the century, but more particularly after World War I. In China, the national bourgeoisie lacked both cohesiveness and strength.

The strong national bourgeoisie in India was able to keep the workers movement subdued until much later. It was able to wage a nationalist struggle without incorporating the workers in the movement. The radical intellectuals, who had organized the Revolutionary Party and the Communist Party, remained aloof from the boycott movement and denounced it as an inappropriate strategy devised by a timid and short-sighted bourgeoisie. In China, the weaker national bourgeoisie saw the need for mobilizing the working people in order to strengthen the nationalist ranks.

These conclusions lead us to further inquiry into the reasons for the different characters of the national bourgeoisie in India and China. This requires a look at the mode of colonization in the two countries. India was a colonial state, where one metropolitan power was firmly entrenched. Furthermore, India had a special place in the British empire. India provided a large army, which was essential to protect the empire in the East. India served consistently and reliably as a market for British manufactured (consumer, and later capital) goods. In the process of feeding and clothing the army, as well as of absorbing British capital, India experienced significant industrialization. The industrial class emerged in alliance with a formidable network of professional and bureaucratic elements that developed to assist in the running of the colonial state. That alliance also included the landed bourgeoisie, which developed in response to world market needs of Indian agricultural products. As a result, the national industrial bourgeoisie was able to pursue its class interest without much difficulty. The colonial state apparatus encouraged the bourgeoisie by granting concessions, while at the same time suppressing more radical forces.

In China the national bourgeoisie lacked cohesiveness due to diverse and contradictory influences of various metropolitan powers in the country. The semicolonial status inhibited the growth of a unified group of upper classes. Fragmented, they went in different directions. The radical intellectuals organized the workers. The bureaucratic class sought the support of the landed elite and turned its party, the KMT, into a highly militarized organization. By the late 1930s, the national bourgeoisie was squeezed between invading Japan, the bureaucratic KMT, and the radicalized agrarian CCP. On the other hand, the workers movement in China found a prominent, if largely symbolic, place in the struggle for national independence primarily because it was able to align itself with the radical intellectuals and the peasantry.

This leads us to an important conclusion. Workers in the periphery, due to the peculiarity of its socioeconomic structures, lack independent power. Proletarian nationalists are much more likely to succeed in a movement that is waged in alliance with other classes, particularly the peasantry. Otherwise, despite the leading role promised them in Marxist ideology, the workers can be ignored, isolated, or neutralized.

REFERENCES

BAGCHI, A.K. (1972) Private Investment in India: 1900-1939. London: Cambridge University Press.

BEAUCHAMP, J. (1935) British Imperialism in India. London: M. Lawrence.

BORG, D. (1967) American Policy and the Chinese Revolution, 1923-1928. New York: Octagon.

BROOMFIELD, J.H. (1968) Elite Conflict in a Plural Society: Twentieth Century in Bengal. Berkeley: University of California Press.

BROWN, J.M. (1972) Gandhi's Rise to Power: Indian Politics 1915-1922. London: Cambridge University Press.

CHAKRABARTY D. and C. BHATTA-CHARYYA (1935) Congress in Evolution: A Collection of Congress Resolutions from 1885-1934 and New Important Documents. Calcutta: The Cook Co.

CHESNEAUX, J. (1968) The Chinese Labor Movement, 1919-1927 (trans. H.M. Wright). Stanford, CA: Stanford University Press.

DUTT R.P. (1940) India Today. London: Gollancz.

HAITHCOX, J.P. (1971) Communism and Nationalism in India: M.N. Roy and Comintern Policy, 1920-1939. Princeton, NJ: Princeton University Press.

ISAACS, R. (1968) The Tragedy of the Chinese Revolution. New York: Atheneum

MALRAUX, A. (1961) Man's Fate (La Condition Humaine, trans. H. M. Chevalier). New York: Vintage Books.

MAZUMDAR, A.C. (1915) Indian National Evolution: A Brief Survey of the Origin and Progress of the Indian Nation. Madras: Natesan.

ORR, C. (1940) A study of Indian Boycotts. Film reproduction of Ph.D. thesis, Ann Arbor, MI.

PHILIP. A. (1932) India: A Foreign View. London: Sidgwick & Jackson.

REMER, C. (1933) A Study of Chinese Boycotts with Special Reference to Their Economic Effectiveness. Baltimore: Johns Hopkins University Press.

TOMLINSON, B.R. (1979) The Political Economy of the Raj: 1914-1947: The Economics of Decolonization in India. London: Macmillan.

VIOLLIS, A. (1930) L'Inde Contre les Anglais. Paris: Editions des Politiques.

NOTES ON THE CONTRIBUTORS

NESAR AHMAD teaches at Friends World College, New York. He was formerly Director of the Third World Studies program at Goddard College and an editor of *Third World Forum*.

GIOVANNI ARRIGHI is Professor of Sociology at the State University of New York at Binghamton. His recent publications include *The Geometry of Imperialism* (1983) and *Dynamics of Global Crisis* (1982) with S. Amin, A.G. Frank, and I. Wallerstein.

CHARLES BERGQUIST is Associate Professor of History at Duke University. He is the author of *Coffee and Conflict in Columbia*. His *Workers in Modern Latin American History* will be published next year.

STEPHEN G. BUNKER is an Assistant Professor of Sociology at the University of Illinois at Urbana-Champaign. He has done fieldwork on rural societies and economies in Uganda, Guatemala, and Brazil, and is currently researching the relations between mining and peasant agriculture in Bolivia and Peru. In addition to articles on development programs, official bureaucracies, and class relations in Africa and Latin America, he is the author of *Underdeveloping the Amazon: Extraction, Unequal Exchange, and the Failure of the Modern State* (1984).

MICHAEL BURAWOY teaches sociology at the University of California, Berkeley.

CHRISTOPHER K. CHASE-DUNN is Associate Professor of Sociology at Johns Hopkins University. He is the editor of *Socialist States in the World System* and the coauthor with Volker Bornschier of *Transnational Corporations and Underdevelopment*. His current research is on the growth of national city systems since 1880.

FREDERIC DEYO is Associate Professor of Sociology at SUNY, Brockport. He has published a number of works on Asian industrialization and labor, including a book (*Dependent Development and Industrial Order*) that traces the implications of export-oriented industrialization for trade unions in Singapore.

RICHARD G. FOX, Professor of Anthropology at Duke University, received his Ph.D. from the University of Michigan in 1965. His publications include *From Zamindar to Ballot Box* (1969), *kin, Clan, Raja, and Rule* (1971), *Urban Anthropology: Cities in Their Cultural Settings* (1977), and a book-length manuscript based on his Punjab research, *The Lions of British India: Culture in the Making.*

ALICE INGERSON is completing doctoral work in anthropology at the Johns Hopkins University on class consciousness under the corporatist dictatorship in Portugal. She has also written on the politics of religion and the arts in Portugal, and plans to pursue further comparative study of cultural change in the world system, especially in textile production and consumption.

WILLIAM G. MARTIN coordinates research programs at the Fernand Braudel Center, State University of New York at Binghamton. He is currently engaged in projects concerning household structures in the world-economy, and southern Africa's role in the world-economy in the long twentieth century.

JUNE NASH is Professor of Anthropology at City College of the City University of New York, and the Graduate Center. She has worked with Maya of Guatemala and Mexico, and with Bolivian tin miners before doing her recent fieldwork in Pittsfield, Massachusetts. Recent publications include, "We Eat the Mines and the Mines Eat Us; Exploitation and Dependency in Bolivian Tin Mines," and *Women, Men and the International Division of Labor,* edited with M. Patricia Fernandez-Kelly.

BEVERLY J. SILVER is a Research Associate at the Fernand Braudel Center at the State University of New York at Binghamton. She is engaged there in collaborative research projects on the world labor movement and on semiperipheral development.

CAROL A. SMITH is Associate Professor of Anthropology at Duke University. She has written extensively on class relations in rural and urban Guatemala. A recent essay, "Local History in Global Context," in *Comparative Studies in Society and History* (April 1984) treats both historically.

LAWRENCE WEISS is President of Friends World College, New York. He is currently preparing a manuscript from his dissertation *Storm Around the Cradle: The Korean War and the Early Years of the People's Republic of China, 1949-1953.*